A GUIDE TO
THE ILIAD

JAMES C. HOGAN received his doctorate in the classics from Cornell University. He has taught at Washington University in St. Louis, the University of Oklahoma, and Allegheny College in Pennsylvania, where he is currently Frank T. McClure Professor of Classics.

This guide is based on the most recent edition of Robert Fitzgerald's translation of the Iliad, published in hard and paper editions by Anchor Press/Doubleday.

A GUIDE
TO
THE ILIAD

BASED ON THE TRANSLATION

By Robert Fitzgerald

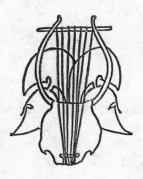

by James C. Hogan

ANCHOR BOOKS
ANCHOR PRESS/DOUBLEDAY
GARDEN CITY, NEW YORK
1979

Permission was kindly granted for an excerpt from *The Making of Homeric Verse* edited by Adam Parry, 1970 © Oxford University Press 1970.

Library of Congress Cataloging in Publication Data

Hogan, James C
  A guide to The Iliad.

  Bibliography: p. 61
  Includes index.
  1. Homerus. Ilias.   I. Fitzgerald, Robert, 1910–
II. Homerus. Ilias. English. 1979.   III. Title.
PA4037.H76   883′.01
Anchor Books Edition: 1979

ISBN: 0-385-14519-5
Library of Congress Catalog Card Number 78–58757

CONTENTS

PREFACE

Today Homer has more readers in English than in Greek. In high schools and colleges students may find themselves reading the *Iliad* with an instructor who has little or no knowledge of ancient Greek. Even teachers who know Homer's Greek text may find themselves devoting more time than they like to the explanation of historical and cultural points which, though pertinent to a specific passage, do not bear directly on larger matters of plot, character, and theme. This companion to Robert Fitzgerald's translation of the *Iliad* aims to make studying the poem more efficient and informed.

That, of course, is the intention of most commentaries on the original text. When the text in hand is a translation, certain problems arise that the Greek scholar does not face. Whereas notes on historical, archaeological, and mythological points can be treated in substantially the same manner for both Greek text and English translation, in matters of style the commentator must determine how much he will say about Homer's Greek and about the differences between the English and the original. To take but one example from the present translation: for good poetic reasons Fitzgerald has not tried to make a word-for-word version, and in translating the numerous repetitions known as noun-epithet formulae he has occasionally varied his phrasing in order to suggest nuance and emphasis, and in some cases he has not translated them at all. I have wanted to give the reader as secure an understanding of the original Greek style as possible. It has not seemed worthwhile, however, to belabor the necessary difference between the Greek and the English, and so in a sense the reader may occasionally feel that the twin goals of efficiency and understanding are at odds. In making the introduction and notes I have assumed the reader will want to

know about Homer's world and art, even when that understanding can be had only through a discussion of matter and
manner not immediately before him in the translation.

I have organized this guide along traditional lines, save that
the pagination on the left of each page refers not to lines in
the *Iliad* but to the page numbers in Fitzgerald's translation.
Where lexical or stylistic points are discussed, the lines of the
Greek text are usually identified. Each note begins with a
brief quotation from the translation. Such commentaries are
necessarily selective, both in the kinds of topics discussed and
in the passages used to exemplify the topics. The emphasis of
this volume falls on style, theme, and the interpretation of intellectual and psychological peculiarities. It is hoped that the
reader will consult the index when questions arise which are
not addressed at a specific point in the commentary. Topics
such as "fate" "divine intervention," "foreshadowing," and
the meaning and use of specific epithets cannot be discussed
on every page.

Bibliography has been a problem. Most scholarship assumes
a knowledge of Greek, and much of it is in foreign languages.
I have assumed that the reader of this guide is unlikely to
have either Greek or German. Only in cases where I felt an
immediate personal debt have specialized or foreign-language
studies been cited. Most of the items cited in the bibliography
will be available to the reader in English. Constant use has
been made of the commentaries of Willcock, Leaf, Ameis
and Hentze, and of Erbse's new edition of the scholia. Whatever the reader may find of value in my notes will in most
cases be the product of generations of Homeric scholarship.

Finally, my thanks to friends and colleagues who have
contributed to the preparation of this volume. Robert Fitzgerald encouraged me from the beginning, read early drafts
which might well have been suppressed, and suggested a number of improvements in style and content which I have happily and tacitly accepted. His generosity and kindness have
made the writing easier and more rapid. At various stages
Gene Bushala, Tom Van Nortwick, Peter Rose, and Cedric
Whitman offered useful suggestions and saved me from several errors. I owe them a special debt, not least because on a
number of critical issues I have perversely disagreed with
them. My wife has saved the reader from numerous obscuri-

ties I had tried to perpetrate. This work was begun during a year in which I held a fellowship from the National Endowment for the Humanities; had it not been for that grant, completion of this project would have been much postponed. During my nine years on the faculty of Allegheny College I have frequently benefited from research and travel grants, the most recent of which enabled me to complete the revision of this work. My sincere thanks to President Lawrence L. Pelletier and to the Faculty Development Committee.

INTRODUCTION

Anger be now your song, immortal one,
Akhilleus' anger, doomed and ruinous,
that caused the Akhaians loss on bitter loss
and crowded brave souls into the undergloom,
leaving so many dead men—carrion
for dogs and birds; and the will of Zeus was done.

When Homer sang these first lines of the *Iliad*, he could assume his auditors knew of Akhilleus, the son of Pêleus, and
how his quarrel with Agamémnon, king of Mykênai, brought
destruction on the Akhaians before Troy. The story of the
Akhaian expedition against Troy belonged to a rich tradition
of oral poetry which both the singer and his audience had
heard since childhood. They knew of Paris' seduction of
Helen, of Meneláos' desire for revenge, of the partisan role
the Olympian divinities played in the ten years' seige of Troy.
So, without program or other preliminaries, Homer's audience
was ready to hear the latest version.

Not only was the Greek audience familiar with what we
call the myth, the Trojan saga, but they were also accustomed
to the poet's manner of telling the story. They knew his verse
form, the kind of language (traditional, ornate, formulaic) he
used, the peoples, places, and customs which he mentioned in
passing. In short, Homer's *Iliad* was a very public sort of
poem, if by public we may mean accessible, familiar, utilizing
the language and custom of his own people.

But that tradition is alien to us: its language is seldom studied, its religion and culture have become "pagan," its myths
have become synonyms for fictions, its history is more remote
and obscure than that of the Christian Dark Ages. In this introduction the nature of Greek oral epic is particularly

stressed; in the remainder of the *Guide* more emphasis is
placed on the story, its characters and themes, and on the culture attested by the poem. At the outset it was necessary to
sketch the Trojan saga, which throughout the *Iliad* and *Odyssey* is assumed to be well known.[1]

The Trojan Saga

The *Iliad* and *Odyssey* describe events relatively late in this
saga. The *Odyssey* treats the homecoming of Odysseus, who
has been away from his native Ithaca for twenty years. Like
the *Iliad*, it constantly looks back on events of the war and
the expedition's effect on the lives of the warriors and those
who remained at home. The action of the *Iliad* takes place
during the last year of the war and assumes that we are familiar with earlier episodes at Troy and prior to the Akhaian arrival. In a sense the plot of the *Iliad* turns on a revenge motif.
This same point applies to the entire expedition, which has its
impetus from Meneláos' desire to reclaim his wife Helen and
to make the Trojans pay for the insult to his honor (see his
speech on p. 318). The Olympian divinities take a personal
interest in the action of both poems, and to understand how
their initial involvement came about we must begin with still
earlier events.

At the marriage of the goddess Thetis (the mother of
Akhilleus) and the hero Pêleus all the divinities were present
except the goddess Strife. True to her name, she appeared at
the door of the wedding hall and threw an apple inscribed
"for the fairest" among the goddesses. They all claimed it.
The finalists, Hêra, Athêna, and Aphrodítê, called upon Paris,
a Trojan prince, to decide the issue. Later allegorists tell how
each tried to bribe Paris, Hêra with power, Athêna with victory in war, Aphrodítê with a beautiful woman. Paris judged
for Aphrodítê, who returned the favor by "giving" him the
most beautiful woman in the world, Helen, daughter of Zeus
and Leda.

But Helen was married, and the gift had to be taken, or at
least seduced. All Greece had been courting Helen, and to
avoid dispute her suitors had sworn to honor Helen's choice
and to protect her marriage. Why she chose Meneláos,

younger brother of Agamémnon, is not obvious from
Homer's description, although Homer presents him sympathetically. Paris journeyed to Sparta and was received with
hospitality in Meneláos' home. Instead of respecting the laws
of guest-friendship, however, he carried off Helen (Homer
offers ambiguous, perhaps even contradictory, evidence on the
question of Helen's willingness). They returned to Troy, and
the Greeks who had sued for Helen's hand were summoned
to avenge the wrong done to Meneláos.

Ten years were required to assemble the armada Homer
describes in Book II of the *Iliad*. Many of the captains, like
Odysseus who feigned madness, were not eager to take up
Meneláos' cause, and a hint of their indifference may be seen
in Akhilleus'

> As for myself, when I came here to fight,
> I had no quarrel with Troy or Trojan spearmen:
> they never stole my cattle or my horses,

> I 152–54 (p. 16)

From the outset the omens, recalled by Odysseus in Book
II, indicated a long siege, and a variety of incidents attended
the sailing and the nine years of fighting prior to the beginning of the *Iliad*. Homer mentions the death of Prôtesílaos,
the first Akhaian to land at Troy, and the abandonment of
the archer Philoktêtês on the island of Lemnos. Priam, king
of Troy, had summoned allies from Asia and Europe. The
war went slowly, for while the Trojans were able to withstand
the siege, they could not repel the stronger Akhaian army.
Finally, in the tenth and last year of the war, Akhilleus
slays Hektor, the foremost Trojan warrior. The duel between
Hektor and Akhilleus is the climax of the *Iliad*.

Though Akhilleus himself is subsequently slain by Apollo
and Paris, Troy without Hektor is doomed. In the *Odyssey* we
hear of the famous Trojan horse: what force of arms could
not accomplish in ten years the guile of Odysseus achieved in
a single night. The Trojans, thinking the Akhaians had aban-
doned the field, brought into their city a monumental horse,
which they believed had been left by the invaders as a sacred

offering. It was filled with Akhaian warriors who during the
night opened the gates to the army and sacked the city
(Troy's last night is told vividly and with Trojan bias in the
Aeneid, Book II). In destroying the city and killing most of
its inhabitants the Akhaians offended the gods, specifically
Athêna, whose temple they desecrated. So the goddess who
had supported their cause throughout the campaign turned
against them with equal vehemence. The departing fleet was
struck by a storm; the worst offender, Aías, son of Oïleus,
died along with many others. For the survivors the homecoming was neither happy nor easy.

These homecomings (*nostoi* in Greek) were the subjects of
several poems, of which the *Odyssey* alone survives. In
Odyssey Book IV Meneláos tells of his own adventures home-
ward and how he arrived too late to help his brother Agamémnon, who had been murdered by his cousin Aigisthos.
Helen appears in the same episode, entertaining Telémakhos
and telling stories of Odysseus' guile and her reluctant part in
the whole affair.

Internal evidence, such as the songs of Phêmios and Demódokos in the *Odyssey* and the allusions in the *Iliad,* implies a
variety of stories pertaining to the Trojan saga. External evidence corroborates this inference. Later antiquity knew a
complete cycle of poems telling the story of Troy from the
marriage of Pêleus and Thetis through the returns of the heroes. These poems presented a chronological account and
were titled *Cypria, Iliad, Aethiopis, Little Iliad, Iliu Persis*
(the *Sack of Ilium*), *Nostoi* (the *Returns*), *Odyssey,* and
Telegonia.[2] Although modern scholars generally agree that
the written and transcribed forms of most of these poems
postdate the *Iliad* and the *Odyssey,* their content seems certainly to have been known to Homer. It has been argued
that scenes from one or another of these poems, or some
version of them, influenced Homer's narrative in the *Iliad.*
The death of Akhilleus in the *Aethiopis,* e.g., may have been
on Homer's mind when he described the mourning for
Patróklos. Little more than brief summaries of their plots
has survived, but the information to be had from later my-
thographers (e.g., the *Library* of Apollodorus) and other
sources suggests the wealth of anecdote and legend available
to Homer.

The Iliad

The scene is the plain before Troy, where for nine years the Akhaians have unsuccessfully besieged the city. A raid on outlying towns has produced booty and captives, among whom is Khrysêis, daughter of a priest of Apollo. Her father, Khrysês, comes to the Akhaian camp offering ransom for his daughter, who has been given to Agamémnon, king of Mykênai and overlord of the army. When his appeal is rejected by Agamémnon, Khrysês prays to Apollo for help, and the god responds by striking the army with a plaque. During an assembly Agamémnon agrees to return the girl, but he also demands compensation from the army. Akhilleus, the foremost warrior among the Akhaians, resists the king's demands. They quarrel, and each feels that he has been publicly insulted by the other. When Agamémnon seizes Akhilleus' prize, the slave Brisêis, the son of Pêleus invokes his mother's aid: he will retire from the fighting while she petitions Zeus to bring honor to her son by defeating the Akhaians and humiliating Agamémnon.

Zeus agrees to Thetis' request and sends a dream to Agamémnon which persuades the king to renew the battle. Books II–VIII describe a variety of scenes drawn from battlefield and city: the units of the two armies are catalogued (II); Meneláos and Paris duel (III); the truce is violated and hostilities renewed (IV); Diomêdês, the young lord of Argos, enjoys great success in battle (V); Hektor visits the city and his family (VI); Aías and Hektor duel (VII); Zeus intervenes to help the Trojans (VIII). Despite some success the Akhaians feel threatened and decide to ask Akhilleus to return to battle. But Agamémnon's apology does not appease his resentment, and the emissaries return frustrated (IX). When the fight is renewed the next day, Agamémnon, Odysseus, and Diomêdês are wounded. Zeus gives Hektor glory for a day, and he threatens to burn the Akhaian ships.

The petition of his friends in IX did affect Akhilleus, and now he sends his friend Patróklos to inquire after the wounded Makháôn. Patróklos is urged by Nestor to appeal once again to Akhilleus, or to come to the aid of the Akhaians himself. In Book XVI Patróklos wins Akhilleus' reluctant consent to go to the aid of the retreating army. Though warned not to pursue the Trojans too far, Patróklos is carried away by his success and continues the fight to the gates of Troy, where Apollo, Euphorbos, and Hektor bring him down. Akhilleus realizes his anger and pride have cost him his dearest comrade.

Akhilleus is warned by Thetis that to kill Hektor, whose success has emboldened him to remain on the field, is to ensure Akhilleus' own death. But Akhilleus' anger against Agamémnon has turned on the killer of Patróklos. Revenge is more important than living. Various incidents precede this duel: Hêphaistos makes new armor for him (Patróklos had worn his); in an assembly he and Agamémnon are formally reconciled; and after driving the Trojans in flight Akhilleus engages the river god Skamánder in a great battle that for some readers has symbolized the fate of Troy. The climax of this section of the poem is reached in XXII when Akhilleus kills Hektor in a duel before the walls of Troy.

But the poem does not end with the death of Hektor. In XXIII Akhilleus continues to mourn his companion, performs the funeral rites, and celebrates games in his honor. All the while the corpse of Hektor has lain outside Akhilleus' tent, desecrated by the Akhaians but protected by the gods. Finally the gods assemble in Book XXIV and Zeus accedes to Apollo's appeal for the return of Hektor's body to his people. Akhilleus agrees to this decision, and Priam, father of Hektor, comes by night to his tent to claim the body. Seeing the pitiful old man, Akhilleus' anger is placated. He gives the body of his enemy to Priam and offers a truce in order that a proper funeral may be arranged for Hektor.

The Odyssey

The *Odyssey* is the only other Greek epic of the archaic era extant. Odysseus, the king of Ithaca, survives the war and returns home. But the gods have not been gracious, for after ten years at Troy his homecoming has been delayed another ten. His wife Penélopê is harassed by suitors and his son Telémakhos, who is just twenty, cannot claim his birthright against their depredations. Athêna takes a hand by encouraging Telémakhos to travel to Pylos and Sparta in quest of news of his father. It is not until Book V that we meet Odysseus, shipwrecked now for seven years on the island of the enchantress Kalypso. On Athêna's plea, Hermes is sent by Zeus to arrange his release by Kalypso. Once again he en- counters trouble at sea (the god Poseidon has sworn to make his journey late and painful) until he is thrown up on the shores of Skheria, the land of the Phaiakians. Here he is re- ceived hospitably and promised a safe transport to Ithaca. During his stay with the Phaiakians he tells the story of his adventures (Books IX–XII). He has seen fabulous lands, monsters, and witches: he is the cunning survivor.

Odysseus does not arrive home till halfway through the poem. Now the problem is to reassert his authority, avenge himself on the suitors, and reunite himself with wife and fam- ily. He tests friend and foe, is recognized by his family and members of the household, and finally takes his revenge on the suitors by killing them all.

The two epics differ in so many respects, in theme, tone, and use of the divinities, for example, that many readers have not been confident they are by the same poet. The folklore of the *Odyssey* belongs to a world of fantasy largely alien to the *Iliad;* some readers feel the character of Odysseus is radically transformed from that of the earlier poem; technical studies have pointed to significant differences in diction and scenic organization. During the classical period Homer was univer- sally acepted as the author of both epics as well as several shorter poems, but beginning with Alexandrian scholarship of the third century separatists have argued for two poets. This controversy obviously implies more than a little ignorance about the poet and the time and place of composition.

Homer and History

Who was Homer? Where and when did he live? How did these poems come into being in an age for which the evidence of literacy is so slight? These questions sum up what is tradi- tionally known as the "Homeric question." There are no definitive answers, nor are there likely to be. But the obscu- rity surrounding author, place, and time has stimulated research, which has at least clarified the issues and done much to illuminate the study of the *Iliad*.[3]

Of Homer the Greeks knew little. He was traditionally said to be a blind bard, a native of Ionia, and a contemporary of the Boiotian poet Hesiod. Many places claimed him, none with more authority than Chios; Semonides of Amorgos (late seventh century) wrote:

> the man of Chios said one excellent thing:
> "Very like leaves upon this earth are the generations
> of men."

The line is from *Iliad* VI, 146 (p. 146). But Chios' claim was not uncontested; numerous cities and islands of the eastern Aegean wanted Homer. Tradition and the predominant Ionic dialect of the poems both point to an Ionian poet, yet where so many places are in contention it is hard to believe anyone had tangible evidence. If Homer was an itinerant bard, he may in fact have lived in many Ionian towns. Ionia was the center of Greek culture in the eighth and seventh centuries, and the demand for a first-class artist might have made a constant traveler of the poet.

The poems reveal very little about the poet. He says nothing in his own person and most comments on character and events appear to be traditional commonplaces. Some commentators have detected the poet's personal judgment, e.g., at XXIII 176:

> but as for the noble sons of Troy, all twelve
> he put to the sword, as he willed their evil hour.

> (p. 541)

This can be construed as condemning the sacrifice of the Trojan youth, yet comparison with other passages shows that the adjective ("evil") does not pass ethical judgment and means only that he intended what would be harmful to them. Other scholars have thought the similes and certain characters, e.g., Hektor and Patróklos, show signs of a sensibility distinct from the rest of the poem. Most of these judgments seem subjective, more the result of contrasts in narrative and dramatic style than the purposeful subjective coloring we find in poets such as Vergil and Ovid.

For various reasons it seems unlikely that Homer should be dated as late as the seventh century. If he had been a contemporary of the poets Archilochus and Callinus, who wrote during the first half of the seventh century, we might expect to know more about him, either from them or their contemporaries. Because of archaeological and linguistic evidence, modern scholars usually assign the epics to the second half of the eighth century. Yet the nature of oral, traditional poetry makes the use of any particular piece of evidence of uncertain value, as we shall see in the following discussion.

History and the Iliad

Though the poet tells us little concerning his own life, the poem does not present a completely fictional world, fabulous in the sense that Books IX–XII of the *Odyssey* obviously are. On the contrary, the poem is realistic and claims to be historical. We find references to small towns and local cultural institutions that substantiate this historical realism. For the historian two aspects of the poem stand out: 1) it is written in a predominantly Ionic dialect and contains scattered allusions to cultural phenomena (e.g., the use of iron, temples for gods, Ionic cults, hoplite tactics in war) which clearly indicate it was composed well after the beginning of the Greek migration to the islands and central coast of Asia Minor (c. 1050 for the earliest migrations); 2) the poem celebrates a culture in which bronze is the principal metal used for shields, swords, and various other tools and implements. Such a culture existed in Greece prior to the so-called Dark Ages (c. 1100–800) and terminated with the invasion and destruction of its major sites (Mykênai, Pylos, Thebes) in the course of the twelfth century. The citadel at Mykênai, first excavated by Heinrich Schliemann, was truly the imposing center of power that the *Iliad* implies. There was a Troy, which modern archaeology (Schliemann made the initial dig; the University of Cincinnati re-examined the site completely) has shown to have been destroyed by fire, not too long before the destruction of the Greek Bronze Age citadels (Troy VIIa designates the city usually associated with the Akhaian expedition). Most ancient Greeks believed in the historical verac-

ity of the Homeric poems; to some extent modern archaeology has corroborated this belief.[4]

Since the poet Hesiod, whom the Greeks thought Homer's
contemporary, this ancient time, when the heroes fought
around the walls of Thebes and Troy, has been called the heroic age.[5] In his *Works and Days* Hesiod lists five ages of
man, four of which are named for metals. Hesiod seems to
have interpolated a heroic age, as if he thought of it as an actual historical epoch for which he had to account, even
though it did not conform perfectly with his allegory. Many
scholars have had problems like Hesiod's: they are inclined to
view the society depicted in the epics as historical, but finding
Homer's model has proven an elusive task. Since it cannot be
denied that to some degree Homer's picture is composite,
claims for the influence of the Mycenaean period, the Dark
Ages, and later Ionia are relative.

Scholars who have argued for the influence of Mycenaean
culture can adduce a few artifacts described by Homer, the
predominant use of bronze for weapons, and some geographical and linguistic evidence in support of their case. But
they must contend with apparent discrepancies in the social
organization of the Homeric and Mycenaean cultures. Most
of our evidence for Mycenaean society derives from the Linear B tablets, the translation of which still presents many
problems. These tablets, which are especially numerous from
Pylos and Knossos, date from the end of the Bronze Age and
reveal some rather unheroic dimensions in that culture. They
usually comprise inventories, lists of people (tenants and su-
pervisors assigned to various occupations and places), types
of goods, herds, and the like. Though Homeric armor can be
illustrated from Mycenaean graves and art, the bureaucratic
regime suggested by the tablets would seem to have slight
affinity with the world of Akhilleus and Odysseus. Homer
knows nothing of the economic and social organization these
tablets imply. On the other hand, the wealth and political
power exhibited by the princes of the *Iliad* do not seem com-
patible with the more restricted economic and political hori-
zons of the post-Mycenaean period.[6]

The list of problems could be extended: the army before
Troy cremates its dead, whereas the Mycenaeans practiced
inhumation; Aías carries a large, tower shield of a type seen

in Mycenaean paintings, but Akhilleus' shield is round, like those of the Ionian period; Homer's warriors use spears of two types, thrusting and throwing, but actual usage is often confused; the chariot in the *Iliad* has the limited function of transporting the warriors to the field of battle, but it seems unlikely that this would have been the only historical use of the chariot in Mycenaean times (the Linear B inventories confirm their use). Finally there is the problem of political geography. It has been claimed that the catalogue of ships in Book II reflects Mycenaean political power. Certainly there are discrepancies between the catalogue and the rest of the *Iliad*, where, e.g., Boiotians, prominent and powerful in the catalogue, are relatively inconspicuous. In general the *Iliad* focuses on individuals whereas the catalogue is concerned primarily with the power that comes from numbers of men and ships. We could hardly have anticipated the role of Aías from the twelve ships and two lines granted him in the catalogue.[7]

It should be emphasized that many of these problems are historical and not literary. From a literary perspective there is no reason that all shields should have the same shape, nor is there anything intrinsically contradictory in Homeric cremation and burial. Homer is free to describe the function of the chariots as he sees fit. Yet the poems clearly claim a realistic and historical perspective, and it is not altogether quibbling to wonder how huge spears may be so easily thrown or why a warrior carries two spears but uses only one. The world described in the *Iliad* refers to peoples and places that did exist; if Homer's information about history is sometimes inconsistent, it is not unreasonable to ask how such inconsistencies entered the poem.

The Composition of the Epics

The Linear B tablets reveal a literate culture keeping detailed records of its business activities, yet Homer hardly seems to know of writing. The single reference to writing in the epics tells how Bellérophontês carried his own death warrant. Some scholars have doubted that Homer himself understood exactly what Bellérophontês brought to Lykia:

> a deadly cipher,
> magical marks Proitos engraved and hid
> in folded tablets.

> VI 168f. (p. 147)

Whether or not the poet is indicating a written message, the evidence for literacy in the eighth century is limited to a few inscriptions incised, or more rarely painted, on pottery. So far as we know, the art of writing was not generally known, and the idea that a poem of almost sixteen thousand lines should have been written in a virtually illiterate period is difficult to accept.

All archaeological evidence suggests that literacy disappeared from Greece with the fall of the Mycenaean states. When writing reappears in the eighth century, a new alphabet, entirely different from the Linear B script, is used. This alphabet, from which classical Greek is derived, is Phoenician in origin. Whether it arrived in Greece as early as the ninth century is debatable, and most authorities prefer the eighth century. If this picture is accurate, Homer's knowledge of Mycenaean Greece must have survived orally.[8]

It is generally agreed that the Greek epic originated in an oral tradition that probably dated back at least to the late Bronze Age. Such a tradition would account for the existence in the *Iliad* of a cultural and historical residue from a time and place an Ionian poet never knew. As we know from studies of modern oral poetry in Yugoslavia and Greece, such traditions are naturally conservative, passing on language, descriptions, and themes from generation to generation. This tradition need not have been disturbed by the fall of the Mycenaean states where it originally flourished, and since its technique and mode of composition were oral and mnemonic, its survival was not contingent upon written transcription.[9]

We have in the eighth book of the *Odyssey* a glimpse of the oral poet at work. Odysseus is feasting with the Phaiakians and sends the herald with a choice cut of meat as a gift for the singer Demódokos. Earlier in the day Demódokos had, unbidden, sung

                                                              a song
of heroes whose great fame rang under heaven:
the clash between Odysseus and Akhilleus,
how one time they contended at the godfeast
raging. . . .

> *Odyssey* VIII, 73–77
> (Fitzgerald's translation, p. 127)

Now Odysseus, who has not yet revealed his identity to his
hosts, calls for a song:

"Demódokos, accept my utmost praise.
The Muse, daughter of Zeus in radiance,
or else Apollo gave you skill to shape
with such great style your songs of the Akhaians—
their hard lot, how they fought and suffered war.
You shared it, one would say, or heard it all.
Now shift your theme, and sing that wooden horse
Epeios built, inspired by Athena—
the ambuscade Odysseus filled with fighters
and sent to take the inner town of Troy.
Sing only this for me, sing me this well,
and I shall say at once before the world
the grace of heaven has given us a song."

> *Odyssey* VIII, 487–98
> (Fitzgerald, p. 139f.)

He is a court poet, singing the deeds of famous men. Sometimes he selects the song himself, but he is also on call. A
harp or lyre accompanies his song, which has the vividness of
an eyewitness' report and moves the audience to tears. The
singer is taught, or inspired, by the gods. From his story
well told he may gain a reputation for divine inspiration.

Demódokos is blind; he has not witnessed the events he
sings, and he probably never traveled from the isolated home
of the Phaiakians. Like Homer he heard songs of famous
deeds and repeated them on festive occasions. No doubt the

vividness which causes Odysseus to weep from recollection came from more than a mere rehearsal of events. The bard dramatized his song, brought it to life, and in so doing he created it anew. When we try to assess the nature and methods of Homer's art, it is necessary to remember that we have only the text, not the performance. A study of that text can tell us much about the language, style, and forms of Greek oral poetry, but it cannot give us the original or final form of our poem. It is always well to return to Demódokos for a glimpse of the living art. We should also remember Telémakhos' response to his mother's criticism of the Ithacan bard Phêmios:

> Men like best
> a song that rings like morning on the ear.
>
> *Odyssey* I, 351f.
> (Fitzgerald, p. 12)

Men like the old songs, but the new one, whatever its theme, charms them too. Old and new constantly merged and interacted in the Greek tradition. The analysis of our texts will reveal something of this process.

Language

If historical problems did not urge the hypothesis that the epics belonged to an oral tradition, their mixed dialect and linguistic peculiarities would compel us to the same conclusion. The language of the *Iliad* and *Odyssey* was never spoken colloquially in the Greek world; it is an artificial, poetic language composed primarily of a mixture of the Aeolic and Ionic dialects. But this poetic speech is not a rough composite of now one dialect, now another, for the poems embody such a thorough blend of various dialectical elements that no attempt to separate them has been successful. Words of a certain Ionic origin use suffixes indigenous to the Aeolic dialect; Aeolic forms have been influenced and reshaped from Ionic models; words and case forms survive from Mycenaean Greek. Because Ionic predominates, it is generally assumed that it was the language of the later stages of oral poetry. But

Aeolic (north Greek) and Arcado-Cypriot (Mycenaean Greek) forms are so deeply imbedded that they can only be accounted for by the supposition that these dialects played an integral role in the evolution of the poetic speech.

A few examples will illustrate this dialectical mix: the poem retains both *pros* and *poti*, which are metrical variants of the same preposition (meaning "toward"); different suffixes are attached to the same stem, e.g., both Pêlêiadao ($--\cup\cup-\cup$) and Pêlêiadeô ($--\cup\cup-$) for "the son of Pêleus"; a variety of suffixes are used to denote the infinitive: *-menai*, *-men* (both Aeolic), and *-nai* (Attic-Ionic); the genitive of the second person singular of the personal pronoun may be spelled *seo*, *seu*, *sethen*, or *teoio*. Such variations show both the contribution of different dialects and phonetic change within dialects over a period of several generations. Within the poetic language itself these dialectical variations interacted to produce artificial forms never used colloquially.

Linguistic differences enable us to distinguish earlier and later strata in the epic diction. For example, when the obsolete digamma—a semi-vowel like "w" no longer written in classical Greek—must be recognized as having influenced the meter, whether to make a short syllable long by position or to avoid hiatus, we can be fairly sure an older word or phrase is present; when, on the other hand, the movable *nu* of later Ionic-Attic is necessarily involved in the meter, we can infer a later stage of the epic diction. Similarly, contraction of vowels was a later phenomenon; uncontracted forms (e.g., genitive -oo for -ou) can be restored in some lines for metrical advantage. There is, however, evidence in the poems of conscious archaizing, so that it is not always possible to discriminate between the authentically old and those words and phrases modeled on the old. And it should always be remembered that Homer's language is such a thorough fusion of linguistic elements that we can never label any extended passage as early or late on the basis of a uniform linguistic texture.

Style and Formula

It is the style of the *Iliad* that most clearly reveals its origins in an oral tradition. Even before Milman Parry's decisive

analyses of Homeric formulae many scholars had perceived
that the high incidence of repeated lines and phrases in
Homeric epic implied a different compositional technique
than is found in the epics of later, literate ages. About one
third of the lines of the *Iliad* are either repeated in their en-
tirety or contain repeated phrases. Repeated phrases usually
occur in exactly the same metrical position. These formulae
often contain artificial linguistic forms and words otherwise
unused in the epics. Parry's studies, though limited to noun-
epithet phrases such as "the Lord Marshal Agamémnon,"
showed that it is not these phrases alone but the *scope* and
economy of the system within which they are found that reveal Homeric poetry to be from an oral tradition. Until
Homer's formulae have been analyzed according to metrical
function, one might assume that "Lord Marshal," "ruler of
the great plain," and "the high commander" are either variations of particular contextual significance or randomly chosen
ornamental epithets. But in fact, these phrases, like the vast
majority of repeated word groups, are never metrically redundant of one another: though all these formulae customarily
stand at the end of the line, none of the three has the same
metrical shape or length as the others. So we may say that the
economy of a formulaic system is seen in the limited number
of phrases present and in the fact that there is no metrical
redundance; the *scope* is seen in the variety of metrical patterns offered.[10]

To understand the function of the formula is is necessary to
know some of the rules governing Homer's verse form, the
dactylic hexameter. This is a quantitative verse, scanned in
long and short syllables:

$$- \cup \cup - \cup \cup - \cup \cup - \cup \cup - \cup \cup - -$$

The spondee $(- -)$ is freely substituted for the dactyl
$(- \cup \cup)$ in the first four feet of the line; the last two
feet almost invariably have the rhythm $- \cup \cup - -$. Certain metrical shapes are excluded from this meter, for example, the cretic $(- \cup -)$ and the tribrach
$(\cup \cup \cup)$. These are not uncommon patterns in Greek
words, and the poet often resorts to artificial metrical length-
ening to fit some words to his meter. Since the primary accent
in Greek depended on a pitch inflection rather than stress, a
quantitative verse does not seem the easiest to accommodate

to the natural rhythm of the language. Yet it is obvious that the hexameter had a long history prior to its use in the Homeric epics: rules governing caesura are firmly established and the line follows a fairly rigorous colometric structure. Thus a word will terminate after the first long syllable or the first short of the third foot, thereby ensuring a caesura between the two halves of the line. The pronounced reassertion of the dactylic rhythm in the fifth foot, after the free substitution of the spondee in the first four feet, is still another indication of metrical rigor. Finally there is the phenomenon of metrical fixity: words of a specific metrical shape, even monosyllables, tend to appear in preferred positions. This localization of metrical word types implies a long history of rhythmic experimentation and refinement; it is surely also connected with the emergence of the formula as the basic element in Homeric verse.

The formulae connected with the name "Agamémnon" will illustrate the interaction of meter and patterns of phrasing. His name occurs eighty-nine times in the *Iliad* as the subject of a sentence. In all but three cases it occurs at the end of the line: Ágamémnōn (localization of word type). Three adjectives or adjectival phrases are commonly used to modify his name in the nominative case:

$$- \; \cup\cup - \cdot - \cdot \; kre\hat{i}\bar{o}n \; \underset{\smile\smile}{Agamemn\bar{o}n} \quad \text{(28 times)}$$
$$\ldots Atreid\bar{e}s \; eurukrei\hat{o}n \; \underset{\smile\smile}{Agamemn\bar{o}n} \quad \text{(10 times)}$$
$$\ldots \acute{a}nax \; andr\bar{o}n \; Agamemn\bar{o}n \quad \text{(30 times)}$$

These are translated by Fitzgerald "Lord Marshal," "the son of Atreus, ruler of the great plain," and "the high commander" (or "the lord marshal"). That the metrical requirements determined by the first half of the line, rather than a special meaning, fix the choice of phrase is shown by the slight variation between *kreiôn* ("ruling") and *eurukreiôn* ("broad-ruling"). Though Homer uses distinctive (characterizing a single person) and particular (chosen for a specific situation) epithets, generic epithets such as *kreiôn* are half again as numerous as distinctive epithets and are easily identified by their use with other nouns of the same metrical type: *kreiôn Agapênôr* (II 609), *kreiôn Helikáôn* (III 123), *kreiôn Elephênôr* (IV 463), etc., all scanned — — ∪ ∪ — — ,and all in the final position.

Different metrical requirements develop, however, when "Agamémnon" is declined into the genitive or dative case: *Agamémnonos* (genitive: "of Agamémnon," scanned ∪∪ − ∪∪·) and *Agamemnoni* (dative: "to Agamémnon," scanned ∪∪ − ∪∪). Since the last syllable in the hexameter is always considered long (the natural pause at the end of each line may account for this), the name at the end of the line would now have the practical scansion ∪∪ − ∪· − , which is impossible in the hexameter. Consequently "Agamémnon" can no longer be used at the end of the line, because the next to the last syllable cannot be short. Two phrases, *Agamemnonos Atreidao* (∪∪ − ∪∪ − ∪∪ − ∪ , which can be used at the end of the line) and *Atreideô Agamemnonos* (− ∪∪ − ∪∪ − ∪·∪ , used internally) appear. They are identical in meaning ("Agamémnon, son of Atreus") but metrically different. The poet obtains this metrical variety by inverting the name and its patronymic and by taking advantage of two different genitive suffixes (*-ao* and *-eô*, both represented in English by "of"), which differ only in their metrical scansion. *Kreiôn* disappears: declined before *Agamemnonos* it would become kreiontos and yield − − ∪∪∪ − ∪∪ ;   declined   after   it ∪∪ − ∪ − − − ∪ . The former presents an impossible succession of three short syllables; the latter contains a cretic.

In the dative case "son of Atreus" is also found, but the poet was able to use two new phrases:

... *Agamemnoni diô*   ("brilliant"; 2 times)
... *Agamemnoni poimeni laôn* ("marshal of the army"; 6
                                                      times)

These phrases could not be given the genitive form because the consonant (in *diô* and *poimeni*) following the last syllable of *Agamemnonos* would make that syllable long, thus creating the scansion: − ∪ − . Metrical coercion is apparent at every turn: *poimeni laôn* and the accusative *poimena laôn* (same scansion − ∪∪ − −) occur forty-four times, always at the end of the line; but no one is ever *poimên laôn* (nominative: − − − −): the phrase then consists of two spondees, acceptable in itself, but not for the last two feet of the line, where the fifth foot is regularly a dacyl.[11]

These noun-adjective formulae are frequently combined with verbal formulae at the beginning of the line. For example, the poet has a pattern consisting of personal pronoun, participle ("answering"), and finite verb which he uses thirty-six times to begin lines. The second half of the line is completed by noun-adjective phrases denoting Akhilleus, Agamémnon, Zeus, Diomêdês, Priam, and Odysseus.

> *ton d'apameibomenos prosephê podas ôkus* (12 times)
>   *Akhilleus*
> ("answering him the runner Akilleus said")
>
> *ton d'apameibomenos prosephê kreiôn* (5 times)
>   *Agamemnôn*
>
> *ton d'apameibomenos prosephê* (8 times)
>   *nephelêgereta Zeus*
>
> *ton d'apameibomenos prosephê polumêtis* (5 times)
>   *Odysseus*

Because the personal pronoun can be varied without metrical change to the feminine (*ton* to *tên*), and the participle can also be changed to the feminine (*apameibomenos* to *apameibomenê*), the formula has the flexibility naturally extended by an inflected language. This answering formula is part of a larger system in which the metrical and syntactical pattern remains constant while the semantic content varies:

> *ton d' apameibomenos prosephê* ("answering him he [she] spoke . . .")
>
> *tên de meg' okhthêsas prosephê* ("angered he addressed her . . .")
>
> *tên d' epimeidêsas prosephê* ("smiling at her he addressed . . .")
>
> *agkhou d' istamenê prosephê* ("standing near she addressed . . .")

The pattern is evident: pronoun, connective (*d'* or *de*), participle (in the second example an adverb supplements the participle), and the finite verb (*prosephê*), which is invariably in the same metrical position. In the last example an adverb (*agkhou*) is substituted for the pronoun and the participle is correspondingly shorter, as it is in the second example. Yet another variant ("leaping up with his spear he spoke") substitutes a noun for the initial adverb. There are about one hundred examples of this pattern in the *Iliad* alone.

The preceding verbal formulae are useful for noun-epithet phrases scanned ∪ ∪ – ∪ ∪ – – . They will not do, however, if the poet wants *anax andrôn Agamemnôn* to conclude his line. In this case he has *ton d' êmeibet' epeita* ("then he answered him"). This latter formulae is more concise but does not give the poet the opportunity to indicate tone or manner, as the participial phrase does. Thus the poet has choices, but once he has used a word in a given phrase, he does not look for new contexts for it. So *êmeibet'* occurs forty-eight times in the *Iliad*, only in this phrase.

The poet is not compelled by versification to make his speech transition in a single-line formula. At I 68ff. he wants to introduce Kalkhas, the next speaker, before giving his actual words:

> Putting the question, down he sat. And Kalkhas,
> Kalkhas Thestórides, came forward, wisest
> by far of all who scanned the flight of birds.

> (p. 13)

Agamémnon has spoken, he sits down, and the next speaker rises to address the assembly: all this is given in a single formulaic line (five times). The name and description of the next speaker are reserved for the following line. Cf. I 101ff.:

> He finished and sat down. The son of Atreus,
> ruler of the great plain, Agamémnon,
> rose, furious.

> (p. 15)

Here the poet could obviously have used the *apameibomenos* formula, but he chose a different locution because he wanted first to indicate Agamémnon's reaction to Kalkhas' speech before giving the actual words. So the poet has choices. Once he selects a particular mode of transition, however, he has ready at hand a formula which he is not inclined to modify. Such formulae greatly expedite composition for a poet who has no text and who is reciting before an audience which expects a continuous narrative. The familiarity of phrasing and technique makes the song easier to follow for the audience, which cannot turn back a page to check its understanding of a line or a speech.

If all the lines in the *Iliad* were composed of such phrases, description of Homer's style would be an easy matter. But there are a great many lines and phrases that are not formulaic in the sense that they are frequently repeated and invariably localized. Consequently "formula" has become a controversial term, so much so that J. B. Hainsworth has noticed eight distinct uses in recent scholarly discussions.[12] Most of these variant definitions are a consequence of the desire to extend the definition in such a way that it will include a larger percentage of the lines and phrases than the strict criterion of verbatim repetition can comprehend. At the same time, while many scholars have attempted to extend the definition of formula, others have sought to show that Homeric style is not so formulaic as is often asserted, and that in any case the poet is certainly not the victim of a purely mechanical compositional technique. The forces at play in these recent discussions merit comment.

In the noun-epithet systems he studied Milman Parry demonstrated a rigorously systematic use of the formula. Though Parry was not primarily concerned with the aesthetic implications of his work, he did not feel that the metrical coercion apparent in the selection of formulae impugned the style of the poems. Originality is not the cornerstone of oral poetry, and "ornamental" was not a dirty word for Parry, who was content to accept the conclusion that Greek oral poetry was stylized and generic. Later scholars, James Notopoulos and Joseph Russo most prominently, have extended the definition of formula to include analogical patterns in phrasing. By stressing the role of syntactical and rhythmic analogy in the creation of new phrases, these scholars have attempted to show that the *Iliad* is more formulaic than is evident from a

mere tabulation of verbatim repetitions. Far from being
troubled by the mechanical aspect of formulaic composition,
this line of study has seen evidence for the poet's creativity
and control of his material in the part played by old formulae
in supplying patterns for new phrases.[18]

If, as Parry argued, most Homeric epithets are ornamental
(i.e., not organic, not designed to characterize a particular
character in a specific context) and generic (capable of application to a variety of characters without regard to context),
then traditional modes of criticism are either invalidated or
severely limited. Homeric style is stripped of much of the
nuance critics have often attributed to it. This view has disturbed many readers, and it may be well to let Milman Parry
speak for himself on this subject:

> In the matter of the generic meaning of the epithet as in
> that of its ornamental meaning, we can conclude that the
> poet was guided in his choice by considerations of versifica-
> tion and in no way by the sense. We now have the alterna-
> tives of believing either that Homer sacrificed his thought
> to the convenience of versification or that he felt an epithet
> used for more than one hero to be applicable to any hero.
> The use of the generic epithet in accordance with its meas-
> ure is quickly demonstrated. *dios* appears in the nominative
> with the names of twelve heroes of which nine are of the
> same metrical value: *Akhilleus, Odysseus, Alastôr, hu-*
> *phorbos, Agênôr, Epeigeus, Epeios, Ekhephrôn, Orestês.*
> The other names are *Alexandros* (thrice), *Menestheus*
> (once), and *Oineus* (once). Against these five usages, we
> find 183 for the nine names with the metre ∪ — —, be-
> ginning with a vowel. *hippota* is yet more rigorously limited
> to names of the same metrical value, being said only of
> *Nestor, Phuleus, Tudeus, Oineus, Pêleus. kreiôn* appears in
> the nominative only with *Agamemnon, Agapênôr, Heli-*
> *kaôn, Eléphênôr, Eumêlos. xanthos* is used only for *Melea-*
> *gros, Radamanthus, Menelaos.* [Parry goes on to empha-
> size that these observations apply to most of the noun-
> epithet formulae he has studied.] Clearly coincidence can-
> not be the explanation of this limitation of the epithet to
> names of a given measure. Homer therefore assigned to his

characters divinity, horsemanship, power, and even blond hair, according to the metrical value of their names, with no regard to their birth, their character, their rank, or their legend: except in so far as these things were common to all heroes.[14]

Parry's contention has not gone undisputed. Some scholars have argued that contextual analysis shows that formulae have specific emotive or semantic content. Thus George Calhoun thought that the frequent formula "he (she) spoke winged words" introduced a speech of heightened emotional intensity. William Whallon has argued that epic themes affected the choice of epithets and that matter and manner evolved together.[15] Generally speaking, arguments against the generic character of the Homeric epithet do not appear to have convinced most scholars. While it cannot be denied that the poet selected theme, character, and plot, and so in a sense controlled the kinds of formulae that he would use, he did not select each formula because of its specific applicability to the immediate situation and character. Akhilleus, then, is "swift" or "noble" at all times, whether he happens to be pursuing Hektor or sitting in his tent, whether he is defending his rights as a warrior or slaying a suppliant. Inevitably some generic epithets seem to us incompatible with a particular character or his actions in a specific situation; this is the sort of risk an oral poet might be expected to run. Far more often, however, the generic and ornamental epithets do not jar, and it would certainly be a mistake to suppose that they constitute mere nonsense filler, sounds filling the line but utterly devoid of sense.

There is in the *Iliad* a remarkable complement to these formulaic phrases, and that is the rare or unique word and phrase. About 25 per cent of the words in Homer's vocabulary occur only once. While many of these words and phrases were almost certainly more familiar to the poet and his audience, they nevertheless give the poem a notable freshness and variety which might not be expected after a study of the noun-epithet formulae. The diction of the similes has attracted special attention in this regard, but more provocative for the whole question of the definition and use of the formula are the rare words used in narrative and dramatic con-

texts. Is the phrase or line that occurs only two or three times
to be put in the same category of generic usage as the *kreiôn*
and *dios* formulae? To illustrate: when Hektor abuses Paris
with

> "You bad-luck charm!
> Paris the great lover, a gallant sight!

> III 39 (p. 68)

the line has a particular appropriateness to character and situation. Hektor uses the line again at XIII 769 (p. 323). Of the
five words in the line three occur only in this formula; one of
these is a pun on Paris' name. The two other words occur in a
familiar phrase (eight times), one which Glaukos turns
against Hektor at XVII 142:

> "Hektor, you are a great man, by the look of you,

> (p. 412)

Obviously, III 39 is not formulaic in the same sense that the
"answering" formula is. It has a limited applicability and is
peculiarly appropriate to the character.

Somewhere between the obviously generic and the unique
phrase is a line like XX 503:

> And Pêleus' son . . .
> staining his powerful arms with mire and blood.

> (p. 489)

This line concludes the book with a powerful image, and in
the notes I have suggested that the imagery associated with
the hands of Akhilleus has been consciously developed by the
poet. Yet the line occurs earlier at XI 169, where it is used of
Agamémnon. Claims for special, organic relevance must be
constantly checked against typical usage.

Discussion of formulae, of types of formulaic phrasing, of
the systems into which noun-epithet phrases and verbal

phrases join, will remain a controversial focal point for Homeric scholarship. Understanding the oral poet's use of these repetitions is central to defining the mode and limits of his control. We do not really know how much is traditional and how much is new in the language of the epics. Comparative studies may yet offer more compelling analogies to the language of Greek epic, and so more specific clues to the nature of Homeric craftsmanship. While it seems well established that Homer tended to think in a stylized, generic, paratactic manner, for which the noun-epithet formulae and their systematic usage are the primary evidence, there is also no doubt of extensive prima-facie evidence in our texts for novel and specifically appropriate language. As yet, efforts to establish a quantitative proportion between these two poles have not produced generally accepted results.

Syntax

Any assessment of Homeric style must begin with the formula. Formulaic composition proceeds by phrase, not by word. Whole-line formulae usually compose a complete thought, though in some cases they provide the subject or object of a verb, or an appositional modifier. In oral poetry the verse-end tends to mark the end of a sense unit, and enjambment (run-over of sense from one line to the next) is less complex than it is among later, literate poets. Clauses are short, so that even those which run over to the next line are soon completed. There is a certain looseness in Homeric syntax, and this is particularly evident in the preference for coordination over syntactical subordination, a phenomenon known as parataxis. Thus Homer prefers "I shall do it; he will follow me" to "I shall do it so that he will follow me."[16]

To illustrate from a brief passage in narrative:

These were the speeches they exchanged. Now Aías	1
could no longer hold: he was dislodged	2
by spear-throws, beaten by the mind of Zeus	3
and Trojan shots. His shining helm rang out	4
around his temples dangerously with hits	5

as his helmplates were struck and struck again;   6
he felt his shoulder galled on the left side   7
hugging the glittering shield—and yet they could not   8
shake it, putting all their weight in throws.   9
In painful gasps his breath came, sweat ran down   10
in rivers off his body everywhere;   11
no rest for him, but trouble upon trouble.   12

XVI 101–11 (p. 380f.)

1) The "Now" is supplied by the translator from the context. 2) The connective, represented by the colon, is the
strongest in the passage, which otherwise uses only a weak
"and" (*de*). 3–4) We may assume that the relation of "the
mind of Zeus" and the "Trojan shots" is *instrumental;* the
poet simply co-ordinates the two. 5) The line adds further
specification from "shots." 6) "As" is used for the Greek
"and" (*de*): further specification from the helmet to the
helmplates. 7–8) A new aspect: the working of the shield
causes his left shoulder to be tired; "and yet" for the Greek
"and . . . not." 9) *Though* they put their weight in throws.
10) The *effect* of their effort on him is now given, after the
details of the attack. In 8 through 10 the Greek changes the
subject (Aías, Trojans, Aías) by changing the verb form,
without expressing the subject in the nominative case. 11)
Because he is short of breath the sweat flows. 12) A variant
(verb for noun) on "In painful gasps his breath came" (10).
The last clause offers an abstract summary of the whole passage.

This is not a difficult passage. To supply connectives may
seem superfluous, but they do illustrate the additive character
of this style. The poet accumulates detail and lets the auditor
infer the logical connectives. He moves back and forth from
the attackers to Aías, building up the scene through a series
of discrete images. There are twelve independent clauses in
these ten lines, more than the average in Homer, but still in-
dicative of the brevity of his sentences.

The negative sentence is common in the *Iliad*. By excluding
certain possibilities negatives indirectly lead to the proper inference. Diomêdês is about to attack Aphrodítê:

                                            —as Diomêdês
moved ahead to attack the Kyprian goddess.
He knew her to be weak, not one of those
divine mistresses of the wars of men—
Athêna, for example, or Enŷô,
raider of cities—therefore he dared assail her

                        V 330–33 (p. 120)

The dashes indicate the digressive character of the observation. "For example" has no counterpart in the Greek, but it accurately reflects the implicit thought. "Weak" strikes the poet as wanting specification: so Aphrodítê is "weak, i.e., neither one of those . . . nor yet Athêna nor Enŷô," which is the Homeric way of saying Aphrodítê does not belong to the same class of divinity to which Athêna and Enŷô belong. Such examples of paratactic apposition occur constantly and in large part explain the length of the poem.

The poet prefers to juxtapose ideas and leave their exact connection, whether, e.g., they are in temporal, causal, instrumental, or adversative sequence, to his auditor. At its most elemental level parataxis is simply a kind of apposition in which the poet modifies a word or phrase by adding a word, phrase, or clause without connective. Often one appositional element calls for yet another, as if the poet were tempted into an infinite regression from his narrative. But a remarkable degree of control can be seen in the parataxis of larger blocks of thought. In more extensive passages in which complementary thoughts or feelings are set against one another, one can see how parataxis is related to the presentation of psychological phenomena. For example, when Paris returns to his house in Troy after the abortive duel with Meneláos, Helen begins her speech by abusing him roundly:

"Home from the war? You should have perished there,
brought down by that strong soldier, once my husband.

She continues in this vein for five and a half lines (III 428–33; p. 82); then suddenly she changes her tone and urges him to remain. The two halves of the speech seem, and in a sense are, contradictory. The paratactic division is Homer's way of displaying Helen's ambivalence toward Paris. (More examples will be found in the index under *parataxis*.)

When parataxis is used on a scenic level, i.e., when scenes or episodes are introduced without any specific recognition of their relationship, the poem may give the impression of a disjointed or fragmentary structure. In older studies of the *Iliad* the student will find extensive discussions concerning the authenticity of various episodes. Nineteenth- and early-twentieth-century criticism viewed many of these apparently irrelevant "digressions" with suspicion. Scholars of the analytical school, assuming the epics evolved from shorter poems into their final, elaborate form, devoted themselves to finding the Homeric in Homer. For these analysts many scenes had no thematic or stylistic affinity with their context, and since they recognized the oral, traditional character of the poems, they concluded that much of the *Iliad* was the product of successive accretions during the process of growth and transmission. Unitarians, those scholars committed to the integrity of the poems and their authorship by a single poet, countered by defending the epics, often with analyses more subtle than convincing. Such controversies are still alive in continental scholarship, but they have generally yielded ground to a critical perspective that recognizes the non-organic compositional technique of Greek epic.[17]

On a scenic level parataxis implies the use of integral juxtaposed scenes with minimal connecting links. In Book VI, e.g., Hektor visits the house of Paris and Helen before going to find his wife Andrómakhê. Both scenes appear to be afterthoughts, since his primary mission in the city is to secure a sacrifice to Athêna. The poet offers little motivation for the first visit (see p. 150) and not much more for the second (p. 153), yet the contrasts between the two couples and between the two men and the two women are effectively highlighted. Helen condemns Paris and her own "harlotry" (VI 356) and invites Hektor to rest; Andrómakhê praises her husband but is anxious for the safety of herself, their child, the city, and Hektor. Rather than ask him to rest, she pleads for a more defensive posture. Without explicit reference these juxtaposed scenes continue the development of thematic lines previously suggested. Hektor faces dilemmas of a moral, civic, and social order. How he reacts to Paris' apathy, to the presence of Helen, whom Meneláos has apparently won back in a fair fight, to his duty to his family and city, and to his own sense of honor as a warrior, all these are present and crucial questions for the plot of the poem. It is Homer's method to dramatize such questions and by their deployment in independent scenes to generate a complex fabric.

Because Homer's transitions are often abrupt and the episodes self-contained, it is an easy matter to excise passages, and analytical criticism did not pass up this opportunity. But once we recognize what B. E. Perry called "the early Greek capacity for seeing things separately," we shall realize that Homeric aesthetics did not demand the kind of organic unity Western art has valued since Plato.[18] The unitarians were hardly less guilty of un-Homeric readings, for they often insisted upon kinds of unity for which the text presents little evidence. It is the very nature of paratactic composition to leave gaps where a more sophisticated sense of closure would modulate the rhythm, whether through the speech of the characters, authorial observation, or scenic description. This technique probably grew out of the conditions of oral recitation, in which the poet needed to keep his mind on the subject immediately before him. In the hands of a skilled poet, however, paratactic composition achieves a different kind of sophistication, one predicated on the balancing of large elements and their thematic integration into a monumental, coherent poem.

Typical Scenes

There is in this paratactic technique an inherent danger of producing a fragmentary, incoherent whole. How does the poet control the larger elements of his story and secure a satisfactory dramatic development? For some time scholars have noticed the recurrent use of "themes" or "typical scenes." Some of these themes are so comprehensive as to include the entire epic: A. B. Lord, e.g., calls "withdrawal and return" a theme common to the *Iliad* and the *Odyssey*. More useful for understanding the oral poet's methods is the comparison of scenes which occur several times in the poem. Scenes of arming, sacrificing, offering a banquet, entering and leaving battle are among numerous types of action for which the poet has habitual forms of procedure. For any given theme there is a usual, and apparently traditional order, a group of formulaic lines and phrases regularly present, and a scheme sufficiently elastic that he can add lines or motifs particularly suited to the context.[19]

The more limited and specific the theme, the more its conformity to regular patterns and formulaic usage is evident. In scenes of arming, e.g., the armor is always put on in the same order (greaves, cuirass, sword, shield, helmet, and spear). Stock formulae describe the arming, but variety may be obtained by noting the appearance of the cuirass or shield, or by adding similes and imagery suggestive of the effect the warrior's appearance will have on friend and foe. In scenes of sacrifice, to take another example, the poet already has a normal order for preparing the animal, cutting up the meat, cooking it, and dining. He always follows the same sequence in these scenes and has a number of whole-line formulae for various stages. He may elaborate the description by adding details concerning the animal, the prayers, and the reaction of the gods. From a nuclear theme, then, the poet elaborates freely. If he desires only the minimal length, he can rely almost exclusively on formulae. If he chooses to elaborate, he can interpolate new elements (similes, biographical details, speeches, etc.). The long stretches of narrative of battle in the *Iliad* provide a wealth of example of both the typical elements in Homeric composition and the variety the poet achieves.

We may illustrate these points with a brief study of the *aristeia,* the Greek term for that period in battle during which a hero gains exceptional distinction. Episodes depicting the *aristeia* vary in length from under a hundred lines to several books. Some, like Hektor's, are ill-defined. Patróklos' *aristeia* is well defined, and included within Hektor's, since Hektor's greatest achievement is the killing of Patróklos. Characteristic features of the *aristeia* include description of the hero's appearance, similes (especially those pertaining to fire, stars, and lions), his arming, a list of enemies killed, an engagement with one or more gods, vaunts, retirement, re-entry, a duel, and the wounding or death of the hero. From this list major items may be excluded or duplicated: Diomêdês engages and wounds two divinities, Aphrodítê and Arês, while Agamémnon in a much shorter *aristeia* (two hundred lines) does not confront a divinity. The arming of the hero may or may not be included: Diomêdês is already armed when Athêna makes him bold; Patróklos borrows the armor of Akhilleus. All these variations serve to characterize the hero and give each *aristeia* a unique relation to the poem. Agamémnon, e.g., is a brutal fighter who gives no quarter. In his *aristeia* at the beginning of Book XI he is given only one speech, and that a brief one in which he denies a suppliant's plea. Diomêdês' *aristeia* (Books V–VI), on the other hand, is both more brilliant in its achievement and more leisurely in its pace.

Careful study of such compositional techniques reveals two complementary facets of Homer's art: the habitual use of standard themes and structures and a flexibility in their application. Bernard Fenik has noticed that in the sequence

1) A throws at B and misses.
2) B strikes A's shield or body armor, but fails to pierce it.
3) A slays B.

"items (1) and (2) are never reversed."[20] There seems no reason for this sequence not being reversible, save that maintaining the order facilitated composition. For all the possible sequences in battlefield duels, only a limited number are actually used. If a duel progresses to the stage at which one warrior throws a boulder, he will be the winner (unless a god intervenes). But of course boulders are not used so often that this habit becomes a cliché. We see another technique for control in ring composition, which has its name from the fact that after a digression or simile the poet returns to a phrase or word used at the beginning of the passage, thus completing the ring. This simple structural device has achieved sophisticated forms in the Homeric speeches, where topics are often organized in concentric patterns (a, b, c, d, c', b', a').

Scenes of arming, entering battle, sacrificing, and dueling are not limited to oral poetry. What distinguishes oral technique is its adherence to regular patterns and its peculiar reliance on formulaic phrases and lines. Once again, *economy* is evident in the poet's use of a regular sequence; *scope* or flexibility can be seen in the expansion or contraction of these scenes and in the manner in which they are elaborated.

Formulae give the poet control and the means of performing a long poem before an audience that is not accustomed to wait for the singer to ponder the next verse or episode. But the formulae may be used mechanically so that they appear clichés and filler. Parataxis enables the poet to integrate whole scenes and episodes into a larger context and to achieve fine thematic effects through surprise and contrast. But parataxis may leave a fragmented and disjointed narrative in which contradiction and irrelevance mar the dramatic rhythm. Typical themes and scenes enable the poet to elaborate his narrative, emphasizing significant details through implicit comparison with the norm (it is a mistake to take any given scene as the norm, but poet and audience, familiar from countless recitations with any given type, know how additions and exclusions affect meaning and tone). But typical scenes may also become clichés, formal routines included more from habit than for artistic purpose. Most readers have found Homer successful in avoiding these dangers while pressing this stylized language and syntax to its maximum extent in the creation of a monumental poem.

For the modern reader it is difficult to grasp how the oral poet, who had to be concerned with the immediate problem of making line after line in a continuing oral performance, was able at the same time to achieve such coherence of plot and characterization over thousands of lines. Assuming Homer did not make use of writing or dictation, we may perhaps speculate for a moment on how the poems reached their present form and were transmitted until they were recorded in writing. We should not forget that the *Iliad* need not have been produced in a single creative effort. Much of it, from formulaic phrases to the idea and elements of the *aristeia,* was certainly traditional, even though we can seldom identify any particular element as necessarily traditional. As a professional singer who had practiced his craft for years, the poet was constantly called upon to present episodes from familiar stories. He had a great deal of time to perfect scenes and years to consider the integration of episodes into a single monumental epic. He had both the experience of live performances and hours of reflection to plan new lines and to revise familiar scenes. More often than not he sang a part (the *aristeia* of Diomêdês, the deception of Zeus, the games at Patróklos' funeral), and it seems doubtful that Homer would have had many occasions for presenting the entire poem. Full recitation would have required at least three days of uninterrupted performances, and one may wonder if such a sustained effort was even physically possible. But over the years a single comprehensive epic did develop, one whose episodes the poet had sung many times. Gradually a firm outline of the story emerged and gained authority from its excellence. Other poets heard and repeated the epic. If it survived through oral transmission for as much as two hundred years, it was probably modified by later generations of singers. Yet there is good evidence to suggest that oral poets are capable of remarkable feats of memory and fidelity to the received song. If a single great poet devoted a lifetime to the perfection of the *Iliad* and *Odyssey* and gave definitive form to these poems, we may reasonably believe that his successors were capable of transmitting his achievement. Since it is obvious that originality per se was not the goal of this tradition, there is little reason to suppose that successive generations of bards would have felt compelled to alter a good thing.[21]

Several objections can be raised to the preceding speculation. The epics were not sacred texts. Why, then, would subsequent bards and rhapsodes have even attempted verbatim transmission of such a long poem? Secondly, the Slavic texts collected by Parry and Lord indicate that subsequent poets alter even those poems they claim to have repeated exactly. Third, archaic Greek literature shares with the *Iliad* an appetitive quality which makes addition of lines, scenes, and episodes a process we would naturally expect, even if we were speaking of the transmission of a written text. Adam Parry and A. B. Lord have argued that our text was dictated by the original poet to a scribe. Thus, at a stroke, the problem is solved and the integrity of Homer's oral poem is assured. It is a bold hypothesis, and probably anachronistic, since it seems so obviously developed from the field work of Parry and Lord in Yugoslavia. The process of creation and transmission will probably remain mysterious, but scholars do not sleep well with mysteries.

Homeric Criticism

Whether or not Homer dictated his text, it is certain that the early Greeks heard the poems; they did not read them. Some scholars have suggested that oral poetry requires a special poetics, one which takes account of the peculiar significance of formula, typical scenes, and the like. So far nothing very concrete has emerged from these suggestions, and Kirk has argued that we have in fact risked too great a distinction between Homer and his literate successors. While this latter point may be overstated, the reader of this volume should remember that though much in oral, formulaic composition is virtually unique to the Greek epics, they share perhaps even more with their heritage. The notes in this volume emphasize repetitions and other idiosyncrasies of oral speech. That much in the *Iliad* is accessible to the reader who may not have such notes is a reminder that Homer's voice is not impeded by his speech.[22]

Any poem of the *Iliad*'s magnitude and artifice requires careful study. The issue is not really one of reading or listening. Practically, our problem in reading Homer comes down to the fact that Homer and his audience were much more familiar with an idiom of traditional poetic speech than we are. That familiarity would save them from the kind of mistake we see in Pope's estimate of the motivation of Hektor in Book XVIII:

> Shall I retreat
> from him, from clash of combat? No, I will not.
> Here I'll stand, though he should win; I might
> just win, myself: the battle-god's impartial,
> dealing death to the death-dealing man."

XVIII 306–9 (p. 445)

Pope comments: "But Hektor is not so far gone in Passion or Pride, as to forget himself; and accordingly in the next lines he modestly puts it in doubt, which of them shall conquer." Pope acknowledges his debt to the Byzantine commentator Eustathius. But if Hektor is modest, then Idómeneus, Sarpêdôn, and several others who conclude speeches in the same vein, with the same lines or lines very like them, are equally modest (see the notes to Sarpêdôn's speech, p. 290). On this point of characterization Pope is mistaken, or at least must find other lines for evidence. The most obvious pitfall for the reader is the possibility of not recognizing what is generic.

There are extensive notes about the typical and generic in the *Iliad*, not because the unique and special are less important, but because we can more readily recognize the former and so gain a surer feeling for the poet's style.

The Poetry and Themes of the Iliad

Certain aspects of Homer's Greek are impossible to translate: the hexameter cannot be reproduced effectively; the variegated linguistic texture would seem odd and recondite in a modern poem; finding equivalents for the formulae while avoiding woodenness and clichés is difficult. But much of the substance and spirit of Homeric poetry can be had from translation. The style is direct, circumstantial, explicit, concrete, in brief, realistic; put negatively, Homer is neither esoteric, private, nor subjective. Ambiguity and complex metaphor are not common features of this style, which aims for direct and complete description. The subject matter is ethical: the poet is interested in people, why they act as they do, the consequences of action, their thoughts and feelings in response to action. He lets his characters speak for themselves and does not include long passages reflecting on the significance of their speech and feeling. So the characters are presented directly and vividly, unmediated by the mind of the poet. Homer may ramble, but he is not vague.

Homer's subject is ostensibly the anger of Akhilleus, and that is the primary dramatic plot of the poem. As any outline shows, however, the scenes in the *Iliad* actually devoted to the quarrel with Agamémnon and its consequences are a small proportion of the total. What, then, is the business of the rest of the *Iliad*? Perhaps it does not go too far to say that Homer's true theme, the real concern of the entire poem, is simply the accurate and comprehensive description of the heroic world. All the particulars of that world absorb him, as his genealogies, catalogues, and anecdotes reveal. The narrator's assumption is that the auditor is not interested in the narrator's opinions but in the facts. So the poet offers as many characters as he can get on the canvas, and they all speak for themselves. Another assumption, as already mentioned, is that the story and the world are known, even familiar. Characters are introduced without fanfare: in Book I

Patróklos is mentioned for the first time as the "son of Menoitios," without his proper name. We have noticed earlier that the abduction of Helen is taken for granted as the cause of the expedition.

The story takes place in the distant past. For the poet and his audience it is history, it is true, and it may properly be celebrated. This last item may seem to us an unhistorical attitude, but since Homer considers the heroic generation literally greater in strength, stamina, and achievement, praise of that era is altogether fitting. This is not to say the poet continually heaps laudations on his characters; he is far too objective for that:

> But Diomêdês
> bent for a stone and picked it up—a boulder
> no two men now alive could lift, though he
> could heft it easily. This mass he hurled
> and struck Aineías on the hip, just where
> the hipbone shifts in what they call the bone-cup,
> crushing this joint with two adjacent tendons
> under the skin ripped off by the rough stone.

> V 302–8 (p. 119)

The past was more glorious because its men were stronger. Diomêdês and his peers themselves regard their fathers and grandfathers as men more able than they are, as Nestor's speeches remind us. Such comparisons are seldom hyperbolic —the factor of two is sufficient. The distance in time has not shrouded the story in a nebulous uncertainty. In this passage, as in many others, the anatomical detail is exact and particular. Such realistic descriptions vouch for the factuality of Diomêdês' feats.

Another aspect of the poet's handling of time and history deserves comment. A number of scenes in the poem, particularly in Books II–VII, seem anachronistic. The marshaling of the troops "by nation and by clan" which Nestor calls for in II (p. 47) turns out to be a catalogue of the ships and contingents which came to Troy. In Book III Helen names the leaders of the Akhaian host for Priam, as if he would not know them well enough by now. Paris and Meneláos duel in order to settle the fate of Helen; this is a sensible arrangement, though the tenth year of the siege seems a late stage for it. Such additions to the story may be explained by invoking the paratactic mentality, but it is also obvious from other aspects of the poem that the poet desired an inclusive and comprehensive view of the heroic world. If Homer's technique is naïve, which it certainly is by comparison with the narrative methods of the *Odyssey*, it is also true that most of these scenes have both an intrinsic interest and a larger thematic relevance.

That relevance does not consist simply in their usefulness in filling out the canvas. In the course of the action the fate of Troy is linked more and more closely with the fate of Hektor. When Hektor kills Patróklos, we hear the death knell for Troy. If Troy's fate is to have any significance, the city and its people must have a life and experience of their own. Homer's technique may not be the most naturalistic or plausible, but it has an aesthetic point, and it works. In effect, many of these anachronisms are flashbacks; the poet cuts to them and back again with great economy. Before we have time to wonder what the outcome of the battle implied in the catalogues will be, Hektor is abusing Paris for being a coward. Paris responds with a willingness to meet Meneláos; Hektor calls for a truce, and the preparations for the duel begin. Once Homer turns to a new action, the pace is fast, the action is vivid and dramatic.

This inclusiveness of the epic appears in other ways. The immediate setting is the plain before Troy, the Akhaian camp on the beach, and the city. This space is geographically limited, and apart from a few landmarks such as the rivers, the tomb of Ilos, and the gates of the city, Homer does not describe it in great detail: at Troy the agents are all important. But his Akhaian army is drawn from all of Greece; descriptive touches concerning the towns and regions of the homeland figure repeatedly in anecdotes and in the formulae. The Trojan alliance furnishes numerous opportunities for allusion to people and places of Asia Minor and the neighboring European continent. Stories related by characters like Nestor, Phoinix, and Glaukos incorporate earlier legendary feats and places like Aetolia and Lykia. There is an encyclopedic quality in these references to the world beyond Troy, as if the more we know of them the better we shall like the story. Many sites mentioned are historically verifiable; smaller and more remote places have not yet been identified, and there is little doubt that Homer included references he had inherited from the poetic tradition.

In a more oblique way the similes also look outward from the poem. With a very few exceptions these comparisons, of which there are about two hundred in the *Iliad*, do not name specific places or consciously invoke another time. Taken together, however, they form a world of their own, one which is in many respects antithetical to the heroic struggle. Their themes are drawn from rural and domestic scenes, from the familiar world of work and man's encounter with nature. Hunting, farming, tending flocks, and the ways of the weather are common subjects. Generally they presuppose a context of peace, though many include images of violent and destructive activity. Some, like the fire and lion similes associated with the *aristeia*, belong to typical scenes. Their variety is impressive in both style and content. They may be relatively static, built up in the manner of a collage:

> and in the dust he reeled and fell.
>
>   A poplar
> growing in bottom lands, in a great meadow,
> smooth-trunked, high up to its sheath of boughs,
> will fall before the chariot-builder's ax
> of shining iron—timber that he marked
> for warping into chariot tire rims—
> and, seasoning, it lies beside the river.
> So vanquished by the god-reared Aías lay
> Simoeísios Anthémidês.
>
>   IV 482–89 (p. 104)

The image of a falling tree is generically appropriate to the warrior toppling to the ground. The details pass from this specific point of similarity to focus on the tree itself, its shape, situation, use, and the man who felled it. Thus the simile, like the interview between Helen and Priam, assumes an integrity of its own.

Weather, good and bad, has always been a favorite topic:

> and the stones showered to earth
> like snow driven by a stormwind thick and fast
> in a murky veil swept over pastureland.
> So missiles came in torrents, . . .

> XII 156–59 (p. 286)

But usually Homer includes man in this world, as the chariot-builder found a place in the poplar simile:

> like agile-waisted hornets
> or bees who build their hives on a stony road—
> hornets that will not leave their homes but wait
> for hunters, and in fury defend their young—
> those two men, two men only, at the gate
> will not give way. For them, kill or be killed!"

> XII 167–72 (p. 286)

There are problems here: are the hunters (formula) hunting hornets? has the poet reduced the hive to two hornets, as the comparison suggests? The simile may be a bit clumsy, but the questions point to the autonomy of the form, a certain independence of narrative context not unlike the paratactic independence of the typical scenes.

Formally, the similes are comparisons. Most of them begin with "like," "as," or "as when." But in theme and tone the world of the similes more often suggests contrasts than similarities with the life of the warrior. While narrative and simile share dramatic values and a sharp focus on detail, in the similes the human struggle engages nature, not man, and often man achieves a harmony with his environment that seems denied the warriors:

> As when in heaven
> principal stars shine out around the moon
> when the night sky is limpid, with no wind,
> and all the lookout points, headlands, and mountain
> clearings are distinctly seen, as though
> pure space had broken through, downward from heaven,

and all the stars are out, and in his heart
the shepherd sings: just so from ships to river
shone before Ilion the Trojan fires.

VIII 555–61 (p. 198f.)

The Trojans pass the night "in brave expectancy" (p. 198),
awaiting the dawn and the opportunity to engage the enemy,
while the shepherd in peace contemplates the brilliance of the
sky.

Homeric realism does not, as we see from the similes, consist merely of accurately painting the struggle, the wounds,
and the agony of war. It constantly looks outward to comprehend the context of the present events. Akhilleus pursues
Hektor:

They passed the lookout point, the wild figtree
with wind in all its leaves, then veered away
along the curving wagon road, and came
to where the double fountains well, the source
of eddying Skamánder. One hot spring
flows out, and from the water fumes arise
as though from fire burning; but the other
even in summer gushes chill as hail
or snow crystal ice frozen on water.
Near these fountains are wide washing pools
of smooth-laid stone, where Trojan wives and daughters
laundered their smooth linen in the days
of peace before the Akhaians came.

XXII 145–56 (p. 520)

The digression describing the springs and their use in another
time reminds us of the human significance of the race for
Hektor's life, yet the language is neither sentimental nor di-
dactic. The facts speak for themselves, and we know, though
the poet will not say, that the Trojan women will never wash
at these fountains again.

Such comparisons of time and place have an autonomous
character because the style does not stress logical, thematic,

and affective connections. The scene, however, like the poem, is coherent and unified. Parataxis has not run amuck. The absence of connectives does not mean that either a sentence or a scene is a non sequitur. We have looked at Homeric style as a function of oral poetry, and now it is time to examine briefly the sources of order and coherence found in the language, plot, and themes of the poem.

The metrical utility of formulaic composition for the oral poet is apparent. What of the aesthetic effect of the formulae? They occur repeatedly, often in predictable situations. They are used by everyone, Trojan, Akhaian, and narrator. Designed for a metrical order, they bring to the poem a comprehensive cognitive order. Strangers and enemies address one another with familiar honorific titles used by peers and comrades. Helen, pointing out the leading Akhaian warriors to Priam, says:

> "That is the giant soldier,
> Aías, a rugged sea wall for Akhaians.
> Opposite him, among the Kretans, there,
> is tall Idómeneus, with captains round him.
> Meneláos, whom the wargod loves,
> received him often in our house in Sparta
> when he crossed over out of Krete.

III 229–33 (p. 75)

There is an almost severe formality in the familiar epithet "whom the wargod loves." Only "our house" suggests their former intimacy. In the same passage Antênor, counselor to Priam, has also described Meneláos as a man "whom the wargod loves" (line 206). Helen and Antênor do not agree on this epithet from mutual consent but because the whole world knows Meneláos as a companion of Arês. So the formulae imply a stability and continuity in the world they describe, and a unanimity of perception among those using them.

The typical scene has many of the same qualities. It asserts a proper mode of action and a sensible form of experience. Not only religious activities such as sacrifice assume a ritual aspect, but most of the routines of life gain a certain shape and rhythm, for the characters and for the reader. Such scenes, evolved by the poetic tradition for their utility in extemporaneous composition, become formal elements in the plot. Their repeated use, particularly the *aristeia*, invites comparison between sequences of action and between the characters in each *aristeia*. Diomêdês and Akhilleus hardly meet in the poem, but the former is celebrated in the first significant *aristeia*, the latter in the last, and several shared components, e.g., the presence of Aineías who duels each of them, also urge us to compare the two young heroes. Such doublets inform the *Iliad* at many levels and, like the generic and ornamental epithets, give it a structure and stability.

Since Aristotle's frequent references to Homer in his *Poetics*, it has been recognized that Homer's methods are dramatic. Aristotle saw that the *Iliad* had an organic plot developed in a few key episodes. Within the dramatic representation of the wrath theme Homer is both more economical and more attentive to cause and effect than elsewhere in the poem. Books I, IX, XVI, XVIII, and XXII give the heart of the action (XIX and XXIV might also be included). Agamémnon and Akhilleus quarrel; Akhilleus retires from battle and rejects a petition to return; he relents a little, and finally lets his friend help the army; Patróklos is killed and Akhilleus vows revenge; with Hektor's death the revenge is accomplished. A few, essential scenes, in which thought and feeling are fully articulated by the agents themselves, form a five- or six-act tragic plot. Whereas the typical scenes, catalogues, descriptive anecdotes, and much else tend to be static and digressive, the wrath theme has a dynamic linear impulse that carries the poem forward. There is nothing paratactic about this dramatic rhythm, which is as organic, logical, and necessary as anything in Greek tragedy.

The characters of the story fall into two groups, gods and men. Men are mortals: they expect death; gods are immortals: for them the dangers of the field are play. When Akhilleus has left the assembly and retired to his tent, he prays to his mother to help him seek vengeance on Agamémnon. To his request that she invoke the aid of Zeus, she responds:

"Alas, my child, why did I rear you, doomed
the day I bore you?

I 414 (p. 25)

"Fate" and "destiny" are recurrent motifs. Their essential
reference is to man's mortal lot. Thetis may sympathize, but
she cannot change her son's destiny, nor is she able to dis-
suade him from decisions that bring it on all the sooner. The
wrath theme is quickly linked to the fate of Akhilleus, Hektor, and Troy, though never in an abstract or mechanical
way. Every agent consciously exercises a free choice in working out his own destiny. The ultimate destiny is certain; how
man acts out his portion is all-important.

The whole concern of the Homeric warrior is honor and
reputation. He fights for booty, since the prize is a token of
victory. He fights for glory, since man's only immortality is
the fame that lives on in song and the report of posterity.
When the embassy reaches the tent of Akhilleus they find him
singing "old tales of heroes" (p. 209). The warrior's honor is
in part a sense of his own merit, a self-esteem or pride, but
honor is also that which others confer. It is the respect, admiration, and esteem of the group. War is the profession in
which these warriors lay claim to prestige; it is difficult to
imagine them doing anything but fighting. They cannot rest,
for if they do, a newcomer may eclipse their achievements.
For them a glorious death in battle is much the best end.
Their profession is social and recognition of achievement is
social: to withdraw from the battle, as Akhilleus does, would
be an occasion for the scorn of his peers if he were a lesser
warrior.

These are the values of Akhaian and Trojan alike, yet the
defensive role cast for the Trojans necessarily carries respon-
sibilities the Greek side does not know. By introducing the
women, children, and old men of Troy, the poet imposes bur-
dens on Hektor and his camp that do not restrict the decisions of Akhilleus and Agamémnon.

One
and only one portent is best: defend
our fatherland!

XII 243 (p. 288)

Thus Hektor rejects Poulýdamas' interpretation of a portent.
He is a civic hero, yet not immune to the call of honor: he
finally faces Akhilleus and certain death because

> I am ashamed to face townsmen and women.
> Someone inferior to me may say:
> 'He kept his pride and lost his men, this Hektor!'

> XXII 105–7 (p. 519)

Shame, the regard for the censure of others, complements the
warrior's regard for the praise of others. Hektor is not so
civic-minded that he can ignore the pressures of shame,
honor, and reputation which surround most of the heroes.
  By describing these values we can stake out the sources of
group and personal conflict for the warrior. But if we turn to
individual men and women, it is the variety of personality and
characterization that impresses, not the uniformity of their
concerns. Consider Paris: he is the source of the trouble over
Troy, but that is not weighing heavily with him:

> My own gifts are from pale-gold Aphrodítê—
> do not taunt me for them. Glorious things
> the gods bestow are not to be despised,

> III 64f. (p. 69)

He has just tried to dodge an engagement with Meneláos, and
has been reminded by Hektor that he would have been stoned
long since, were the Trojans not such cowards. Paris does
meet the cuckold Meneláos, and would be killed except
for Aphrodítê's intervention. Back in his rooms with Helen he
dismisses the defeat and suggests:

> Let us drop war now, you and I,
> and give ourselves to pleasure in our bed.

> III 441 (p. 83)

Paris will later do some good work in battle, but his casual
self-indulgence is fixed forever. Since Paris is incapable of

bearing the moral responsibility for his folly, Hektor must. This is a brilliant stroke: Hektor is not guilty though he accepts responsibility. He recognizes that Paris and Helen ought to be thrown out, but since neither he nor his father nor the city will go so far, they must live with Paris and accept the consequences. Hektor knows what they are:

> Long ago I learned
> how to be brave, how to go forward always
> and to contend for honor, Father's and mine.
> Honor—for in my heart and soul I know
> a day will come when ancient Ilion falls,
> when Priam and the folk of Priam perish.
>
> VI 444–49 (p. 155)

He is replying to his wife's plea that he retire into the city. Contrast the bravado of his vaunt over the fallen Patróklos:

> "Easy to guess, Patróklos, how you swore
> to ravage Troy, to take the sweet daylight
> of liberty from our women, and to drag them
> off in ships to your own land—you fool!
> Between you and those women there is Hektor's
> war-team, thundering out to fight! My spear
> has pride of place among the Trojan warriors,
> keeping their evil hour at bay.
> The kites will feed on you, here on this field.
>
> XVI 830–36 (p. 402)

Like most warriors Hektor falls victim to the fury of battle, a mad exaltation that has just led Patróklos to his death. We may sympathize with Hektor, but it ought to be noticed that in the frenzy that accompanies success he is just as determined to see Patróklos' body mutilated as Akhilleus will be to desecrate Hektor's corpse.

Our response to Akhilleus is complicated by several factors. Clearly, he is a winner: no one claims equality with him, though it is a measure of Hektor's folly that, in the scene just cited, he responds to Patróklos' prophecy of Akhilleus' revenge with:

> "Why prophesy my sudden death, Patróklos?
> Who knows, Akhilleus, son of bright-haired Thetis,
> might be hit first; he might be killed by me."
>
> XVI 859–61 (p. 403)

In the event he runs in terror from Akhilleus. Akhilleus is conscious of his own merit. He is a proud man who bitterly resents Agamémnon's insult. However excessive his anger and revenge may seem, it is important to realize that Agamémnon does wrong him when he takes Briseis, Akhilleus' prize (see Nestor's speech, p. 20f.). When his friends appeal to him in Book IX, they do not censure him for having retired from battle, but they do think that Agamémnon's restitution ought to appease his anger. Akhilleus is moved by their friendship:

> And yet my heart grows large and hot with fury
> remembering that affair: as though I were
> some riffraff or camp follower, he taunted me
> before them all!
>
> IX 646–48 (p. 223f.)

From this point we sense that, if he is not in the wrong, he still takes risks by indulging his humor.

To Akhilleus' credit he admits responsibilty for Patróklos' death, but he has earned the spiritual anguish he suffers. Homer has woven this crisis and its tragic consequences out of the clash of individualism and social obligation. Heroic society values individual self-assertion beyond all else. Life is competitive, and to win is to triumph over the will and effort of others. So long as such competitive energy is turned outward against a foreign enemy, society is not endangered. But when the individual's self-esteem is discredited within the group, his honor can only be avenged at the expense of his own society. The Trojans have tacitly admitted Paris' right to do as he pleases, and he keeps Helen to the cost of all Troy.

To humiliate Agamémnon Akhilleus endangers the entire Akhaian army. As Nestor says, "Akhilleus . . . alone gains by his valor" (XI 763; p. 274). Patróklos has elected to help his friends, and in persevering in his anger Akhilleus has placed his own honor ahead of his friend's safety.

When he returns to battle Akhilleus is so overwhelming and brutal that he seems daimonic. He has accepted death as the price of revenge, and we know there is no hope for Hektor. Had Homer concluded the poem with Book XXII (the death of Hektor), we would have to conclude that Akhilleus has lost all the humanity we see in his grief for Patróklos in Book XVIII. But in the final scene of the *Iliad* Homer depicts a hero not merely mollified but actually responding sympathetically to the grief of Priam. It is too late to undo the suffering, and he never regrets his decision or the killing of Hektor, yet it is not too late to reassert elemental bonds of human kinship symbolized by his recognition in Priam of the grief Pêleus must now experience.

Our perception of the human struggle is not simplified by the role the gods play. As if to underscore Akhilleus' superiority, in the final duel Athêna deceives Hektor and helps Akhilleus by retrieving his spear for a second cast. Such aid, especially for the naturally superior hero, seems to us unfair. But not so to Hektor, who realizes that "Athêna tricked me" (XXII 299; p. 525) but still closes for one last desperate effort,

> some action
> memorable to men in days to come."
>
> XXII 305 (p. 525)

Similarly, Patróklos chides Hektor for having been only the third, after Apollo and Euphorbos, involved in his death. These are momentous occasions for character and plot. The divinity's influence is so compelling that many readers feel the course of events is determined exclusively by divine power. Since few significant events in the poem are unaffected by the gods' interest, it may be useful to survey briefly their attributes and role.[23]

The gods are immortal and they are powerful. These attributes do not exhaust their interest, but they do isolate their most distinctive differences from men, who are regularly described by Homer as "mortal," i.e., subject to death, and as dependent upon the divinities for their success in battle, in games, in speaking. Their immortality separates them from man and leaves them, relatively, free from suffering. Their power brings them closer to man in that it is used almost exclusively to aid or impede human projects. Some have sons on the field of battle, whom they may save from death for a time or grieve for when their death-day is at hand, but finally Apollo speaks to the profound separation when he says to Poseidon:

> "Lord of earthquake, sound of mind
> you could not call me if I strove with you
> for the sake of mortals, poor things that they are.
> Ephemeral as the flamelike budding leaves,
> men flourish on the ripe wheat of the grainland,
> then in spiritless age they waste and die.
> We should give up fighting over men.
> Let men themselves contend with one another."

XXI 462–67 (p. 508)

Divine power manifests itself in a variety of forms. The gods are sometimes so narrowly identified with an aspect of life that we may safely say Arês is simply "War," or Aphrodítê "Sexual Desire." Hêphaistos may appear as fire, burning the plain and scalding the river (god) Skamánder; or as the god of the forge and its craft he may be the appropriate power for the making of Akhilleus' armor (p. 450ff.). But in his first appearance he is a fully personalized mediator between his quarreling parents, who belittles himself to make the other gods laugh and forget their differences (p. 30f.). According to legend Aphrodítê helped Paris win Helen, and so it is fitting that she should save him from the avenging Meneláos (p. 80). But she is really not a proper divinity for battle, as we see when Diomêdês wounds her in Book V (p. 120). Aphrodítê and Hêphaistos illustrate not so much a con-

fusion in Homer's thought as a range of representations. The
gods manifest themselves in different ways, and to the
believer such epiphanies are not contradictory. A Greek
would naturally understand a fire sweeping across the plain as
the power of Hêphaistos, just as he would look upon a finely
made shield as an artifact worthy of divine craftsmanship,
i.e., made with the help of Hêphaistos.

The most significant dramatic function of the gods is found
in their influence on the decisions and actions of mortals.
When a warrior is successful in casting his spear, it is because
of a god's help; when he fails, that too is attributable to divinity. All the world is inhabited by gods, and they affect every
action. Achievement in any area, whether it is a foot race or
winning a bride, signifies divine favor. Man does not scorn
such aid, for it never comes to the mean and humble. The
gods help those who help themselves: it is just because
Akhilleus is the best warrior that Athêna stands by his side
during the duel with Hektor. Diomêdês chooses Odysseus as
his companion for the night raid with two thoughts in mind:

> Shrewd as he is, and cool and brave, beyond
> all others in rough work. Pallas Athêna
> loves that man.

> X 244f. (p. 237)

Odysseus' shrewdness and Athêna's aid are reciprocal. Man is
not a puppet racing or stumbling at the whim of the god, for
the gods favor the strong. Man is free to seek the aid of divinity and to resist divine power, but there is no guarantee a
prayer will win favor, as Meneláos learns (p. 79f.), and re-
sistance entails risk, as Helen discovers (p. 82).

If the god were either names for powers or fully anthropo-
morphic agents, the *Iliad* would be an easier poem. But in
many cases the intervention of the deity takes an ambiguous
form that blends various modes of presentation, with the result that we wonder what has really occurred. Not infre-
quently they seem projections of psychological states, and the
dialogue between mortal and immortal has the quality of
dramatized reflection. For example, when the quarrel be

tween Akhilleus and Agamémnon has reached mutual recrim-
ination and insult, Akhilleus debates:

> should he draw
> longsword from him, stand off the rest, and kill
> in single combat the great son of Atreus,
> or hold his rage in check and give it time?
> And as this tumult swayed, as he slid
> the big blade slowly from the sheath, Athêna
> came to him from the sky.

I 189–95 (p. 17f.)

No one else sees her. Akhilleus asks her if she has come to
see him insulted. She urges him to check his rage, though he
may insult Agamémnon as much as he likes. If he will agree,
she promises "winnings three times as rich" and "requital for
his arrogance." He acquiesces:

> Honor the gods' will, they may honor ours."

I 218 (p.18)

Because Homer tends to externalize and objectify psychological phenomena—the personifications of Terror, Rout, and
Hate (p. 103) illustrate this—we naturally are inclined to in-
terpret such a dialogue as a record of Akhilleus' ambivalence
and the considerations which led him to spare Agamémnon.
Athêna does not command: she says "if you will listen" (I
207; p. 18). We might say he had an epiphany, or that he
was inspired with a better plan, for in the next speech he
takes an oath that

> a day will come when every Akhaian soldier
> will groan to have Akhilleus back. That day
> you shall no more prevail on me than this
> dry wood shall flourish—driven though you are,
> and though a thousand men perish before
> the killer, Hektor.

I 240–43 (p. 19)

He has made a better plan, a fuller revenge for this dishonor. Athêna does not give him the plan; it has evolved during their brief conversation.

Such manifestations of divinity that show the process of, or explain, psychological and intellectual phenomena fall between Athêna as "Intelligence" and Athêna as the agent who picks up and returns the miscast spear (p. 524). Homer, of course, never offers these epiphanies as "explanations"; we use this terminology by way of understanding the qualitative differences found in his representation of the divine. We might look at this last scene from the point of view of the assembled army. They saw how angry Akhilleus was and saw him start to draw his sword. But he did not, and after a moment he began to abuse Agamémnon and concluded with an oath of revenge. Wondering what checked him, they naturally attributed his restraint to a divinity. All extraordinary and momentous actions partake of divine influence: this is the view of the narrator and of his characters.

Yet another type of epiphany involves the impersonation of a mortal by a divinity. In Book II Odysseus has given Thersítês a good blow and stands to address the assembly again:

> But the raider of cities,
> Odysseus, with his staff, stood upright there,
> and at his side grey-eyed Athêna stood
> in aspect like a crier, calling: "Silence!"
> that every man, front rank and rear alike,
> might hear his words and weigh what he proposed.
>
> II 278–82 (p. 44)

Why should Athêna impersonate a herald? The soldiers have just been entertained by Odysseus' handling of the upstart Thersítês. Now they are laughing and chattering, and it seems a poor time for a speaker to claim their attention. Yet Odysseus is heard by the farthest ranks, a fact that can only be explained by a remarkable call to order. So effective is the crier that (we would say) he seems to have the authority of a divinity. Homer simply says Athêna was the herald. In Book XIII Poseidon, intent upon rallying the Akhaians, takes the

form of Kalkhas and encourages the two warriors named
Aías. Having urged them on he departs:

> The god who girdles earth, even as he spoke,
> struck both men with his staff, instilling fury,
> making them springy, light of foot and hand.
> Then upward like a hawk he soared—

XIII 59–62 (p. 301)

Aías the son of Oïleus recognizes the divinity:

> It was not Kalkhas, not
> the reader of birdflight; from his stride, his legs
> as he went off, I knew him for a god.
> The gods are easily spotted! As for me,
> I feel more passion to do battle now;
> I tingle from the very soles of my feet
> to my finger tips!"

XIII 70–75 (p. 301)

The rationalistic explanation would be that Aías has taken
renewed energy and determination from the exhortation of
Kalkhas. But the Greeks view such an access of strength as
the gift of the gods. So the god was there, first as Kalkhas,
then departing "like a hawk." In a moment (p. 302) Poseidon is encouraging the other Akhaians. Homer does not say
he has returned nor is he said to take the form of Kalkhas for
his next speech. But the army rallies, and the natural explanation is that a god has renewed their will to fight. Most reversals in the flow of battle are explained by some kind of divine
intervention.

The variety of forms the divine presence takes attests to the
Greek belief in the omnipresence of divine power. Since the
gods are often fully personalized, their absence or lack of attention may explain why the Olympian partisans for the other
side are able to have their way. At the beginning of Book
XIII, for example, Homer says Zeus turned his attention to
the north, ignoring the battle. This explains why Poseidon, a
lesser god who acts against the orders of Zeus, is able to rally

the Akhaians. When Zeus attends to the course of battle again, Poseidon is told to leave the field, and consequently the Trojans, with Apollo's aid, are once again victorious.

There is nothing mechanical in Homer's representation of the gods, though they are the means of implementing so many turns in the action. It is sometimes said that the gods are subject to fate, but even if the Greeks of the Homeric era thought so, the divinities of the *Iliad* so often act from purely personal and spontaneous motivation that the idea of a fated order and hierarchy hardly seems to determine their decisions. The same may be said of men, who never renounce personal responsibility even when they blame the gods. Sometimes this dual accountability seems a contradiction, or at least a redundancy. What finally frees all Homer's agents is the dramatic method, i.e., the fact that we see and hear them reasoning to the ends of action. Akhilleus speaks of his "two possible destinies" in Book IX (p. 216), but no god tells him how to respond to Odysseus. The gods do tell him to return the body of Hektor (Book XXIV); when Priam actually reaches his tent, however, there is no perfunctory transfer but a scene of supplication and persuasion that moves Akhilleus to a generosity of spirit comparable to his battle fury. In the same fashion Homer tells us Zeus consults the scales of fate to determine whether the death-day of Akhilleus or Hektor is at hand (p. 522). Yet Hektor has already rejected Priam's plea that he escape into the city, and he has admitted to himself that Akhilleus is the better man (p. 518f.). In fact, the warrior's character is his fate.

Notes

In these notes scholars are cited by name only; full reference will be found in the bibliography. Titles are cited when more than one item occurs in the bibliography. The following abbreviations are used throughout this volume:

AJP	*American Journal of Philology*
CP	*Classical Philology*
HSCP	*Harvard Studies in Classical Philology*
JHS	*Journal of Hellenic Studies*
TAPA	*Transactions of the American Philological Association*
YCS	*Yale Classical Studies*

1. See the account of the following events in the epitome of the *Library* of Apollodorus (III.2.ff.).

2. Lesky discusses the epic cycle and its relation to the Homeric poems, pp. 79–84.

3. Most critical studies of Homer begin with a discussion of the Homeric question. See Lesky, pp. 32–41; Kirk, *Homer and the Epic*, pp. 190–201; Nilsson, *Homer and Mycenae*, pp. 1–55; and Adam Parry's introduction to *The Making of Homeric Verse*, pp. x–xxi.

4. G. S. Kirk has treated this subject sensibly (*Homer and the Epic*, pp. 33–62). M. I. Finley continues to argue for the influence of the Dark Ages. See the criticism offered by A. M. Snodgrass, "An Historical Homeric Society?" *JHS* 94 (1974), 114–25. John Chadwick's *The Mycenaean World* offers a comprehensive study of that era and a chapter skeptical of Mycenaean influence on Homer ("Homer the Pseudo-historian," pp. 180–87).

5. In the *Works and Days* (lines 109–201), Hesiod describes the five ages: Gold, Silver, Bronze, Heroic, and Iron.

6. Chadwick's book contains a full account of the tablets and their relevance to the understanding of the Mycenaean era.

7. D. L. Page has argued strongly for the Mycenaean origin of the catalogue in Book II. Cf. the reservations of Kirk, *Songs of Homer*, p. 118.

8. For the evidence pertaining to writing and literacy see Lilian H. Jeffery's "Writing," pp. 545–59, in Wace and Stubbings, *A Companion to Homer*.

9. On oral epic see Kirk, *Homer and the Epic*, pp. 1–32, where he discusses both the oral nature of the Homeric poems and the modern Slavic epic. Good, too, is his "Homer: the Meaning of an Oral Tradition" in *Homer and the Oral Tradition*. The standard work on the modern Slavic epic is A. B. Lord's *The Singer of Tales*.

10. Milman Parry's work has been collected and edited by Adam Parry in *The Making of Homeric Verse*. If the reader will look at pp. 10–16 of Milman Parry's "The Traditional Epithet in Homer," the function and significance of the Homeric formulae will be vividly impressed on his mind. Parry's conclusions have not gone uncriticized: M. W. M.

Pope, "Athena's Development in Homeric Epic," *AJP* 81 (1960), 113–35, and "The Parry-Lord Theory of Homeric Composition," *Acta Classica* 6 (1963), pp. 1–21. For a more recent rejection of the implications of Parry's views see Norman Austin, *Archery at the Dark of the Moon* (Berkeley, 1975), Chapter I, "The Homeric Formula," pp. 11–80.

11. For verse and formulae see Kirk, *Homer and the Epic*, pp. 4–9, or *The Songs of Homer*, pp. 59–68.

12. *Homer*, p. 19. Hainsworth's discussion is brief (pp. 19–25) but valuable. He concludes: "But what right have *ton d'apameibomenos* . . . and the like to be thought typical? In fact they constitute a very small class of very frequent lines. I have taken their ossified usage to be a function of their frequency." (In this last sentence he refers to his study, *The Flexibility of the Homeric Formula* [Oxford, 1968].)

13. J. A. Notopoulos, "Homer, Hesiod and the Achaean Heritage of Oral Poetry," *Hesperia* 29 (1960), 177–97. Joseph A. Russo, "The Structural Formula in Homeric Verse," *YCS* 20 (1966), 219–40. Their extension of the use of "formula" has not won general acceptance (see Hainsworth 20f.), though their claims seem modest when compared to those of Michael Nagler (*Spontaneity and Tradition: A Study in the Oral Art of Homer* [Berkeley, 1975]).

14. From "The Traditional Epithet in Homer," p. 149f. of *The Making of Homeric Verse.*

15. G. M. Calhoun, "The Art of Formula in Homer—*epea pteroenta,*" *CP* 30 (1935), 215–27. See Parry's reply, "About Winged Words," pp. 414–18 of *The Making of Homeric Verse.* William Whallon, "The Homeric Epithets," *YCS* 17 (1961), 97–142.

16. Enjambment is necessarily a technical topic which can only be treated in the Greek. Still, the first pages of Kirk's "Verse-Structure and Sentence-Structure in Homer" (*Homer and the Oral Tradition*, p. 146ff.) give a clear account. For parataxis see J. A. Notopoulos, "Parataxis in Homer: A New Approach to Homeric Literary Criticism," *TAPA* 80 (1949), 1–23. My estimate of the importance of parataxis is not accepted by all contemporary critics.

17. See the discussion of Nilsson, *Homer and Mycenae*, pp. 2–19 and 30–35, and E. R. Dodds, "Homer," pp. 1–13. The unitarians seem to have survived the cogent criticism of

F. M. Combellack, "Contemporary Unitarians and Homeric Originality," *AJP* 71 (1950), 337–64.

18. B. E. Perry, "The Early Greek Capacity for Seeing Things Separately," *TAPA* 68 (1937), 403–27.

19. On thematic composition see Kirk, *Songs of Homer,* pp. 72–80; Fenik, *Typical Battle Scenes in the Iliad;* J. I. Armstrong, "The Arming Motif in the *Iliad,*" *AJP* 79 (1958), 337–54.

20. Fenik, p. 6, where he notices other patterns of this sort.

21. For the past twenty-five years a lively discussion on the original composition and transmission of the poems has occupied some of the most distinguished scholars in the field. Two important papers are reprinted in *The Language and Background of Homer:* A. B. Lord, "Homer's Orginality: Oral Dictated Texts," which first appeared in *TAPA* 84 (1953), 124–34; G. S. Kirk, "Homer and Modern Oral Poetry: Some Confusions," which first appeared in *Classical Quarterly* 10 (new series, 1960), 271–81. Lord believes the texts were dictated by Homer to a literate scribe; Kirk is skeptical. See also Lord's *Singer of Tales,* p. 149ff.; Adam Parry's "Have We Homer's *Iliad?*" *YCS* 20 (1966), 177–216, to which Kirk replied in "Homer's *Iliad* and Ours," reprinted in *Homer and the Oral Tradition.*

22. G. S. Kirk, "The Oral and the Literary Epic," in *Homer and the Oral Tradition.* Kirk offers bibliography. Good to read on this topic are F. M. Combellack, "Milman Parry and Homeric Artistry," *Comparative Literature* 11 (1959), 193–208; J. B. Hainsworth, "The Criticism of an Oral Poet," *JHS* 90 (1970), 90–98.

23. In making the following notes on Homer's gods I have profited from M. M. Willcock's recent article, "Some Aspects of the Gods in the *Iliad,*" *Bulletin of the Institute of Classical Studies* (London University), no. 17 (1970), 1–10.

BIBLIOGRAPHY

All citations in this volume are abbreviated to the author's name, except for those scholars with more than one item listed below. For abbreviations of journals see Notes to the Introduction. Bibliographical surveys:

E. R. Dodds, "Homer" in *The Language and Background of Homer* (see G. S. Kirk), reprinted from *Fifty Years of Classical Scholarship*, Oxford, 1954.

J. B. Hainsworth, *Homer* (*Greece and Rome*, New Surveys in the Classics No. 3), Oxford, 1969. A brief, discriminating discussion of recent trends in Homeric scholarship.

James P. Holoka, "Homeric Originality: A Survey," *Classical World* 66 (1973), 257–93. Good documentation and critical evaluation of oral theory and practice since Milman Parry.

The following studies and sources will be useful for the understanding of the *Iliad*. Most of them translate the Greek.

T. M. Andersson, *Early Epic Scenery*, Ithaca, 1976.

Apollodorus, *The Library*, edited and translated by James G. Frazer in the Loeb Classical Library (2 volumes), Cambridge, Mass., and London, 1921.

S. E. Bassett, *The Poetry of Homer*, Berkeley, 1938.

Charles R. Beye, *The Iliad, the Odyssey, and the Epic Tradition*, New York, 1966.

C. M. Bowra, *From Virgil to Milton*, London and New York, 1945.

———, *Heroic Poetry*, London, 1952. Both volumes show the student of comparative epic and heroic poetry at work. Good on Homer and the tradition.

———, *Tradition and Design in the Iliad*, Oxford, 1930. More recent critical studies tend to translate the Greek, but in this early study Bowra did not.

Rhys Carpenter, *Folk Tale, Fiction and Saga in the Homeric Epics,* Berkeley and Los Angeles, 1946. The first four chapters are recommended.

John Chadwick, *The Mycenaean World,* London and New York, 1976. Chadwick tells the story of the Linear B tablets and describes the Mycenaean period. He is skeptical of Mycenaean influence on Homer. Good illustrations in an authoritative study.

E. R. Dodds, *The Greeks and the Irrational,* Berkeley and Los Angeles, 1951. A landmark in the study of Greek thought. Chapter 1, "Agamemnon's Apology," is required reading.

Bernard Fenik, *Typical Battle Scenes in the Iliad,* Wiesbaden, 1968. This is heavy going, but useful for the student who wants to know more about Homer's composition by theme and typical scene.

M. I. Finley, *The World of Odysseus,* revised edition, London and New York, 1977.

Hermann Fränkel, *Early Greek Poetry and Philosophy,* translated by Moses Hadas and James Willis. Oxford, 1975. Stimulating for his interpretations of intellectual and psychological topics.

W. K. C. Guthrie, *The Greeks and Their Gods,* London, 1949; reprint, Boston, 1955. Chapter IV, "Gods and Men in Homer."

Hesiod, *Hesiod, The Homerica Hymns, and Homerica,* translated by Hugh G. Evelyn-White in the Loeb Classical Library. London and New York, 1954.

G. S. Kirk, *The Songs of Homer* (SH), Cambridge, England, 1962.

————, *Homer and the Epic,* Cambridge, England, 1965. This is a shortened version of *The Songs of Homer* and is designed for use by students reading in translation. Kirk's studies are comprehensive and skeptical of special theories. Especially recommended for his treatment of historical problems and oral composition.

————, *Homer and the Oral Tradition,* Cambridge, England, 1976.

———— (ed.), *The Language and Background of Homer: Some Recent Studies and Controversies,* Cambridge, England, and New York, 1964. This collection includes: C. M.

Bowra, "The Meaning of a Heroic Age"; Adam Parry, "The Language of Achilles"; A. B. Lord, "Homer's Originality: Oral Dictated Texts"; Sterling Dow, "The Greeks in the Bronze Age"; G. S. Kirk, "Homer and Modern Oral Poetry: Some Confusions."

Albin Lesky, *A History of Greek Literature,* translated by James Willis and Cornelis de Heer, New York, 1966. An excellent introduction to the Homeric epic (pp. 14–79).

C. S. Lewis, *A Preface to Paradise Lost,* London and New York, 1942. Lewis discusses Homer and Vergil on his way to Milton. Good on the epic tradition.

Hugh Lloyd-Jones, *The Justice of Zeus,* Berkeley and Los Angeles, 1971. Chapter I on the *Iliad,* for a different view of Homeric gods and men.

A. B. Lord, *The Singer of Tales,* Cambridge, Mass., 1960. The standard work on the Slavic epic, which is treated in Part I (The Theory), but Lord's singer is Homer (Part II, The Application).

H. L. Lorimer, *Homer and the Monuments,* London, 1950. A discussion of the archaeological evidence relevant to the Homeric epics.

J. V. Luce, *Homer and the Heroic Age,* New York and London, 1975. Maps, illustrations, and photographs vividly present the "world of Homer."

Gilbert Murray, *The Rise of the Greek Epic,* 4th edition, Oxford, 1934, and since reprinted. Much in this book seems dated, but Murray was a lively, intelligent, literate scholar who somehow managed to write about the *Iliad* before oral theory and its attendants.

Martin P. Nilsson, *The Mycenaean Origin of Greek Mythology,* Berkeley, 1932.

———, *Homer and Mycenae* (HM), London, 1933. The title reveals the bias, but this remains a good introduction to the *Iliad*.

———, *A History of Greek Religion* (HGR), 2nd edition, translated by F. J. Fielden, Oxford, 1952. Reprinted in the Norton Library, New York, 1964. Very good on the complexities of Homeric man's spiritual and cognitive life is Chapter V, "The Homeric Anthropomorphism and Rationalism" (pp. 134–79).

E. T. Owen, *The Story of the Iliad*, Ann Arbor, 1966. A reprint of the 1st edition, Toronto and New York, 1947.

D. L. Page, *History and the Homeric Iliad*, Berkeley and Los Angeles, 1959.

Milman Parry, *The Making of Homeric Verse: The Collected Papers of Milman Parry*, edited by Adam Parry, Oxford, 1971.

Alexander Pope, *The Poems of Alexander Pope*, volumes 7 and 8, *The Iliad*, edited by Maynard Mack et al., London and New Haven, 1967.

James M. Redfield, *Nature and Culture in the Iliad: The Tragedy of Hector*, Chicago, 1975.

John A. Scott, *The Unity of Homer*, Berkeley, 1921. Written in the days of the analytical hegemony, this study led the unitarian resurgence. "Hektor . . . is the creation of the poet who conceived the idea of the *Iliad*" (p. 226).

R. Hope Simpson and J. F. Lazenby, *The Catalogue of the Ships in Homer's Iliad*, Oxford, 1970.

W. B. Stanford, *The Ulysses Theme*, Oxford, 1954; reprint Ann Arbor, 1968.

C. G. Thomas (ed.), *Homer's History: Mycenaean or Dark Age?* New York, 1970. An anthology of essays: politics, economics, archaeology, and history.

A. J. B. Wace and F. H. Stubbings, *A Companion to Homer*, London, 1962. Several prominent scholars contributed the articles to this volume, which has been my constant companion. The Poems (language and style), Homeric Criticism, The Setting, The Rediscovery of the Heroic World, Social Culture, and Material Culture.

T. B. L. Webster, *From Mycenae to Homer*, 2nd edition, New York, 1964.

Cedric H. Whitman, *Homer and the Heroic Tradition*, Cambridge, Mass., 1958, reprinted in the Norton Library, 1965.

Commentaries:

Hesiod, *The Theogony*, edited with introduction and commentary by M. L. West, Oxford, 1966.

Homer, *Homers Ilias*, edited by Karl F. Ameis and C. Hentze, Leipzig and Berlin, 1906.

————, *The Iliad*, edited by Walter Leaf, the second edition (2 volumes), London, 1900.

Malcolm M. Willcock, *A Companion to the Iliad* (based on

the translation of Richmond Lattimore), Chicago and London, 1976.

A number of articles on Akhilleus, his values, and his motivation in the epic are available to readers in English:

D. E. Eichholz, "The Propitiation of Achilles," *AJP* 74 (1953), 137–48.

A. L. Motto and J. R. Clark, *"Eĩsê daís.* The Honor of Achilles," *Arethusa* 2 (1969), 109–20.

Adam Parry, "The Language of Achilles," *TAPA* 87 (1956), 1–7 (reprinted in *The Language and Background of Homer*).

William Sale, "Achilles and Heroic Values," *Arion* 2 (1963), 86–100.

Cedric Whitman, "Achilles: Evolution of a Hero," which is Chapter 9 in *Homer and the Heroic Tradition*.

The following studies have been useful to me though they are rarely cited in the notes.

A. W. H. Adkins, *Merit and Responsibility: A Study in Greek Values,* Oxford, 1960.

J. Th. Kakridis, *Homeric Researches,* Lund, 1949.

D. Lohmann, *Die Komposition der Reden in der Ilias,* Berlin, 1970.

Paul Mazon, *Introduction à l'Iliade,* Paris, 1967.

R. B. Onians, *The Origins of European Thought About the Body, the Mind, the Soul, the World, Time and Fate,* Cambridge, England, 1951.

W. Schadewaldt, *Iliasstudien,* 3rd edition, Darmstadt, 1966.

Bruno Snell, *The Discovery of the Mind,* translated by T. G. Rosenmeyer, Cambridge, Mass., 1953.

FOREWORD

by Robert Fitzgerald

We imagine with good reason that the original composer of
this work was also the original performer. The precise nature
of his performance—ceremonious, formal, and traditional but
at the same time animated and inventive—could hardly be
conveyed in translation even if we could quite grasp or evoke
it, and we cannot. We do not know how Homer sounded as
aoidos, when or to what extent he recited or chanted and
when or to what extent he imitated voices and gestures,
played the roles he created. As to this last point, however, we
know that among rhapsodes in later centuries who memorized
and delivered these tales there were some who had mimetic
powers and used them; probably Homer did too. But what the
performer accomplished through expressive timing and intonation can at least be suggested in English rendering.

Spacing, for example, may mark a natural pause in narra-
tion or speech, a change in mood or focus—either between
one part of a divided line and another, or between whole
lines. To space in this way is to take a slight liberty with the
Greek "text." Slightly greater liberties are conceivable. As
Homer had a fondness for "epexegesis"—the explanatory or
parenthetical aside—the translator thinking of performance
may resort to a form of this now and then by inserting a brief
stage direction, as it were: e.g., on page 318, "Then in a

lower tone/he said, etc." The general principle, of which
these are applications, is that by appropriate means the shift-
ing action of the poem and the responses of the actors, originally a matter of oral performance, should be made clear in
the medium of print.

Translation can at most only suggest the Greekness of
Homer and the formulaic character of his style. As to the
Greekness: proper nouns, for example, can be given in their
Greek forms, not in the Latinized versions that Latinizing
centuries gave them. This is the general rule in the present
translation. Spelling and accentuation are used to suggest the
Greek sound. Aías, Eye-as, is not known as Ajax. The
Akhaians, Ah-kye-ans, are not Achaeans. The name of the
hero is not Achilles but Akhilleus, three and one half sylla-
bles, Ah-kill-eoos. Agamémnon, accented on the third syllable, is the son of Atreus, two and a half syllables, Áh-treoos.
Zeus is one and a half, Zeoos. On each long vowel perches a
circumflex acent: Lêto, Láy-toe; Khrysês, Khreé-sayce;
Khrysêis, Khree-sáy-is; Hêra, Háy-ra; Hêphaistos, Hay-fýce-
toss; Thersítês, Ther-seé-tayce; Pêneleôs, Pay-neh-leh-óhce;
Skôlos, Skoé-loss; Eteônos, Eh-teh-ówn-oss; Astyokhê, Ah-
steé-oh-khay. The umlaut sets its syllable apart: Danääns,
Da-ná-ans; Peiríthoös, Pay-rí-tho-oss; Asïa, Áh-zee-ah.

The reader should refuse to be intimidated by these proper
nouns, even when they come by dozens or in hundreds, as in
Book II. He should collar each, pronounce it slowly and
boldly, and savor every syllable.

There are a few deliberate inconsistencies. Helen, Priam,
and Troy have their eternal names. She is not, as in Greek,
Hêlênê, Hay-láy-nay; he is not Priamos, Preé-ah-moss; the
place is not Troiê, Troí-yay. The island of Crete is Krete not
Krêtê, Kráy-tay. The names of Patróklos and Meneláos are
accented in the familiar way, not as they are in the Greek
nominative: Pátroklos, Menélaos. A few such concessions to
common sense only make the rule of transliteration more evident. The Greek spellings are a slight strangeness to which
the ear should soon become accustomed, and they have the
effect of removing a Roman screen from between ourselves
and Homer.

Greekness of a more fundamental kind can hardly be
revealed by the mere removal of that screen. The truth is

that Homer's language and English are so remote from one another that many local effects of one are not to be reproduced in the other. The present translator once remarked that the Homeric poems, considered strictly as aesthetic objects, can no more be translated into English than rhododendron can be translated into dogwood. A little amplification of this may be in order. With respect to the shapes and phonetic qualities of language a comparison of the first three lines of the *Iliad* with the first three of *Paradise Lost* will yield certain facts and ratios. In the three Greek lines there are seventeen words to forty-five syllables, or far more than two to one in favor of polysyllables; in Milton's lines there are twenty-three words to thirty syllables, or far more than two out of three monosyllables. In the Greek there are twenty-nine single-consonant sounds out of thirty-four consonant occurrences, or more than four out of five single consonants; in Milton's lines there are six single-consonant sounds out of twenty-eight consonant occurrences, or far less than a quarter single consonants.

The Greek is therefore, first, relatively polysyllabic, and second, relatively lightfooted and fast-moving. Greek words with rare exceptions terminate in a vowel or in s (sigma), r (rho), or n (nu). English words often end in whacking or thudding consonants impossible as terminations in Greek, and liquid or nasal terminations are comparatively rare in English.

How about the way the languages construct meaning by the order of words and by the morphological twists given to words to interrelate them? In the three Greek lines, for example, three objects in the accusative precede their verbs, and one participial adjective is separated by four other words from its noun. These constructions would strain English if they were possible to it at all, and none like them appear in Milton's lines. There is no need to labor this difference between the inflected and the uninflected language.

A third, and important, point of comparison is rhythm. Homer's metrical line had six measures of which five could be and often were dactylic. This rippling line keeps its élan by variation of caesura and cola, not to mention the rich tones of vowels and diphthongs. For the original auditors there was also a melodic rise and fall of pitch, since almost every word owned a pitch intonation. English words have stress intonation, a quite different thing. But pitch intonation is scarcely more alien to English than regular dactylic meter as a norm in serious verse. Lightfooted, polysyllabic, undulating, Homeric Greek fell naturally into dactyls; hard-hitting, monosyllabic, level English does not. A good ear for quantity and a shrewd mixture of spondees may charm us briefly as we hear of harpers hoar with beards that rest on their bosoms, but in reading *Evangeline* we soon feel that this rhythm is too overtly foisted on us, the meter submerges its matter, and in the end it cloys and bores.

So remote is the Homeric medium from true English. If English is to remain English its words cannot be highly inflected, cannot often be polysyllables, cannot so often be joined with liquid neatness and rapidity, cannot happily take the dactylic meter. The quality of the Greek is not reproducible. It can no more be translated into English than rhododendron can be translated into dogwood. In saying that, the translator had in mind two types of flowering, but the two words themselves exemplify the linguistic difference: rhododendron is a polysyllabic Greek compound, dog and wood English monosyllables terminating in hard-bitten mutes, as no Greek word could. The conditions are forbidding, but the translator, all the same, will feel an irrepressible wish to make his version resemble the original; he will try at least for rhythmic variety and a lightfooted quality in his English to match that rapidity that Matthew Arnold found in Homer.

It would be convenient for the student if every line of Homer were rendered in a single line of English. In the long run, though, fidelity of this kind may conduce to infidelity on a more serious plane. As the inevitable slight instances of padding and contorted syntax accumulate, they may tire the reader and choke the life out of the poem. Homer's poem sang steadily ahead without awkwardness, and so, if possible, should an English rendering.

The largest and at the same time the subtlest problem in Homeric translation is what to do with Homer's formulae. The problem can be briefly stated: since from one point of view they are striking and important and from another point of view they are neither, how can one do justice to both aspects?

The composer making up his tale without benefit of reading or writing disposed of a traditional metrical language in which a great many phrases and lines were repeatedly useful with various slight modifications or none at all. He and his auditors assuredly heard nothing odd in this. But when the language of oral composition died out and the *Iliad* and *Odyssey* became texts, as they mysteriously did, the invariable epithets and repeated lines became noticeable to readers literately brought up on literary work. They are noticeable now to anyone reading the Greek of Homer for the first time.

There is, however, a further experience at a further stage: to the practiced reader of Homer the formulae become, with familiarity, less and less noticeable, until in the end one is barely aware of them; they are conventional signs in a language made up of conventional signs as all languages are. Their literal meanings are less important than their incantatory and ceremonious quality, and this in turn is less important than the sense they gradually convey of a self-consistent and stable universe.

The present translator hoped to bring Homer's thought and action to life at every point in English verse as fully English as Homer's Greek was fully Greek. Our language is not a language formed by an oral and metrical tradition, it is not formulaic, and we would tamper with English itself if we seriously tried to make it so. What was functional and usual in Homer would become, in our version, artificial and odd. The translator's ear alone can determine how far he should go in identical rendering of identical passages. To this translator it seemed sometimes effective to do so. On the other hand it often seemed practically irrelevant that lines n-n in a certain book=lines n-n in another book many hundreds or thousands of lines away, when the immediate context, the action in hand, required rendering in English (non-formulaic) as it had once required composition in Homeric Greek (formulaic). Likewise with Homer's ornamental or characterizing epithets: since they were often used for purely metrical convenience in the Greek, purely metrical convenience might dictate their omission in English.

When the translator does see fit to render the formulae, how should he do so? Here it is useful to remember that all languages are idiomatic and that only idiocy comes of render-

ing idioms literally. Homeric epithets rang true for his auditors. To take one, he repeatedly referred to the army before
Troy as *euknemidas Akhaious,* literally "well-greaved Akhaians." This "well-greaved" looks and sounds like an idiom
that literal rendering will betray. For one thing, we have no
ready conception of what leg armor meant to a man otherwise protected only by his helmet and breastplate and by a
shield that covered him down to the thighs. In our humble
street-fighting tradition a kick in the shins can disable a man;
how much more thoroughly would a spear-thrust or a sword-
cut? To be accoutered in greaves or leggings meant to be in
a state of combat readiness, to be prepared for battle. In the
present translation "well-greaved" is rendered by an equally
well-worn English idiom, "under arms."

For a thousand matters of great interest not touched on
in these brief remarks the reader will find Professor Hogan's
Guide invaluable. An English rendering of the *Iliad,* insofar
as it is readable, will stir curiosity as to the world the poem
presupposes, the world from which it came, and the heroic
world of its imagining. A great deal of learning, old and new,
is presented here freshly and judiciously for the satisfaction of
curiosity and the enlightenment of reading.

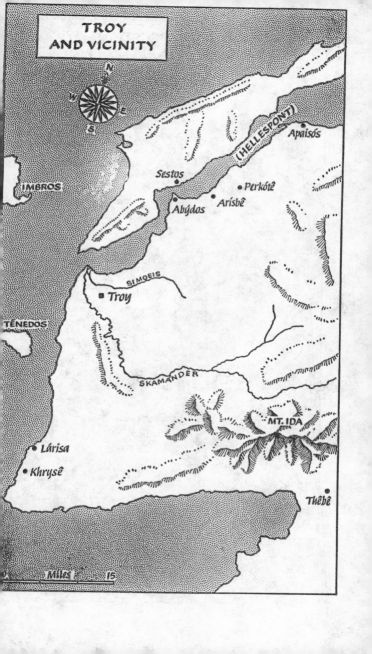

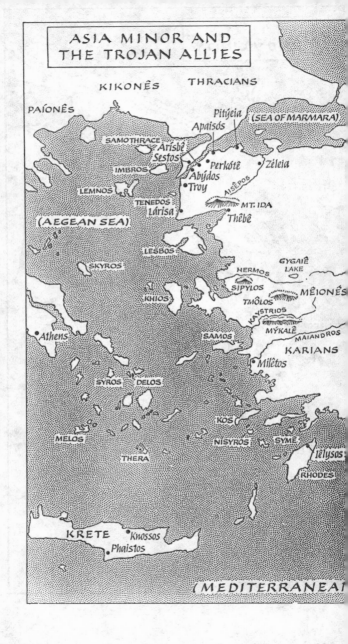

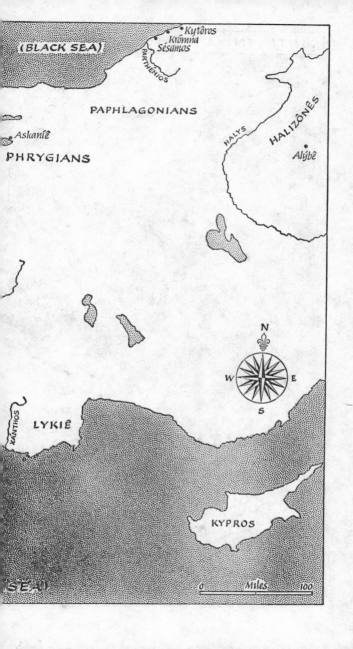

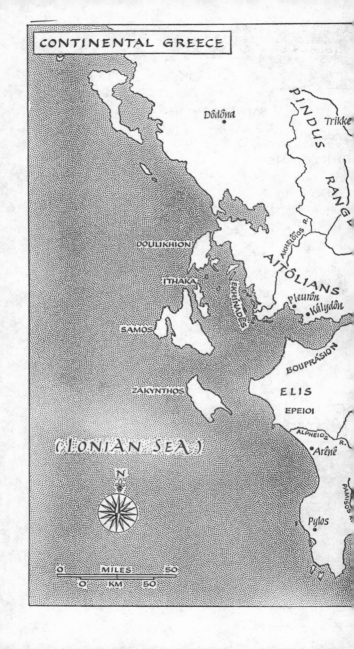

BOOK ONE

🝰🝰🝰🝰🝰🝰🝰🝰🝰🝰🝰🝰🝰

QUARREL,
OATH, AND PROMISE

Agamémnon, king of Mykênai, has received as his share of
the booty from a recent raid, Khrysêis, daughter of a priest of
Apollo. When the king refuses to return the girl and accept
ransom, Apollo sends a plague upon the army. Akhilleus calls
an assembly to consider remedies. Advised of Apollo's wrath
by the seer Kalkhas, Akhilleus urges the girl's return. When
Agamémnon insists on a substitute prize, the two men quarrel, and only Athêna's intervention persuades Akhilleus to
wait and accept "winnings three times as rich" (p. 18).

Akhilleus swears to have revenge, and retires to his tent.
Agamémnon adds to the public insult by sending heralds to
take Akhilleus' prize, Brisêis. Akhilleus asks his mother, the
goddess Thetis, to intercede with Zeus in his behalf. Zeus re-
luctantly agrees to make Agamémnon pay for dishonoring her
son. The last scene shows Hêra complaining of Zeus's fa-
voritism toward the Trojans.

Much about this quarrel, both in social context and the values at issue, will be clearer if the following description of the typical heroic society is kept in mind: "In every heroic society the chief and his associates work closely together, and it is to this degree aristocratic, though the chief may have titles and the prestige of kingship. From his point of view the seizure or the maintenance of power demands the service of men hardly less eminent than himself, to whom he must give his complete confidence and not grudge position and fame. Without them he would never attain his full ambitions, and without him they might never rise from obscurity. Legend is emphatic on this point. A heroic age is one in which the ruler is surrounded by remarkable men who go their own ways in considerable freedom but remain, even if with reservations and misgivings, under his command. . . . The rulers command in battle, but they could hardly win their full successes without the help of men almost as redoubtable as themselves. It is this co-operation of ruler and his supporters in a single military caste which provides the essential structure of a heroic age as posterity sees it. Respect for individual prowess has been extended from a single man to a company of men, who may not have his position or authority, but are his equals in worth and honour and by contributing to his glory gain their own." (C. M. Bowra, "The Meaning of the Heroic Age," *The Language and Background of Homer,* p. 32)

Homer assumes such a social context as this and creates a story by exploiting the structural weaknesses latent in the society. Individual honor and standing are reflected in the prizes distributed after battle; the prizes are material tokens of public esteem, and to be without a prize or to lose a prize is felt to taint honor and reputation. The hero depends upon the group for honor; the group is always represented in battle by individual warriors, never by anonymous platoons and battalions.

Book I is almost totally dramatic, and it is probably by his genius for dramatization that Homer chiefly distinguished himself from other Greek epic poets (see Aristotle, *Poetics,* Chapter III). Both Homeric epics quickly develop a problem which is elaborated through much of the poem until it is finally resolved by the protagonist's decisive action.

11   **Anger be now your song, immortal one:** the poet invokes the Muse. According to Hesiod, who was probably Homer's contemporary, there were nine Muses, daughters of Zeus and Memory (see Hesiod's *Theógony,* 75ff.). See I 603f. (p. 31*) for their singing on Olympos and compare the invocation at II 484ff. (p. 51).

       loss on bitter loss: for the present the consequences of his anger are only vaguely suggested. The poet becomes more specific as the poem progresses (see, e.g., the prediction of Zeus on p. 196). The loss will finally touch Akhilleus himself, but until Book XVI it is the army that suffers. Cf. Akhilleus' curse of his anger at XVIII 107 (p. 439).

       the Akhaians: Homer refers to the Greeks before Troy as the "Akhaians" (i.e., of Akhaia, in later times limited to the district along the north coast of the Peloponnesus), the "Danääns" (the descendants of Danaus, an ancient king of Argos), and the "Argives" (the people of Argos). Since the three names are used synonymously, it is apparently their different metrical shapes which account for the retention of all three.

       the will of Zeus: an allusion to Zeus's promise to Thetis to avenge the honor of her son (p. 28).

12   **Atreus' son:** characters are most fully identified by a personal name and their father's name, sometimes with the name of the grandfather. Since all the important agents are well known, some are introduced only by reference to the father, e.g., "the son of Zeus by Lêto," i.e., the god Apollo. A better example, illustrating the auditor's presumed familiarity with the story, can be found at I 307 (p. 21), where Patróklos, the comrade of Akhilleus, is mentioned casually and only by his patronymic, "the son of Menoitios"; (Fitzgerald makes it easier for the English reader by substituting Patróklos' own name for the patronymic). On p. 12 we find the

---

* Unless "Introduction" is prefixed, all page numbers cited in this volume refer to the pages of Robert Fitzgerald's translation. So XIII 389; p. 311 means Book XIII line 389 of the *Iliad,* page 311 in Fitzgerald's translation. The reader will note that each page of Fitzgerald's version represents about thirty lines of the Greek text. If this is kept in mind, citations of the Greek lines will be more readily located.

plural of the patronymic form in "Atreidai," i.e., "the sons of Atreus" (Agamémnon and Meneláos).

Khrysês: the priest of Apollo at Khrysê, a village near the south coast of the Troad. His name and his daughter's are derived from the name of the place, a rather mechanical procedure. Below he prays to Apollo of Ténedos (an island just off the coast) and the "holy towns" (named in the Greek text as Killa and Khrysê). For possible sites see Leaf, *Troy, A Study in Homeric Geography,* 216f. and 223ff.

The gods who hold Olympos: a formulaic phrase. The gods live on Mount Olympos in Thessaly, from which they observe the war and may intervene in a moment.

Sminthian: this unique epithet apparently means "the mouse god" and is perhaps used here in reference to the god's ability to bring plagues. In the following lines the more familiar conception of Apollo as the archer god takes hold. Like most prayers in the *Iliad,* this one is pragmatic: the priest has served the god well and now asks for a favor in return.

13   Phoibos: "the brilliant one." Apollo kills with his arrows (see below, "the Archer God"), but the death spreads through the army as a plague might; striking first the animals, then the men. Though Apollo is the most important divinity active for the Trojans in the battle scenes, his action here is conceived simply as a personal favor to his priest.

pyres burned night and day: fire is one of the most common motifs in the *Iliad.* Helmets gleam like fire (p. 109), sacrifices are consumed by fire, corpses are burned (p. 175), or refused the grace of fire (p. 541), the ships are threatened with fire (p. 372), and fires roar through the forests of the similes (e.g., p. 50). See the narrative and simile concluding Book VIII and the index (fire, imagery).

Akhilleus called all ranks to assembly. Hêra . . . moved him to it: see the analysis of divine motivation of human actions in Introduction, pp. 51ff. Plausible human actions are often attributed to a divinity as well as to a human agent, thus producing a kind of redundant motivation. Akhilleus' summons is crucial, and the Greek naturally assumes the gods have a part in it. The gods do not help nobodies: a hero must have the capacity for achievement before the gods take an interest in him. Among the divinities Hêra is the most bitter and unrelenting enemy of the Trojans.

a failure/in vows or hekatombs: a hekatomb is literally a sacrifice of a hundred oxen, used figuratively of any large offering. Akhilleus naturally connects the plague with a god. Nothing is a matter of chance: any success or failure will be attributed to the gods.

Kalkhas Thestórides: -ides denotes "the son of," so Kalkhas, the son of Thestor. He is the chief seer for the Akhaians. In Book II (p. 45) Odysseus recounts Kalkhas' interpretation of an omen at Aulis, before the fleet sailed for Troy. Such interpreters were honored for their skill, but were not necessarily considered infallible (cf. Hektor's rejection of Poulýdamas' counsel on p. 288). Kalkhas anticipates Agamémnon's anger and seeks protection from Akhilleus, one of many signs throughout Book I of the army's loose organization. Despite Agamémnon's recognized leadership he does not have absolute command; other chieftains may call assembly, initiate proposals, and withdraw from action without consulting him. Although the assembly of all ranks convenes and has its voice, Homer portrays an aristocratic society in which the barons are virtually the equals of the overlord.

14 **spurned his gifts:** this is a significant theme in the *Iliad:* defeated warriors supplicate the victors and offer ransom; Agamémnon tries to appease Akhilleus with gifts (Book IX); they are offered again in Book XIX and received with indifference; in Book XXIV Priam pays ransom to Akhilleus. Gifts are the tangible evidence of honor and esteem; cf. the reconciliation of these two men at the end of Book XXIII (p. 563).

15 **a prize of honor for me:** Brisêis and Khrysêis are considered little more than prizes, i.e., tokens of the honor conferred upon their chieftains by the army. In the Greek the two names have the same metrical shape and both are accompanied by the same adjective, as if to suggest their identity as prizes (cf. the note on Diomêdê p. 224). Despite Agamémnon's apparently romantic preference for Khrysêis over his wife, we see a different sort of value judgment in the last line of this speech: the clause Fitzgerald translates "my girl goes elsewhere" would more literally be "my prize goes elsewhere." Both hero and king are prone to speak of the girls as chattel. Cf. Akhilleus in IX: "as in my heart I loved/ Brisêis" (IX 342f.; p. 214) but also "my prize" (IX 367; p. 215).

16   **Aías, Idómeneus, or Prince Odysseus:** all are heroes of Akhilleus' rank who will have prominent parts in the
poem.

      Phthía: Akhilleus' native district, adjacent to
Hellas (see p. 57 and p. 216) in northern Greece.

      for your brother's sake: a reference to Meneláos
and his seduced wife, Helen. Like the two prizes of Akhilleus
and Agamémnon, Helen has become a symbol of her husband's (lost) honor, which the expedition has undertaken to
reclaim. But neither Akhilleus nor any other chieftain has a
personal stake in the issue, and there is relatively little national pride in the Argive camp. The tone and resentment are
similar in Book IX (p. 213ff.)

17   **battalion of Myrmidons:** Akhilleus' men take their
name from the Greek word for <u>ant. Seeing that his son
Aiakos, Akhilleus' grandfather, was alone on the island of
Aígina, Zeus created men from ants to be his people.</u> See p.
499.

18   **Athêna/came to him from the sky:** generally divine intervention has a personal rather than political motivation, as in the case of Apollo's response to Khrysês' prayer.
Athêna and Hêra, however, regularly move to help the Argive cause as well as individual heroes, but more out of animosity toward Troy than from love of the Argives (see p.
88f.). Usually Athêna is the actual agent, Hêra the instigator.
Akhilleus is not surprised to see her, and his tone may even
be a bit abrupt and tactless, whereas the goddess diplomat-
ically suggests future compensation if he will follow her immediate advice. See the discussion of this scene in Introduction, pp. 53ff.

      To see/the wolfishness of Agamémnon: the word
hubris has gained popular currency in English and is often
misunderstood. In this line (203) Akhilleus speaks of the
hubris of the king, and in line 214 Athêna repeats the noun,
concurring ("for his arrogance"). *Hubris* means arrogance in
action, i.e., the abuse of another person verbally or physically.
Threatening Akhilleus, belittling his contribution to the army,
and taking Brisêis, all these are hubristic acts.

      winnings three times as rich: his reply tacitly ac-
cepts these terms. Later we learn the "requital" he demands
entails the humiliation of Agamémnon. It has been asserted

that Akhilleus is, or becomes, indifferent to prizes and material rewards; the evidence is mixed (cf., e.g., the notes to p. 215).

19 **this great staff:** Homeric descriptions often include details concerning the origin and descent of the object: at II 100ff. (p. 38) the owners of Agamémnon's staff from its maker Hêphaistos are named; at X 261ff. (p. 237) the earlier owners of Odysseus' helmet are listed. If an object has had only one owner, the poet may describe the source of the materials or the way it is put together, as in the case of Pándaros' bow (IV 105ff.; p. 91).

I swear/a day will come: Akhilleus binds himself by a public oath and thus restrains future action: cf. his reply to Aías (IX 644ff.; p. 223), where he also foresees the devastation of "killer Hektor" (for this formula see the note on p. 583).

20 **Nestor:** king of Pylos, an old counselor often praised for his good advice (cf. pp. 47, 98, and 207). In a long speech at XI 656ff. (pp. 271–76) he persuades Patróklos to bring aid to the Akhaians, which is crucial for the plot of the poem. For other instances of the "when I was a young man" motif see VI 133ff. (p. 165f.), XI 668ff. (p. 272), and XXII 629ff. (p. 555).

Peiríthoös . . . Theseus: these heroes of an earlier generation figured in the battle of the Lapiths and the centaurs (see p. 59), a common subject in Greek sculpture. Homer's Greeks and those of later generations looked to the past for ethical paradigms. These exemplary tales are frequently used for argument, both to provide analogy, as at IX 524f. (p. 220):

we learned this
from the old stories of how towering wrath
could overcome great men;

and as appeals to authority:

And I repeat: they listened to my reasoning,
took my advice. Well, then, you take it too.

I 273f.

No one vies in honor: for Agamémnon's heredi-
tary kingship see II 100ff. (p. 38). Akhilleus' response to
Phoinix at IX 607ff. (p. 222) may be thematically significant:

Honored I think I am by Zeus's justice.

22   his charming Briseís: on the adjective see the note
to p. 15. The poet constantly uses fixed epithets for mortals
and immortals when the qualifying noun or adjective has no
specific relevance to the immediate context (cf. "Akhilleus,
fast in battle": 58 [p. 13] and "Hêra/whose arms are white
as ivory": I 55 [p. 13]). Homer usually characterizes his
agents by physical rather than moral attributes. Sometimes, as
in the case of Akhilleus' swiftness of foot, the attribute anticipates a significant event in the poem (Akhilleus pursues Hektor—but does not catch him!—around the walls of Troy in
Book XXII).

23   his mother: Thetis, daughter of Nêreus ("her old
father"; cf. "the Old One of the sea," p. 29), the immortal
mother of Akhilleus, who lives in the depths of the sea with
the other Nêrêïdês.

          that . . . town of Eëtíôn called Thêbê: on the bay
of Adramyttion below Troy, and also the home of Andrôm-
akhê, wife of Hektor (see p. 154f.). Akhilleus uses a
number of lines in this speech which occurred earlier in the
description of the coming of Khrysês. Oral poetry often
repeats long passages verbatim; here Akhilleus abbreviates a
good deal.

24   in Father's house: Pêleus, the father of Akhilleus
and moral "husband" of Thetis. "the son of Krónos" is Zeus.
The rebellion alluded to is otherwise unknown, and Willcock
has suggested that the poet has invented a part for Thetis in
aiding Zeus during a rebellion so that she may have a legitimate claim on his thanks. As we see in Khrysês' prayer, quid
pro quo is the rule in petitions, and Willcock's suggestion
makes sense in light of this kind of thinking. Violence among
the divinities is common enough (cf., e.g., Hêphaistos' story
on p. 31). Hesiod tells in his *Theogony* how Krónos mutilated and overthrew his father Uranos, and how in his turn
Zeus deposed Krónos. Briareus (Aigaion: see the note on p.
339) is one of three giants "with a hundred arms" who according to Hesiod aided Zeus in his war with the Titans

(*Theogony* 617ff.). Zeus's power and knowledge are greater than that of other divinities, but he is neither omnipotent nor omniscient (see p. 334ff.). On this and other possible inventions by the poet see M. M. Willcock, "Mythological Paradeigma in the *Iliad*," *Classical Quarterly* 14 (1964), 141–54.

25   doomed/the day I bore you: apparently a reference, like Akhilleus' own "as my life came from you, though it is brief" (I 352; p. 23), to the "two possible destinies" which Akhilleus explains to the embassy in Book IX (p. 216). The motif reappears at the beginning of XVI (p. 378f.), in XVIII (p. 438), and in XXIII (p. 538). Cf. "Doom for him/of all men comes on quickest" (I 505; p. 28).

25   the Sunburned: the Aithiopians, who in the *Odyssey* (I 22–26) are identified as the

most remote of men, at earth's two verges,
in sunset lands and lands of the rising sun
                    (p. 2 of Fitzgerald's translation)

take his knees: the usual attitude of a suppliant.

still burning for the . . . girl: resentment, not passion, seems to be indicated, but cf. his rather self-contradictory reply to Odysseus in IX, where he speaks of his love for Brisêis but still refers to her as a prize and refuses Agamémnon's offer to return her (IX 334–44 [p. 214]; IX 367f. [p. 215]).

25–26   Odysseus . . . the great tactician: the hero of the *Odyssey*, famed for his guile and clever speech (see the description offered by Priam, Helen, and Antênor, p. 74f.), is one of the most fully developed and individual of Homer's characters. See Chapters II and III of W. B. Stanford's *The Ulysses Theme*.

When prayers were said: for Homeric sacrifice see the note to p. 49.

27   Meanwhile unstirring and with smoldering heart: Akhilleus will be off-stage until Book IX; he reappears briefly in XI, and then in XVI he sends Patróklos into battle. Finally, in Book XVIII, he re-emerges as the central dramatic figure of the poem. Apart from his actual presence, the speeches and actions of the other agents keep him before us as the pivotal character in the *Iliad*. The translation brings out the contradictory nature of Akhilleus' action: to secure revenge for his sullied honor he retires from battle, thereby denying himself the opportunity to contend for honor in the ranks of the fighters. To win glory he must fight; to be avenged on Agamémnon he refuses to fight. His problem is not merely that of an egotist caught in his own machinations, for the values he holds (regard for his honor, unwillingness to suffer insult, pride in his achievements) are those of his society. Furthermore, Nestor has advised Agamémnon not to take Brisêis from him, and if Akhilleus has gone too far in public insult of the king, he still has some legitimate complaint (as Agamémnon himself will admit at II 377ff. [p. 47]). The present impasse is of a kind that will inevitably arise in a culture as competitive and as devoted to reputation as the Homeric culture was.

28   how low in your esteem/I am of all the gods: the Homeric divinities are just as conscious of their honor as mortals, and just as quick to take offense. As the old man Phoinix observes later, the gods too have their interest "in bravery, in honor and in strength" (IX 498; p. 219).

Here is trouble: the poem repeatedly turns to Olympos for scenes of bickering, deceit, abuse, and threats of physical violence (see, e.g., p. 87ff., 181ff., 334ff.). As often as not the tone is light: Zeus is represented as father, not king, who must fend for himself against the wiles of a wife who will have her way at any cost (p. 89), a daughter, Athêna, all too ready to conspire with Hêra, and a brother, Poseidon, who has his own reasons for wanting Troy leveled (p. 281f.). Nowhere is Homeric anthropomorphism more evident than in these quarrels, which often serve as a foil to mortal striving.

30–31 Hêphaistos' mediation is more successful than Nestor's, but the divine mediator is a clown as well as a "wondrous artisan." Homeric man respects the power and authority of the gods, but he does not attribute altruistic motives to them. A good example of this follows in Book II when Zeus sends "Sinister Dream" to Agamémnon, who, as Nestor has said, "holds authority from Zeus."

30   Hêphaistos,/master artificer: the god of metalworking and fire is best-known in the *Iliad* for the making of the armor of Akhilleus (XVIII), yet he can also manifest his power as fire, burning the river (god) Skamánder (p. 504). Like many good clowns he utilizes self-ridicule, both in the reference to his fall to Lemnos (p. 31), an island sacred to Hêphaistos, and in his apprehension of the adulterous Arês (see Demôdokos' song in *Odyssey* Book VIII).

We do not know when or by whom the division of the *Iliad* into books was accomplished. Many, like Book I, are complete episodes. Often indications of self-conscious splicing are present; e.g., at the beginning of II the idea that Zeus is asleep is retracted. A poem the length of the *Iliad* was not recited in toto very often. Self-contained episodes would have been useful to a poet who needed material for two or three hours of entertainment in the evening. So there is good reason to assume that many of these divisions go back to the time of composition. For further discussion see the notes to p. 299.

BOOK TWO

𐊀𐊀𐊀𐊀𐊀𐊀𐊀𐊀𐊀𐊀𐊀𐊀𐊀𐊀𐊀𐊀

ASSEMBLY AND
MUSTER OF ARMIES

Zeus sends a false dream to Agamémnon, who is led to believe he can now take Troy. He decides to test his assembled
troops, but they flee to the ships and must be rallied by Odysseus. Nestor suggests that the army be mustered under its
chieftains; a catalogue of Akhaian and Trojan forces concludes the book.

Despite the fact that the first scene of II initiates the plan
of Zeus and thus moves the action along, as far as Akhilleus
and his honor are concerned, the balance of this book tends
to retard the action. This happens frequently in the *Iliad*. The
poet begins a theme, interrupts it with another, and later returns to fulfill the initiated theme. With a story that was familiar to his audience, this mannerism permits the poet to
develop dramatic tensions through postponement, surprise,
and contrast. Here, e.g., Agamémnon accepts the dream and
we assume the trick of Zeus will be effective shortly. But in

fact the king almost foils Zeus's scheme by abruptly proposing to test the army. This testing precipitates flight; the army
is in no mood to continue a long, apparently futile siege.
Braking the army's flight, in turn, leads to a scene in which
Thersítês vilifies Agamémnon for having insulted Akhilleus.
The poet's indirection becomes clear when we realize that
Thersítês is a vulgar version, a burlesque, of Akhilleus himself; yet he also reflects the army's indignation that their
foremost warrior has been publicly insulted. Odysseus rebukes
and thrashes Thersítês, a show the soldiers receive with
a certain ambivalence. At least the rout has been stopped
by Odysseus and Athêna. In order to restore discipline and
morale Nestor advises that the army be marshaled by nation
and clan. The catalogues, fully half the book, follow.

So the efforts of Zeus do not come to much, and that is the
case until Book VIII. Meanwhile we find sufficient references
to Akhilleus to know he is not forgotten. As early as p. 47 we
have a partial apology from Agamémnon, and in the flight of
the army and Thersítês' impudence we may see the defeatism
that eventually leads the Akhaians to build a defensive rampart. But for a while the poet is more concerned to expand
his canvas, introduce his characters, and look back on earlier
events than he is to rush his story to the intensity of later episodes.

For examples and a brief discussion of retardation see
Scott, pp. 257–59. Carpenter (pp. 78–85) analyzes the
primary plot and "counterplots" in terms of Aristotle's poetic
theory and fifth-century dramatic practice.

35   **Sinister Dream:** cf. the personification of Strife at
XI 1ff. (p. 251) and of Sleep in XIV (p. 337). See the note
to p. 103.

36–37   Repetition of instructions, especially in a messenger's speech, is common in Homer, but this triple use (of
five lines) is out of the ordinary. Cf. the repetition of Hêra's
instructions when Athêna speaks to Odysseus (p. 40f.; 176–
81=160–65).

37   let me test them first: why Agamémnon adds this
proposal is hard to say. He seems to anticipate the army's
flight, and the testing only proves how low morale actually is.
Fitzgerald is right to call it a "curious plan" (p. 38), but his
comment amplifies what is at best tenuous in Homer's words.

On two other occasions (see pp. 204 and 331) Agamémnon proposes retreat, yet in battle he is more savage than most. Homer may have assumed his changeable temper was well known. On the Homeric portrait of Agamémnon see Whitman, pp. 156–64.

38   **thick as bees:** there are about two hundred similes in the *Iliad* of an average length of three to four lines. They are mostly drawn from nature and from the life of farmer and shepherd. The similes are usually framed by a repeated word or phrase (here "thick as bees" to "like bees innumerable"). This stylistic device is called "ring composition" and is used to structure speeches and to mark the limits of descriptions and digressions. The similes appear most frequently in the battle scenes. More comment on their content and function will be found in the notes to Books XI–XV.

       Hermês: the divine messenger, he is not as prominent in the *Iliad* as the goddess Iris, until in XXIV when he guides Priam safely into the camp of Akhilleus.

       Pélops To Atreus . . . Thyestês: Pélops, the grandfather of Agamémnon, won his wife Hippodamia in a chariot race. His sons Atreus and Thyestês, later famous for their mutual hatred, apparently enjoyed a peaceful succession according to the author of this passage.

39   **the son of Krónos has entangled me/in cruel folly:** this is only the first time Agamémnon will blame Zeus for his "folly" (cf. II 375ff. [p. 47], IX 115ff. [p. 207], and especially the speech beginning at XIX 78 [p. 460f.]). For the Greeks, whose gods are not identified with moral laws, there is no blasphemy in "blaming" the divinity. To assign responsibility to the gods is a way of recognizing that the plans of a human agent have gone wrong. Later Priam will say to Helen:

> You are not to blame,
> I hold the gods to blame for bringing on
> this war against the Akhaians, to our sorrow.
>
>   III 164–65 (p. 73)

Though man tends in this fashion to separate himself from his failures, he also attempts to rectify his mistakes. So Agamémnon tries to appease Akhilleus with gifts (p. 207) and Antênor suggests the Trojans should return Helen (p. 172f.). See the discussion of Nilsson, *HGR,* p. 163ff.

40   **Ikarian deeps:** the northeastern Aegean sea, named for Ikaros, the son of Daidalos, who fell into the sea after disregarding his father's warning not to fly too high.

          overriding their own destiny: the basic meaning of destiny (or fate) in Homer is "portion" or "lot," and the primary reference is to a quantitative measure, usually length of time, and, for the individual, length of life. Hence Thetis refers, hyperbolically, to Akhilleus as having the swiftest fate of any man. From this conception destiny is extended to include the content of a man's life, whatever good or bad fortune he may experience. Since Homeric man views the gods as constantly interfering in human affairs, his "fate" is susceptible to sudden, unexpected change: things happen contrary to man's desires and plans. But because the heroes retain a good respect for their own strength, they shrink from assigning to divinity full control for all events. Hence contradictory expressions like "overriding their own destiny" recognize a tendency of events (based on human impulse and decision) as well as the power of the gods to affect, often radically, that tendency. See Nilsson, *HGR,* pp. 167–69, and the notes to p. 183. Fränkel (pp. 56–58) suggests that the contradictions pertaining to fate ought to be seen in light of the tension between the received poetic tradition (historically real for the poet) and Homer's personal aesthetic design.

          Tireless/daughter of Zeus who bears the shield of cloud: the epithet here translated as "tireless" (the traditional meaning) is used only of Athêna (three times in this formulaic line). Its specific applicability to the goddess, like its etymology, is uncertain. Based on hints in the text, Fitzgerald translates *aigis* as "shield of cloud" and "shield of storm" (p. 93). This supernatural weapon with "raveled tassels" (pp. 50, 132) is usually associated with the sky god, Zeus, though Athêna and Apollo also use it (cf. especially pp. 357–60).

42   **crooked-minded Krónos:** the epithet (eight times) is applied only to Krónos. The Homeric poems offer no explanation for its meaning, but his rough and devious handling of his children in Hesiod's *Theogony* may be the story alluded to. In his commentary on the *Theogony* (see 453ff.) M. L. West suggests that the original meaning was not "crooked-planning" but "Kronos of the curved sickle" (p. 158). Its application to Prometheus and analogical formations show that the new meaning was well established by Hesiod's time.

Thersîtês: this is his only appearance in the *Iliad* and the one occasion on which a common soldier speaks in assembly. His appearance suits his manner. In Greek, things or people who are "fine" or "beautiful" tend also to be considered "good"; the ugly are morally repulsive (cf. Plato, *Republic* 401a). His abuse of Agamémnon contains charges made by Akhilleus in Book I, and his last line ("you'd never abuse . . ." p. 43) was used by Akhilleus at I 232 (p. 19), so that he appears a burlesque of the great hero. The first two lines of Odysseus' rebuke (246f.) also recall the quarrel in Book I: 246b adapts a phrase describing Nestor at I 248 ("the Pylians' orator, eloquent and clear"; p. 20); 247 ("Will you stand up to officers alone?") recalls Nestor's language at I 277 ("Akhilleus, for your part, do not defy/your King and Captain"; p. 20). Though the language is formulaic, and thus these repeated phrases may be simply a matter of chance, the concentration and thematic point perhaps imply a poetic design.

43 **father of Telémakhos:** Odysseus' only son, born just prior to the departure of the expedition. He is the central character in *Odyssey* I–IV.

44 **the raider of cities:** Odysseus shares this generic epithet with three heroes and two gods. His association with Athêna, which is particularly stressed in the *Odyssey*, is already a feature of the *Iliad*. Cf., e.g., Diomêdês' praise at X 242ff. (p. 236f.) and her aid during the race in XXIII (p. 559). His reputation as a speaker and counselor is secure, but he is not always so effective as he is here (cf. Antênor at III 204ff. [p. 74] for praise and Akhilleus' violent rebuff at IX 308ff. [p. 213]).

to let you seem disgraced: Odysseus appeals to three values in this prologue: 1) loyalty: will they let their commander suffer disgrace, which would also touch them? 2) obligation to the oath; 3) courage: don't play the coward now.

45 **at Aulis:** it is in Boiotia opposite the island of Euboia. Homer does not mention the sacrifice of Agamémnon's daughter, Iphigenia, at Aulis (see the note to p. 208).

46   **Nestor/lord of Gerênia, charioteer:** in antiquity Gerênia was thought to be a town or river, but the meaning was disputed even then. Nestor shares the generic epithet "charioteer" with Phyleus (p. 55), Tydeus, Oineus and Pêleus; "lord of Gerênia" is reserved exclusively for him (25 times).

47   **to avenge the struggles and the groans of Helen:** line 356=line 590 (p. 54). Does the line mean that Helen has struggled and groaned, or that they would avenge their sufferings on behalf of Helen? Both views (subjective and objective genitives) were advanced by Alexandrian scholars. At III 172ff. (p. 73) Helen seems to suggest that she left home voluntarily.

48   **senior captains:** Idómeneus leads the Kretans (p. 56); Aías (Ajax in the more familiar Latinized form), the son of Telamôn, is the most formidable warrior after Akhilleus; Aías (the "lesser" Ajax), son of Oïleus, leads the Lokrians (p. 52); the son of Tydeus is Diomêdês, apparently the youngest of the great captains.

49   This is the second time a sacrifice is described (seven of these lines were used on p. 26f.) and is the fullest account in the *Iliad*. The "barley strewn" refers to the practice of scattering grain between the horns of the animal before cutting its throat. When the animal has been skinned, pieces are cut from the thigh bones ("joints"), which are wrapped in fat and covered with strips of meat, apparently to produce a mock fillet. All this constitutes the portion for the gods which is burned over the fire together with the "tripes," or inner organs, the latter being eaten ("kidneys had been tasted"); then the rest of the victim is cut up and roasted for the banquet. The portion offered to the gods reminds us of Prometheus' deception of Zeus when the custom of sacrifice was first instituted at Mekone: by wrapping the bones in fat Prometheus succeeded in tricking Zeus into taking the poorer portion (see Hesiod's *Theogony* 535ff.).

50   Five similes anticipate the catalogue of ships. Each simile emphasizes a different aspect of the scene: the glitter of the weapons, the noise of the army, their numbers, the guidance of their leaders, and finally Agamémnon's overlordship.

> **Asia's meadowland . . . Kaystrios:** when places are named in the similes, they are regularly Ionic and Asiatic.

> **beside Skamánder:** the chief river of the plain, which is also called Xánthos (cf. XX 74; p. 475).

51   all those who sailed . . . and number all the ships: the catalogue of ships, which extends to p. 60, presents a number of problems both for the *Iliad* itself and for the history of Greek epic poetry. Only the main issues will be summarized here. 1) In the course of his advice Nestor suggested the troops be marshaled by nation and clan, preparatory to the day's battle. But in fact Homer offers us a list of the ships which came to Troy nine years prior to the events of the *Iliad*. The procedure seems both clumsy and anachronistic. 2) If a comparison is made between the catalogue and the rest of the *Iliad* on such points as numbers of troops sent, the political divisions described, and the leadership provided, inconsistencies and contradictions immediately appear. For example, the Boiotians, mentioned so conspicuously at the beginning of the catalogue and given a very respectable complement, have almost no place in the action of the *Iliad*. Elsewhere there is the strange division of the Argolid between Agamémnon, who rules from the fortress of Mykênai (p. 54), and Diomêdês, who rules Argos itself, Tiryns, and the whole plain below Mykênai (p. 53). No such historical division is known, nor is such a state as is here attributed to Agamémnon particularly easy to account for; and other passages (II 108; p. 38) suggest Agamémnon is "lord of all Argos." 3) A number of details, such as the explanations concerning Prôtesílaos (p. 58) and the absence of Philoktêtês (pp. 58–59), have seemed to many scholars crude interpolations designed to adapt the catalogue to the present situation. 4) Numerous places mentioned in the catalogue were not in existence in the eighth century, and a good number cannot be identified at all.

This situation has confused ancient and modern commentators alike, so that opinions concerning the origin and authenticity of the catalogue have varied enormously; some consider it a poetic fiction, others view it as a virtually exact historical record of a muster of ships in Mycenaean times.

While the truth is probably to be found somewhere between
these extremes, modern consensus seems to be that much of
the geographic and political information of the catalogue survives from Mycenaean or sub-Mycenaean times. In the opinion of these scholars, the oral poetic tradition to which
Homer was heir preserved, and no doubt modified, an early
list of heroes, cities, and ships which the poet of the *Iliad* saw
fit to integrate into his poem. Catalogue poetry was much admired in archaic Greece. This appreciation alone might have
sufficed as reason for the inclusion of these 365 lines and of
the Trojan catalogue which follows to complete Book II. In
Fitzgerald's view, its artistic function is to widen the world
of the poem, otherwise confined to a beachhead.

Students who wish more archaeological and historical information than can be found in these notes should consult *The
Catalogue of the Ships in Homer's Iliad* by R. Hope Simpson
and J. F. Lazenby. For the view that "the Catalogue is
substantially a Mycenaean composition" see Chapter IV
("The Homeric Description of Mycenaean Greece") in D. L.
Page's *History and the Homeric Iliad*.

Pêneleôs: he is mentioned in four later passages,
having a little success in XIV (p. 345) before being wounded
by Poulýdamas in XVII (p. 426), where Lêitos is also hit.
The other captains of the Boiotians are killed in XIV and XV.

The catalogue begins with Greece north of the isthmus of
Corinth, starting with the Boiotians, then moving north-
ward to "Minyan/Orkhómenos" (p. 52), northwesterly to
Phôkians, east to the Lokrians, then to the island of Euboia,
and on to Athens and Sálamis (p. 53), south of the Boiotians
(thus making the tour a spiral).

The number of fighters per ship varies from 50 to 120;
even if the lower figure is used, the number of troops in an
expedition of over 1,100 ships reaches a size incredible for
Mycenaean Greece, and far greater than would have been
required to besiege the rather small city of Troy.

52   **rocky Pythô:** Delphi; the only other reference to
this famous site of Apollo's oracle is in IX (p. 216).

Aías . . . Oïleus' son: "Aías the Short" to be distinguished from "Aías the Tall," both major heroes who fight
together in XII and XIII (e.g., p. 291ff.).

53   **Athens:** despite its later fame, the city of Erékhtheus (a mythical king for whom the Erekhtheum on the Athenian acropolis was named) has no conspicuous part in the *Iliad*. The Athenian captain Menéstheus appears in a short catalogue in XIII (p. 320), and in three other passages of slight consequence for the story.

Great Aías led twelve ships: Aías (Ajax) the son of Telamón, after Akhilleus the greatest of the Akhaian warriors. This brief description, seemingly denigrating his stature and suggesting a dependence upon Athens, was suspected even in antiquity as an interpolation, usually attributed to some Athenian of the sixth century who desired poetic justification for Athenian claims (against those of Megara) to the island of Sálamis. As we learn from later passages (e.g., p. 188), Aías' camp occupied the place of honor on one flank of the Akhaian line, Akhilleus' camp holding the other end.

Argos . . . Tíryns: the catalogue passes to the Peloponnesus, where the "massive walls" of Tíryns remain to this day, an impressive reminder of Mycenaean power. Tydeus (the father of Diomêdês), Kapanéus, Mêkisteus, and Adrêstos (p. 54) all participated in the famous expedition of the Seven against Thebes. A large section in Book V (p. 109ff.) is devoted to the success of Diomêdês on the battlefield.

54   **Mykênai:** Agamémnon's fortress, the remains of which are illustrated in many books on Greek archaeology, is curiously near Argos, seat of Diomêdês, and access to the sea would seem limited to the Gulf of Corinth to the north. But the size of the armament is in keeping with Agamémnon's status as "most kingly." See the note on Períphêtês, p. 369.

Lakedaimôn: in south central Peloponnesus, to the east of Pylos, the kingdom of Nestor. The boundaries of Pylos are disputed, in part because of a passage in IX (p. 208) where Agamémnon offers Akhilleus as a marriage gift "seven flourishing strongholds . . . all lying near the sea in the far west/of sandy Pylos." Apparently Agamémnon had prerogatives over cities in the Pamisos valley, between Lakedaimôn and Nestor's kingdom.

Thamyris/the Thracian: Greek mythology offers a number of stories in which mortals foolishly contend with the immortals; in this respect the minstrel Thamyris is kin to King Lykourgos (p. 145) and Niobê (p. 587), and to

Sisyphus and Tantalos, whose sufferings in Hades are recorded in Odyssey XII. The harp (or lyre) is the instrument usually mentioned as providing music for song (see Akhilleus p. 209 and the harvesters p. 453). For references to the flute see p. 229 and p. 451.

55   Because the Arcadians occupy the land-locked central plateau of the Peloponnesus, they are loaned ships by Agamémnon. Elis (occupied by the Epeioi) is to the west of Arcadia, along the coast north of the kingdom of Pylos. From here the catalogue turns to the islands of northwestern Greece (the kingdoms of Megês and Odysseus), then to Aitolia on the north shore of the Gulf of Corinth. Like Aías, son of Telamôn, Odysseus leads a rather small squadron compared to his personal prominence in the fighting and in the councils.

56   **Thoas:** a fuller, though difficult, account of the misfortunes of the family of Oineus, and especially of Meléagros, will be found on pp. 220–22.

Idómeneus . . . led the Kretans: The description now turns to the island kingdoms, beginning with Krete, moving east to Rhodes, then back north (Kos), and finally to the continent again and the states in the north of Greece. Most archaeologists believe Knossos was destroyed no later than the early fourteenth century; consequently the prominence of the Kretan contingent in a war dated two centuries later has raised a serious discrepancy between literary and archaeological evidence for the historical antecedents of the Trojan war. Both Idómeneus and Meríonês appear repeatedly in the poem.

Tlêpólemos, the son of Herakles: Tlêpólemos is killed by Sarpêdôn in V (p. 129f.); like Meléagros, he has killed an uncle. Homicides within a family, accidental or intended, are a common cause of migration. Cf. the simile describing Priam before Akhilleus, p. 583, and homicide in the index. Hêraklês figures often in the thinking of Homeric characters. As the foremost hero of the preceding generation, he offers examples of achievement and suffering to a culture which looks to the past for moral guidance (see, e.g., XVIII 117ff. [p. 439] and XIX 95ff. [p. 460f.], where the story of Hêraklês' birth to Alkmênê is told by Agamémnon).

57   **Argos of Pelasgians:** a brief invocation inaugurates the final section of the Akhaian catalogue, which is perhaps the most difficult section for precise geographical definition. The whole area lies to the north of Thermopylae and the kingdom of the Lokrians listed previously. Pelasgian Argos is thus distinguished from the Argos of the Peloponnesus and has been identified with the district along the Sperkheios River. Of the places mentioned in the kingdom of Akhilleus only Trekhis has been confidently identified (later Trachis). Akhilleus usually refers to his home as Phthía, but the exact relation of Phthía, Hellas (a district), and Pelasgian Argos remains uncertain.

Lyrnessos and Thêbê are in the same area. In XIX (p. 466) Brisêis says Akhilleus killed her husband and sacked the city of Mynês. Apparently Mynês was king of Lyrnessos, and perhaps the husband of Brisêis. Whether Akhilleus "burned for her" or "because of her," i.e., because she had been taken from him, may be debated (the same verb is translated at IX 567 [p. 221]: "when *in* her *anguish over* a brother slain"). One version does not exclude the other, however.

58   Prôtesílaos: "his bride" is Laodamia; the story and the manner of its addition suggest, once again, an adaptation of the catalogue to its present situation. Homer begins by noticing his death, then his bride's grief, and later the cause of his death. According to tradition the Greeks had received an oracle that the first man ashore would perish. Prôtesílaos gallantly accepted that fate. His kingdom was north and east of Phthía, along the coast and below that of Eumêlos, son of Admêtos and Alkestis, the subjects of Euripides' *Alcestis*.

58–59   Philoktêtês, the great archer: Fitzgerald's "had been commanded" suggests by its tense a more naturally integrated account than Homer actually gives. In the Greek lines 721ff. seem to be an addition which explains the absence of the famous archer (and subject of Sophocles' *Philoctetes*). The Akhaians "remembered and called him back" when, in the last year of the war after Akhilleus had been killed, it was learned that his presence was necessary for the fall of Troy. Philoktêtês had his bow as a gift from the dying Hêraklês, and used it to kill Paris.

59   two sons of old Asklêpios: these are the physicians to the Akhaian army as well as soldiers; Makhaôn is wounded in XI (p. 267), and Akhilleus sends Patróklos to inquire after him (p. 270). These "men of Trikkê" and also the "soldiers from Orménios" occupied western and northern Thessaly, along the Pindus Mountains.

      Peiríthoös: cf. Nestor's allusion p. 20. His son Polypoitês is mentioned four times, most significantly in XXIII (p. 561f.), where he achieves some success in the games. His kingdom is identified with territory to the south of Mount Olympos, including a stretch of the river Pêneios.

59–60   The kingdom of Gouneus, apparently inland, has eluded exact definition. Dôdôna, in Epiros, is well to the west and across the Pindus range. The Titarêssos River has not been identified with certainty.

60   **a branch of Styx:** the river of the underworld by which the gods take their oaths (see note on p. 338). Underground rivers which surface in full flow are often identified with branches from the rivers of the underworld.

      the Magnêtês: the problem is that their territory is too small, but at least they have access to the sea, more than can be said for the people of Gouneus and other Thessalians.

      of all the men and horses/who were the finest: in the answer the horses precede the men. This figure is called *hysteron proteron* ("last first") and was especially associated with Homer because of his habit of taking the last (*hysteron*) item in a series and treating it first (*proteron*) in the subsequent series. So in the speeches the respondent often begins with the last of a series of questions or arguments and proceeds from there in reverse order of their introduction. See Bassett, pp. 120–28.

      Phêrês' pastures: Phêrês is the father of Admêtos, and grandfather of Eumêlos, who, despite his excellent team, takes only a consolation prize in the games of XXIII. Apollo spent a year as servant to Admêtos, a punishment imposed by Zeus for his killing of the Kyklopes, who had made the lightning bolts for Zeus. Those bolts were used against the last great enemy of Zeus's reign, Typhôeus (see p. 61).

61   **Typhôeus:** this monster is associated with Kilikia in southeastern Asia Minor. Einárimos: the first syllable is probably a preposition, but whether the second element refers to a people or a place is uncertain. See Hesiod, *Theogony* 820ff. for Typhôeus (or Typhôn, as it is also spelled).

Iris: the first appearance of the messenger of the gods; she has little personality and regularly impersonates a mortal. As in her next appearance (p. 71), she assumes the form of a mortal who might do naturally what Homer has chosen to implement through divine motivation. Cf. the note to p. 13 and Introduction p. 51ff.

All city gates, wide open,/yawned: the poet wants a Trojan catalogue to complement the Akhaian, and the battle will be fought on the plain. But Hektor's obedience runs contrary to past tactics:

As long as I was in the battle, Hektor
never cared for a fight far from the walls;
his limit was the oak tree by the gate.

Akhilleus at IX 352ff. (p. 214)

62   **Briar Hill . . . Myrinê's tomb:** cf. Aigaion/Briareus, p. 24. There are four such instances of double names in the *Iliad*. The difference may be between traditional poetic naming and normal usage in the poet's own time.

The Trojan catalogue is shorter and briefer in its descriptions. Although some scholars have argued for the great antiquity of the list, our archaeological information about the sites mentioned is less complete and, otherwise, certain severe objections to this view can be raised (e.g., Milêtos, a Greek city, is said to be occupied by the Karians). Until more information on the geography and history of the Near East in the second millennium comes to light, it is best to withhold judgment. For discussion see Hope Simpson and Lazenby, pp. 176–81, and *A Companion to Homer,* pp. 300–6.

Hektor: Priam's eldest son, greatest warrior among the Trojans as well as their strategist.

The Dardans . . . Aineías: Aeneías, hero of Vergil's *Aeneid,* gives the genealogy of the house of Priam when he faces Akhilleus in XX (p. 480). The Dardans are named for Dárdanos, who founded Dardániê, a town near Troy, which is itself named for Trôs, grandson of Dárdanos. Trôs's son Ilos (cf. Ilion) accounts for the last place-name commonly used by Homer for the city and the area near it.

Zéleia . . . Ida: the poet begins each section of the Trojan catalogue with the place nearest Troy, then proceeds on a line away from the city. Mount Ida, frequently mentioned in the poem, lies to the south and east of the Troad; the Aisêpos River extends from its slopes to the Propontis.

sons of Mérops Perkôsios: four lines here are found again in XI (p. 261), where these sons are killed by Diomêdês.

Perkótê . . . Arísbê: cities along the Hellespont.

63 tough Pelasgians: apparently a part of the same tribe mentioned on p. 57, which had migrated eastward, but cf. *A Companion to Homer*, p. 302.

Thracians . . . Kikonês . . . Paíonês: tribes living on the north side of the Hellespont ("Hellê's rushing water").

Paphlagonians . . . Halizônês: the former lived on the south shore of the Black Sea, the latter perhaps beyond them, though the location of Alýbê was a mystery even in antiquity.

Mysians . . . Phrygians: inland tribes of Asia Minor. The battle at the river takes place in XXI, after Akhilleus' return to battle, where, however, Énnomos is not explicitly mentioned.

63–64 Mêionês . . . Karians . . . Lykians: they are along the coast of Asia Minor, from north to south. Sarpêdôn and Glaukos are by far the most important of the allies so far as the *Iliad* is concerned.

64 Akhilleus/Aiákidês: Akhilleus is the grandson of Aiakos. Nástês is not mentioned in XXI when Akhilleus kills so many Trojans in the river.

BOOK THREE

~~~~~~~~~~~~~~~~~~~~~~~~~~~~~~~~~~~~

DUELING FOR A
HAUNTED LADY

The battle is about to be joined when Meneláos challenges
Paris to single combat. Preparations are made for this duel,
and the scene changes to the walls of the city, where Helen
tells Priam of the Greek leaders. Paris is saved by Aphrodítê
and returned to the city. The book concludes with a scene between him and Helen.

A modern reader will expect a full-scale battle after the catalogues, and the opening lines of Book III, with their imagery
of noise and clouded confusion, seem to announce as much.
But even during the general engagements of the *Iliad* Homer's
focus is on individuals, so that his auditor would not expect at
this point a description of companies, battalions, and divisions
maneuvering in battle. After a battle begins, many chance encounters are narrated. These may be preceded by a challenge,
but they are often limited to the cast of a spear, comment on
its effect, and response (speech and/or action) from the other

side. The duel between Paris and Meneláos is distinguished
from such engagements by its formality: the challenge and response (p. 70), truce, sacrifice, oaths (p. 77), prayer (p. 78),
arming (p. 79), and the actual fight, which, typically, has several stages. What surprises us and seems anachronistic is not
that they fight, but that all this has the air of happening for
the first time, and not after years of war. The impression that
the scene is transposed from an earlier period is heightened
by the scene on the wall of Troy. Cf. the duel between Hektor and Aías in Book VII.

Though the duel aborts, decisive impressions have been
added: 1) the Trojan elders condemn the war; 2) Paris is
despised by his brother, wife, and community; 3) a second-
rate Akhaian prince will (usually) beat a second-rate Trojan
prince.

Contrasts of various kinds contribute to the thematic coherence: Paris, dressed in a leopard skin and without armor,
meets the armed and eager Meneláos, "a hungry lion"; the
Trojan elders are unsympathetic to Helen, with whom Priam
sympathizes; Meneláos prays to Zeus but Aphrodítê intervenes to save Paris. There are opposed stylistic forces at work
here also. A linear impulse prompts the addition of item after
item. Helen appears, then the counselors' opinion of her, then
Priam's (contrasting) opinion, then Helen's opinion (self-
reproach). Helen is the mediating figure, but the poet is silent
about the relation of Priam to his counselors. We are left to
ponder this tacit division within the Trojan council until Book
VII (p. 172ff.), where the implicit issue is faced although not
resolved. Consequently, it seems fair to say that contrast,
which is an aspect of parataxis, pulls us back, i.e., against the
linear impulse, since it calls for comparison of items (here,
opinions) each of which is presented as a complete, discrete
unit. Meanwhile the narrative moves from scene to scene till
we notice that the book has "progressed" from battlefield to
boudoir.

The duel between Paris and Meneláos and the view from the
wall (called the "teichoscopia") are in a sense anachronisms;
an annalistic tradition would have placed such scenes at the
beginning of the war. Homer has expanded his canvas to include these and other scenes which a strictly historical or
chronological method would exclude. While the paratactic

style frees the poet from the restraints of a logical, organic economy, it also carries the danger of infinite regress and structural chaos. In his *Rhetoric* (III 9) Aristotle commented on this style: "The running style is the ancient one. . . . By a 'running' style I mean one which has no end in itself, until the sense comes to an end. It is unpleasing on account of this indefiniteness; for everyone wishes to descry the end." (Jebb's translation). Yet Homer controls this process and style, gives it an "end," and keeps the end in view, a poetic achievement we might better appreciate if more examples of Greek epic survived.

67   **the streams of Ocean:** according to Homer the world is flat, surrounded by the river Ocean; cf. p. 109 for the rising of the sun from Ocean and p. 443 for its setting in Ocean. See the note on p. 336. Here the reference is to the southern boundary of the world and to a Pygmy people (of Africa) with whom the cranes supposedly waged war annually. Mythological allusions are rare in Homer's similes.

68   **Aléxandros:** this is another name for Paris and means "he who wards off men." It has been found to be a proper name in the Mycenaean period. In origin Paris is not a Greek word; Apollodorus (III. 12.5) says he got the name Aléxandros from successfully defending his flocks.

      A hungry lion: Fitzgerald has allowed himself variety in phrasing the introductions to the similes, which in Greek word; Apollodorus (III.12.5) says he got the name . . ."

      Hektor: means "Holder" or "Defender." As in Book I, the poet assumes all his characters are familiar to his audience. Though Paris' taking of Helen occasioned the war, Hektor is the leader of the Trojans and the single hero upon whom Troy's survival depends. His rebuke (a common type of speech in the poem) of Paris clearly defines his own sense of the Trojan guilt: they ought long ago to have stoned Aléxandros to death (p. 69).

69   **pale-gold Aphrodítê:** the daughter of Zeus and Diônê is prominent in Books III–V. Her other special epithet is rendered by Fitzgerald "she who smiles on smiling love." Homer assumes we know of the judgment of Paris and thus the reasons for Aphrodítê's protection of this Trojan hero (see notes to p. 13). Hektor concludes by taunting Paris for the gifts of Aphrodítê, which is the topic Paris turns to first, before he speaks of the duel (*hysteron proteron*: see notes to pp. 60 and 115).

   wishing will not bring them: this translation makes sense in the context, but the clause is ambiguous. Whitman's interpretation ("No one would choose them willingly": see on p. 223) is the more natural translation of the clause, though it seems a little strained in light of the rest of the passage. Cf. Fränkel, p. 67f.

70   **Hektor, there in the flashing helmet:** the phrase translates a single compound epithet, used thirty-eight times of Hektor and only one other time, of Arês (XX 38). On this same page we find "Meneláos, clarion in war": the epithet is used sixteen times of Meneláos, twenty-one times of Diomêdês, two times each of Aías and Hektor. Such modifiers easily become generic when, as in the case of the Greek forms of Meneláos and Diomêdês occurring at the end of the line, proper names have the same metrical shape. So Meneláos shares "whom the wargod loves" (p. 76) with three other warriors. Fitzgerald has varied his translation of such epithets, sometimes omitting them altogether.

   as the iron enters/deepest in me: i.e., since the pain of this business especially pertains to me.

71   **Earth and Hêlios:** Hêlios is the sun. So they will sacrifice to deities below and above and to Zeus, god of oaths. See p. 77 for Agamémnon's prayer which explains the choice of deities.

   Hektor meanwhile had sent two runners: this language is echoed at 245ff. (p. 76: "Meanwhile . . . the criers came/with sacrificial sheep"). The ring composition defines the limits of the "digression." Helen's appearance is thematically more relevant than a description of the heralds' errand. The teichoscopia ("view from the wall") constitutes a scenic parataxis: they fight because of Helen, so she is presented, as is the attitude of the Trojans toward her. But Homer does not explain the scenic shift; he simply makes it.

   The temporal continuum (something is always happening, so that there is no dead time or lost time) is maintained despite the errand. As the heralds are dispatched Helen is introduced; when Helen's scene is finished, the heralds have reached the city and can summon Priam. The intervening scene acts as a bridge, though one with significant content. Thus for Homer these events are simultaneous and co-extensive, whereas a more realistic technique might note that the heralds required more time for their mission than actually elapsed on the wall. Even when Homer notes a temporal gap, e.g., the twelve days the gods spend "among the Sunburned" (Book I, pp. 25 and 27), his agents and actions remain unaffected by the lapse of time. The poet will not say: "meanwhile Akhilleus had thought the matter over and had resolved to . . ."

72   **Aithrê, child of Pittheus:** this is a curious and unexplained anachronism. Aithrê was the mother of the Athenian hero Theseus (Nestor's reference, I 265; p. 20). The story was that Theseus abducted Helen, then her brothers raided Attica and recovered her, carrying off Aithrê in reprisal. By now she is very old.

his counselors: Pánthoös has sons prominent in the battle, and Antênor opposes the war in council (VII 348ff.; p. 172), but the rest are unimportant to our story, even though three are brothers of Priam (see p. 480).

Skaian Gates: the western gates of the city.

72–73   **"We cannot rage at her . . . Ah, but still:** an example of parataxis within a speech. The old counselors express their appreciation of Helen's loveliness, which makes the war "no wonder"; then they reverse themselves and wish she were returned to Meneláos. Then Priam speaks to Helen but responds to their judgment. See Introduction, p. 31, and the notes to Agamémnon's speech p. 93.

73   **Unearthliness. A goddess/the woman is to look at:** a man in his power is like a god; so a woman's beauty or distinction is compared to the female divinities. Cf. Akhilleus at IX 389f. (p. 215).

You are not to blame: nether Akhaian nor Trojan hesitates to blame the gods (see the note to p. 39). In her response Helen seems to accept responsibility for following Paris.

The poet does not expect his audience to mind, or even notice, the anachronism of this scene in which Priam asks the identity of warriors who have been besieging his city for years, one of whom has actually visited his city on an embassy (p. 74). Much admired for its poignancy, the scene has also been condemned as a late interpolation by those who demand a more organic aesthetic development than the *Iliad* evinces.

       or was that life a dream: Leaf notes five other occurrences of this trope. See the note to p. 581

74   **Phrygia:** to the east and inland from Troy. The Sangarios flows north from what is now central Turkey into the Black Sea. The Amazons figure in the adventures of a number of Greek heroes (see the story of Bellérophontês, p. 147).

75   **Kastor . . . Polydeukês:** Helen's mother, Leda, was loved by Zeus and gave birth to two sets of twins, Helen and Klytaimnestra (p. 15), and Kastor and Polydeukês, known as the Dioskouroi ("sons of Zeus").

76   **life-bestowing earth:** the phrase is also used at XXI 63 (p. 495):

>   or will the fertile earth
> detain him, as it does the strongest dead?"

Helen's self-reproach and sense of loss win her a sympathy not always granted by the later tradition (cf. Aeschylus, *Agamemnon*, 224ff.). Cf. her speeches on pp. 152f. (self-reproach, abuse of Paris, sympathy for Hektor) and 592f. (self-reproach and lament for Hektor).

       Idaios: critics often note Homer's objectivity. This speech, although not an authorial comment, illustrates this trait. Poet and characters tend to use the same descriptive words and phrases for the same things (here, e.g., the formulae "Trojan breakers of horses," "Akhaians mailed in bronze," "Meneláos, whom the wargod loves," "the grazing land of Argos," and "Akhaia, country of fair women"). Thus the formulae have an aesthetic dimension: everyone perceives the world in the same way. And they have a comparable rhetorical function: everyone talks about the world in the same way. This shared style of speech and thought creates the illusion of a stable world, the experience of which is shared by all. Cf. the speech of Sôkos p. 264, and the note there.

77   **O powers underground:** apparently the Furies, explicitly mentioned in XIX (p. 460), and best-known as "chastisers of dead men" from Aeschylus' *Oresteia*. See the

note to p. 217. For punishment after death see *Odyssey* XI
576ff., where Odysseus witnesses the punishment of Tityos,
Tantalos, and Sisyphos.

In the *Iliad* men do not look to an afterlife for either rewards or punishment, nor do the deities show much interest
in exacting punishment for moral failings in this life, let alone
in Hades. Zeus, viewed here and elsewhere as the god most
interested in the sanctity of oaths ("the peace of Zeus," p. 71,
might also be translated "the oaths of Zeus"), is also the god
who "would not abide [i.e., fulfill]/by what they swore" (p.
78; cf. II 419; p. 49). Thus while passages like this and
XXIII 581ff. (p. 553) imply a firm belief in the efficacy of
oaths, the poet clearly shows time and again the failure of
oaths, often because of the gods' indifference to them. That
Zeus does not bind both parties to their word does not keep
mortals from appealing to him as the god most likely to
avenge broken faith (so Agamémnon at IV 234ff. [p. 96] and
IV 160ff. [p. 93]; cf. the attitudes of Antênor [p. 172f.] and
Hektor [p. 163]).

79   **buckled on his armor:** notes on an expanded version of this typical scene will be found in the analysis at p.
252. Since Paris wore a leopard skin (p. 68) when he left the
city, he must change to armor. Clothing and armor reveal
the man: Paris was not ready to fight. Now the poet can add
the formal description of arming to the ritual of the duel.

80   **treachery to a host:** Zeus is the god of guest-
friendship, i.e., the divinity who oversees the relations between host and guest. Meneláos offered hospitality ("love")
in good faith, which Paris violated by carrying off his wife
and property. Trojans and Akhaians alike agree that Paris is
guilty. It is noteworthy that Zeus remains well disposed toward the Trojans and does nothing in the *Iliad* particularly
calculated to avenge Meneláos' honor (cf. the note to p. 77).

          he laid hold/of the horsetail crest: the preceding
elements in this are fully typical, but the following details are
unique in the poem. So the actual manner of death, the place
or way the weapon enters or strikes, the effect on the part of
the body hit, etc., all these terminal and anatomical matters
are treated with the greatest precision and variety.

81-82   **had Aphrodítê . . . not perceived him:** she becomes the first divinity to intervene in the fighting. Lines

380f. (top of p. 81) are used of Apollo saving Hektor at XX 443f. (p. 487). Such frequent manipulation could lead us to conceive of man as the puppet of the gods; that mortals, for all their sense of omnipresent divinity, do not so understand their situation is well illustrated by Helen's rebuke of Aphrodítê and her attempt, however futile, to reject the will of the goddess. As we see from "Better not be so difficult . . ." Aphrodítê achieves her objectives by threats rather than simple power. Were Helen willing to risk the hatred of both Trojan and Danáäns, she could persevere in her initial refusal ("shaped by heaven" does not mean "influenced" but "descended from Zeus").

Hesiod tells us that "Eros is the fairest of the immortal gods; he relaxes the limbs and conquers the mind and thoughtful counsel of gods and men alike" (*Theogony* 120–22).

83   **Kranaê Island:** unknown, but sometimes identified as Kythera, the home of Aphrodítê between the Peloponnesus and Krete ("kranaê" simply means "rocky," little help in selecting a particular Greek island).

BOOK FOUR

᠎᠎᠎᠎᠎᠎᠎᠎᠎᠎᠎᠎

A BOWSHOT
BRINGING WAR

Book II promised a general engagement and produced, in Book III, a duel. At the beginning of IV Zeus playfully proposes peace, and by the end of the book the battle has begun. This is accomplished in four scenes: the council on Olympos (pp. 87–90), the violation of the truce (pp. 90–95), the inspection of the troops (pp. 95–102), and finally the battle (pp. 103–6).

Conferences on Olympos also begin Books VIII, XV, XX, and XXIV. They are always scenes of discord. Mockery, teasing, threatening, and ridicule are common. Here, e.g., Zeus "with oblique intent to ruffle Hêra" proposes that they accept Meneláos' victory. By baiting her he manages to arrange for the violation of the truce (Zeus himself never descends to the plain; another divinity always acts for him). Hêra is humorless and morbidly hates the Trojans. Athêna serves as Hêra's agent but lacks Hêra's vigorous malice.

It is no wonder that Plato was offended by these divinities. All the charges brought against them in *Republic* III are true: they lie, swear falsely, are petty and craven, and will betray a friend if it serves their personal ends (cf. Hêra's willingness to trade Mykênê, Argos, and Sparta in return for revenge: IV 51ff.; p. 89). Of course Homer had no intention of supplying moral paradigms for Plato. If anything, his gods are somewhat below the moral standard set by the heroes. We should not suppose, however, that the religion of Homer's day, or the religion of the poetic tradition, was morally bankrupt. Homer's gods are not religious figures but dramatic agents to whom the poet looks for comic relief and for sources of power beyond that possessed by his mortal agents. These characters on the Trojan plain, however, do not have the same view of the gods as the reader (auditor), and for good reason the Trojans and Akhaians take the gods seriously.

One reason the divinities may seem comic is that, while their values are the same as those of mortals, their power is so much greater that regard for honor and reputation on their part appears petty. Hêra has the same interest in her honor as Akhilleus has in his. The difference is that for Akhilleus honor, reputation, and what immortality a mortal may aspire to, i.e., that of fame in the report of posterity, are intimately connected, while for Hêra immortality is a literal fact. Hêra's vendetta against Paris is bound to succeed because her power so surpasses that of Paris and the Trojans. Akhilleus' vendetta, on the other hand, might possibly be frustrated, though in fact he is successful. A deeper difference between mortal and immortal agent may be seen in the taint associated with Akhilleus' humiliation of Agamémnon: Akhilleus feels responsible for the death of Patróklos and knows that his pride has cost his friends dearly; Héra, on the contrary, has no friends. Her selfishness is complete, her power is able to satisfy her ends, and so she takes no risk.

Thus, such scenes as begin Book IV are comic per se, yet their influence on the plain of mortal striving is such that they also appear threatening and malignant. The extraordinary power and knowledge of the gods enable them to exploit human weakness, as we see in Athêna's impersonation of Laódokos (p. 90f.). Athêna (Laódokos) appeals to Pándaros'

greed and desire for recognition and so tempts him to wound
Meneláos and break the truce. She is also responsible for saving Meneláos, a further manipulation of the scene that under-
scores the vulnerability of human effort. Homer's human
agents are fully aware of this parallelism and intersection of
human and divine values. Since their values are the same, we
see in divine decision and action the image of what human society would be like if man had the power to achieve the implicit and explicit values he holds.

87   **Hêbê:** the daughter of Hêra and Zeus, she appears
again only at V 722 (p. 132) and 905 (p. 138). Her name
denotes the strength and beauty of youth, and she is depicted
as the cupbearer to the gods. In Greek myth she became the
wife of the deified Hêraklês.

     Guardian in Boiotia: the line and epithet are used
in one other passage (V 908; p. 138). In neither passage does
the epithet have any particular point.

88   **At this proposal, Hêra and Athêna:** these five lines
(IV 20–25) appear again at VIII 457–62 (p. 195f.) after Zeus
mocks the two ladies. The traditional character of such scenes
and of the relations between Zeus and Hêra is implied by the
repeated use of line 25 ("Your majesty, what is the drift of
this?), which occurs in five other passages (pp. 29, 196, 340,
391, and 447). Though the occasion for her remonstrance
varies, most of these scenes show Zeus purposefully teasing or
provoking Hêra.

89   **Ilion/stood first in my esteem:** the piety of the
Trojans is noticed several times by the gods: cf. p. 568f.
(Apollo and Zeus) and Hektor's manners p. 150.

     Our father,/Krónos of crooked wit: the marriage
of brother and sister is usually explained as the mythical result of a compromise in religion reached between the predominantly male divinities of those people who invaded Greece at
the beginning of the second millennium and the female divinities of the indigenous folk. See Guthrie, p. 66.

90   **Zeus, who holds the keys:** see the note to p. 183.

     Pándaros: he tells his own story at V 192ff. (p.
115); cf. also the catalogue p. 62.

91   **every man would praise you:** Homer makes it
clear that Pándaros is a fool (line 104); Athêna can persuade
him because of his simple-minded greed ("glittering gifts").

Lykian Apollo: the adjective is probably connected with Lykia in southwestern Asia Minor, but it may refer to Apollo as a "wolf-god," a title appropriate to him as the god of shepherds. See Guthrie, p. 82ff. On p. 112 Pándaros indicates he is from Lykia, but elsewhere he is captain of the Trojans, and the catalogue locates his home on the slopes of Ida. Perhaps a district near Troy was also known as Lykia.

92   **the arrowhead of iron:** one of the rare references to iron; cf. the ax in the simile at IV 485 (p. 104).

Athêna,/Hope of Soldiers: the epithet is used six times of Athêna. She is the "Hope of Soldiers" because she brings booty. There is a parallel to Athêna's double role in this scene in her deception of Hektor and aid for Akhilleus in Book XXII (p. 522ff.).

a Mêionian/or a Karian woman: districts in southwestern Asia Minor. Like "Asïa's meadowland . . . Kaystrios" (p. 50) this has been taken as evidence for the Ionic provenance of the poet.

93   **The truce I made:** Agamémnon's speech illustrates several mannerisms of Homeric rhetoric, as well as the king's character. (The reader should remember that the Homeric text is not paragraphed; Fitzgerald has used this device to indicate more clearly sequences of thought and changes of tone.)

Meneláos looked for the duel and was not "sent" by his brother, but the entire speech concentrates more on the king's ego than on the condition of his brother. Turning from the occasion for the wound he recalls the elements of the ritual and reflects on the ways of Zeus. This leads to a confident assertion that eventually Zeus will punish the Trojans for their bad faith. Then he returns to Meneláos' probable death and reflects on alternative consequences ("Backward in depths of shame . . ."). In contrast to the first half of the speech this section is completely pessimistic, predicting first their shameful retreat and then the added shame that will come from Trojan boasts over the grave of Meneláos. Both alternatives are predicated on Meneláos' death, but they lead to radically different surmises. Typically, the speaker sets the two prospects side by side rather than correlating them even with a minimal disjunctive construction (i.e., "either violating the truce will prove their undoing, for Zeus will ultimately punish the wicked; or perhaps your death will lead to our disgraceful return to Argos").

94 **In my mind's eye:** the heroes frequently imagine the future opinion or report of posterity. Cf. Diomêdês at VIII 148ff. (p. 186). Hektor, more than most, seems given to this sort of reflection. See VI 459ff. (p. 156) and 479ff. (p. 156), VII 87ff. (p. 164), VII 300ff. (p. 171), and XXII 106ff. (p. 519), where the motif is particularly significant for his motivation.

Makháon,/son of Asklêpios: see the notes to p. 59 and Idómeneus' appreciation of the physician's art p. 267, where Makháon has been wounded. Asklêpios is the father of Greek medicine and son of Apollo, who is a god of the healing arts in addition to his other attributes.

95 **Kheirôn:** the "best of centaurs" was the teacher of several Greek heroes, including Akhilleus (see pp. 277 and 382).

to bring the war-car up: the Akhaian warriors use their chariots for transportation and do not fight from them. When Nestor marshals his troops in the following review (p. 98) he sends the "teams and cars . . . forward," a disposition more plausible for war than the use actually made of them. Homer keeps the equipment of earlier days long after the tradition has forgotten its tactical function. Nestor's advice to fight in line, avoiding solitary engagements, is not the way of the heroes.

97 **Like a dark cloud/a shepherd from a hilltop sees:** the solitary person (shepherd, traveler) is found elsewhere in the similes (cf. VIII 555ff.; p. 198f.).

with Telamônian Aías and the other: Greek uses a dual or plural form for the two men named Aías. They seem to have nothing in common save the name, though some scholars have judged they were originally a single hero. Since migration is a common motif in Greek mythology, the same figure might have left his name in different localities. Nilsson, *HM*, p. 257.

98 **great Ereuthalíôn:** Nestor gives a long account of this adventure at VII 136ff. (p. 166).

99 **the great tactician:** Agamémnon's rebuke of Odysseus is harsh, and the charge of "guile and greed" seems mis-

placed here (cf. Akhilleus' language at I 149; p. 16). Odysseus, given little opportunity to employ his guile, is less at
home in this epic than in his own *Odyssey*. The descriptive
epithets used here ("great tactician," "wily field commander,"
"master mariner and soldier," each of which translates a single compound adjective used almost exclusively of Odysseus)
suggest the contrary of Agamémnon's charges.

100   **the father of Telémakhos:** of the heroes at Troy
Odysseus alone identifies himself by his relation to a member
of his family (cf. II 260; p. 43).

101   **Your father did not lag like this:** Tydeus the
Aitolian, son of Oineus of Calydon (XIV 114ff.; p. 333), migrated to Argos and became one of the Seven against Thebes,
who tried unsuccessfully to restore Polyneikês, son of Oedipus, to the throne of Thebes. Eteoklês, Polyneikês' brother,
had refused to share the rule with him. The Asôpos is a river
south of Thebes, whose people are called Kadmeíans after
the founder of the city, Kadmos. The anecdote on p. 101 tells
of an incident prior to the invasion of the Seven. Other references to Tydeus as father of Diomêdês, and a model for him,
may be found on pp. 113, 134f. (same story), 238, and 333.

The sons of the Seven were finally successful in taking
Thebes, as Sthénelos retorts, but most heroes would agree
with Nestor that earlier generations produced superior men.

102   **As he said this he bounded from his car:** the description which follows promises action, but the poet turns to
the general engagement. Book V will begin with Diomêdês
"putting his mind on valor."

The Trojans were not silent: cf. the similes beginning III (p. 67) with the same contrast between the noisy
Trojans and the silent Akhaians.

103   **Terror and Rout, and Hate:** these companions of
Arês are not so much divinities or spirits as personifications
of the conditions of war; Arês himself is often, as here, little
more than a personification of War. Cf. XI 3ff. (p. 251),
where Strife (=Hate here) is described as a goddess. She is,
however, certainly a creation of the poets, like Rout and Terror (pp. 308, 353); cf. the personified powers on the shield of
Zeus (p. 132). See Fränkel, pp. 60–62.

**Antílokhos/was the first man to down a Trojan
soldier:** the son of Nestor appears now for the first time. This

is also the first of numerous catalogues of those slain in battle.
No major hero ever dies in such a list. They seem designed to
suggest the scope of the battle and to enhance the prestige of
the major heroes (e.g., at V 144ff. [p. 114] Diomêdês alone
kills eight Trojans). Even though many of the names in these
lists appear only once, the poet takes the time to give a sub-
stantial amount of anecdotal material about them. In his
study of these lists C. R. Beye considers the important themes
of the anecdotes to be "1) social position and wealth of the
hero; 2) birth; 3) place of origin; 4) marriage; 5) migration
to avoid blood vengeance; 6) a seer's prophecy" (p. 358 of
"Homeric Battle Narrative and Catalogues," *HSCP* 68
[1964]). The next lists occur on pp. 110–12, then on p.
114, pp. 126–31 (relatively long, with more dramatic incident and longer anecdotes), and pp. 141–43. Beye's article
offers a detailed analysis.

    Ekhepôlos/Thalysíadês: many names in these lists
were apparently invented for the occasion, and sometimes
they turn up again: cf. Ekhepôlos Ankhísiadês, a Greek despite the patronymic (Ankhísês is the father of the Trojan
hero Aineías), p. 544.

    Agênor: the son of the counselor Antênor makes
his first appearance. The struggle over the body of Elephênor
is the first of numerous similar contests which culminate with
the prolonged fight for the body of the dead Patróklos in
Book XVII. Stripping the body of its armor brings spoil and
additional honor, while failing to bury your own dead is a disgrace for the companions of the dead warrior. Proper burial
rites are necessary for passage to the land of the dead (cf.
Patróklos' appeal for burial p. 537).

104   **Simoeísios:** named for the river Simóeis; the boy's
father's name is akin to the Greek for "flower" or "blossom."
Homer constantly supplements the battle narrative with
varied information and description. A familiar anecdote tells
something of the victim's antecedents or family; cf. Demó-
koön, "who had come down from Abýdos [near Troy on the
Hellespont]/where he kept racing horses." So "To his dear
parents . . ." is used again at XVII 301–3 (p. 416), where
Aías has killed Hippóthoös. For the motif see also pp. 408,
585f., and 592.

105   **Pergamos:** this is "Troy's high citadel . . . where [Apollo's] own shrine was built" (p. 123).

    Tritogeneía: three times of Athêna. The first element (*trito*) of this compound has been variously interpreted: 1) as referring to Lake Triton in Libya, or to a stream or lake of that name; 2) as an illusion to Athêna's birth from the head of Zeus (*trito* being an Aeolic word for "head"); 3) as third-born, i.e., after Apollo and Artemis, an interpretation Fitzgerald follows at VIII 39 (p. 182), where he renders it "third born of heaven."

    Diorês: p. 55.

    Thoas: pp. 56, 167, and 358f.

BOOK FIVE

𝍏𝍏𝍏𝍏𝍏𝍏𝍏𝍏𝍏𝍏𝍏𝍏𝍏𝍏

A HERO STRIVES
WITH GODS

Increasingly the poem is now dominated by the fighting. The poet might have described one great battle after which the defeated Akhaians sought Akhilleus' aid. Instead he prolongs the fighting by focusing on individual warriors and by giving both sides limited successes as well as defeats. Virtually all of the major warriors hold center stage someplace in the poem. Sometimes the spotlight is on them for less than a hundred lines; for others this period of glory and distinction, known in Greek as the *aristeia,* lasts for one or more books. During the *aristeia* the warrior experiences an access of strength and valor so that he is able to sweep the field of his enemies and challenge even the gods to combat. Described as "mad" or "furious," he seems to forget his mortality; frequently, in fact, the *aristeia* terminates with the death or wounding of the hero. (A more detailed analysis and a comparison of the *aris-*

teiai of Diomêdês and Agamémnon will be found in the notes to Book XI, esp. p. 254.)

The *aristeia* was undoubtedly a traditional theme for oral poets. Structurally, however, it poses certain problems. In Book V Diomêdês in his "hour for great action" is so successful in repulsing the Trojans that they are driven to offer a special sacrifice to Athêna, to see "if she will relent" (p. 144). Not only does the youthful hero slaughter numerous Trojans, but he wounds, with the aid of Athêna, Aphrodítê and Arês. This victorious career is at odds with the plan of Zeus, for the Akhaians now have a champion more formidable than Akhilleus (the opinion of Hélenos, VI 99; p. 144), whose predictions of disaster in his absence are hardly fulfilled by this episode.

First we should note that the poet's plan and Zeus's plan need not be equated, though the equation is assumed in much criticism. The real problem is that in Books VII and IX the Akhaians talk and act as if they are losing and need Akhilleus, when we have seen Diomêdês (in V) and Aías (in VII) effectively replace him. For Book IX, at least, we have the intervention of Zeus (in VIII) to explain Akhaian defeatism. From these facts, however, we may infer that the poet was not indifferent to plausible motivation: the Akhaians do talk as if they need Akhilleus, and Zeus's aid to Hektor in VIII gives that talk substance. The question, then, is how the successes of Diomêdês and Aías fit into the poet's plan.

It is perhaps not sufficient to explain this long retardation in terms of dramatic diversity and suspense. As sometimes happens in the *Iliad*, the significance of a particular scene or speech is not clear until a subsequent, and complementary, scene or speech follows (e.g., Akhilleus' stipulation at IX 650ff. [p. 224] may constrain him in XVI [see note p. 379]). For all of their shared elements, the *aristeiai* differ, and in the peculiarity of Diomêdês' career we may find the reason for its inclusion. Though the hero of any *aristeia* is in a sense a man possessed, Diomêdês' brilliance is characterized by a restraint, in word and deed, which makes it unique. Personally modest as these warriors go (cf. his rebuke of Sthénelos p. 102), he is guided through his glory by the attendant Athêna. How different he is from Akhilleus, who is driven by hatred and desire for revenge, will not be clear till much later. We may even suppose that when he attacks Apollo (p. 123), the poet aptly describes the warrior as "beside himself" (V 438; p. 123); yet later we shall see Patróklos also engage the god and, unlike Diomêdês, continue his demonic attack until Apollo strikes him (pp. 398–401). Diomêdês' sense of decorum is seen most memorably in the interview with Glaukos in Book VI (p. 145ff.), a scene which concludes his *aristeia,* not with the usual wounding or death, but with a friendly exchange of gifts. But particularly relevent to this present point is his reluctance to attack the gods unless directed so by Athêna ("I simply bear in mind your own commands": V 818ff.; p. 135). When he mistakenly assails Apollo, he heeds the god's warning and retires until Aineías is spirited away. He advises caution before Hektor's advance and waits for Athêna's help before he attacks Arês. All this slows the tempo of his progress. The parallels with the *aristeiai* of Patróklos and Akhilleus only tend to show how much more impetuous and frenzied they are.

So despite all that is typical in this first great *aristeia,* it seems abnormal in its (relative) propriety. Diomêdês is closer to a model of chivalry than any other of the Akhaians. Since it comes first, Homer may have thought of this *aristeia* as the norm, against which all subsequent achievements are to be judged. Later *aristeiai* exhibit greater intensity and power, and so reap greater glory for their heroes; Diomêdês' success is tempered by circumspection, restraint, and civility. Thus many commentators have thought Homer intended a contrast between Akhilleus and Diomêdês. It is certainly curious how little they have to do with one another and how different they are. Only at the end of the embassy does Diomêdês comment on Akhilleus, whom for a while he seems to have replaced (see IX 697ff.; p. 225).

See Bowra, *Tradition and Design,* p. 204f.; Nilsson, *HM,* pp. 258–60; Owen, pp. 45–48; Whitman, pp. 166–69; and the notes to p. 506.

If the preceding considerations explain the reasons for the particular modality of Diomêdês' *aristeia,* they do not ease the structural and motivational problems. The simple fact is that Akhilleus is thought by the Akhaians to be indispensable; like Aías (p. 169), they seem more conscious of his absence than of their success. Moreover, Hektor is on the field, no longer fettered in the city as he has been for years (see p. 214). Lastly, the very restraint of Diomêdês' *aristeia* makes the continued Trojan presence more plausible than it would be were he to run amuck.

109   she kindled fire: a typical motif in the *aristeia:* cf. the description of Hektor p. 301 (and notes) and of Akhilleus p. 442.

         two sons: Homer often presents his warriors in pairs, whether as brothers or companions. Cf. the "two Lapith spearmen" (p. 285), the twin sons of Dioklês (p. 126f.), the sons of Mérops Perkôsios (p. 261). Akhilleus and Patróklos, Sarpêdôn and Glaukos, Meneláos and Agamémnon are other pairs whose mutual loyalty and kinship offer opportunities to develop pathos and motivate action. The love of a friend or kinsman competes with honor for primacy in motivating Homeric agents in battle. Of course they fight in pairs because one must care for the chariot and team while the prime warrior dismounts to face the enemy, but Homer's use of fraternity goes well beyond this technical convention.

110   unless Hêphaistos had performed the rescue: cf. Aphrodítê's rescue of Paris (p. 80), and the salvation of Aineías later in this book, first by Aphrodítê (p. 119), then by Apollo (p. 120).

         Arês: clearly there is little motivation for this address to Arês, who has had nothing to do with the preceding events. Later he will help the Trojans. Athêna remains close to Diomêdês.

         every captain killed his man: names were naturally a potential problem in creating these lists. Of the names here Beye (*HSCP* 68, p. 359) observes: "of the victims, Odíos, last in the Trojan catalogue, will reappear as a Greek herald (IX 170); the Trojan Hypsênor returns as a Greek (XIII 411), and of the remaining four, who appear only here, three are place-names elsewhere (Phaistos, Skamándrios, and Pedaíos)."

111   Artemis herself: so Phéreklos (below) learned his carpentry from Athêna. Every human activity has its special divinity, and success in any sphere signifies divine favor. Artemis, sister of Apollo, is mentioned on only eight other occasions, and actually appears only in XXI (p. 508f.).

         Pallas Athêna: this epithet for Athêna, in later

times also used as her name, probably means "maiden" and thus points to the same attribute as Parthenos, "the virgin goddess."

112 **like an April torrent:** cf. the similes ("a stream in flood") pp. 128 and 502.

113 **Oh hear me, daughter of Zeus:** typical elements in the Homeric prayer include 1) invocation, 2) basis for the claim (former service or association), 3) the problem, and 4) request for help. The prayers of Odysseus and Diomêdês (p. 238) are similar to the present passage, while Glaukos' prayer p. 393 gives much more attention to the problem (his wound). Contrast the terse prayer of Odysseus in the games (p. 559, a single line).

Several aspects of the present scene suggest a comparison of Akhilleus and Diomêdês: 1) Athêna will aid Akhilleus though he does not pray for her assistance; 2) Diomêdês recalls his father Tydeus, with whom he is compared (usually not favorably), while Pêleus, the father of Akhilleus, is much on his son's mind late in the story (see note p. 470); 3) contrast the tone of Akhilleus' prayer when he is threatened by Skamánder (XXI 273–83; p. 502); 4) whereas Akhilleus disregards Skamánder's warning (p. 500), Diomêdês is content with Athêna's stipulation: "be sure you are not the man/to dare immortal gods in combat."

blood-lust/three times as furious took hold of him: the goddess enhances the power and energy (Greek *menos*) already present in the warrior. This increased energy may be recognized by the recipient (cf. the exchange between Aías Telamônios and the son of Oïleus at XIII 68–80; p. 301f.), but it regularly leads to "madness" ("this crazy charge," line 185; p. 115) and comparison of the warrior to a wild animal. The warrior seems, in the full intensity of such power, to forget himself. So even Diomêdês

> charged Aineias
> though he knew well Apollo had sustained him.
> He feared not even the great god himself,

> V 432–34 (p. 123)

See the notes to pp. 144, 388, and 398.

Think of a lion: the most popular animal in the

similes, the lion epitomizes strength, fury, and daring. Other examples of the lion or other wild animal attacking the untended flock will be found at X 485 (p. 244) and XV 630 (p. 369); cf. XV 323 (p. 360) and XVI 352 (p. 388). More frequently the lion finds himself engaged by the herdsmen (cf. the "two young lions" p. 127).

114   First he killed/Astýnoös and . . . Hypeirôn: Diomêdês kills four pairs. In this list the name of Polýeidos ("who sees much") is appropriate to the son of an "old interpreter."

115   looks very like Diomêdês: Aineías had asked 1) why Pándaros is not using his bow and 2) who this raging warrior is. Pandaros reverses the order and answers that 1) it is Diomêdês and 2) his bow has been pure futility today (*hysteron proteron:* See notes to pp. 60 and 69).

116   these horses of the line of Trôs: Aineías gives a full genealogy of the "line of Trôs" on p. 480. As we learn on p. 118, Trôs was given this stock "in fee for Ganymêdês." Ganymêdês was stolen by Zeus, who took this "handsomest of mortals" (p. 480) to be his cupbearer. Diomêdês alludes to the capture of this team at VIII 108 (p. 185).

118   his weapon being guided by Athêna: there is no explicit suggestion in the text that Pándaros is paying for having violated the truce. In her capacity as agent for Hêra, Athêna persuaded him to hit Meneláos; now as protectress of Diomêdês she has a part in Pándaros' death. The incident would seem to be an example from a subplot of A. W. H. Adkins' contention that "Though right triumphs in the main plots of both *Iliad* and *Odyssey*, it does not do so *because* it is right." (*Merit and Responsibility,* p. 62)

119   a boulder/no two men now alive: this line formula occurs again at XII 449 (p. 294). Lines 302–4=XX 285–87 (p. 482), where they are used of Aineías. Cf. XII 381ff. (p. 292).

**   Aineías . . . his mother . . . shepherding Ankhísês:** the story of their courtship is recorded in the Homeric *Hymn to Aphrodite.* Aineías is prominent in this book, again in XIII (pp. 313–16), in XVII (p. 417ff.), and in XX (p. 476ff.).

120   to attack the Kyprian goddess: Aphrodítê, identified closely with the island of Cyprus because, according to the *Theogony* (193), the goddess came to that island soon after her birth. In the *Iliad* she is called the Kyprian only in this book. Homer thinks of her as the daughter of Zeus and Diônê (a name built on the same stem as Zeus's own name, and meaning "goddess"; see p. 121), whereas Hesiod tells of her birth from the mutilated genitals of Uranos. A battle with a god or goddess seems to have been a typical feature of the *aristeia*: cf. p. 401 and pp. 500–4.

        Enyô: she first appears here, and later is a companion of Arês (p. 128), who is himself called Enyálios ("warlike"); Enyô is simply a feminine personification of War (cf. *Theogony* 273, where her sisters are the Graiai and the Gorgons).

        the Graces: they are said by Hesiod (*Theogony* 64) to live with Desire, next to the Muses; so they are often associated with song and dance, and with all that is lovely and elegant. Cf. p. 409: "hair, fair as the Graces'"; on p. 338 Hêra bribes Sleep with "one of the younger Graces,/Pásithea, that one I have desired/all my living days." For the singular see XVIII 382 (p. 447).

        ichor: mentioned only here and p. 122 as the "blood" of the gods.

121   **please let me take your team:** the divinities do not always use a team for transportation. For the motif, however, cf. Hêra's complaint about the wasted effort of her "winded horses" (p. 88) and see the preparations of Zeus p. 182f. and Poseidon p. 300.

        lover of smiling eyes: Aphrodítê's qualities (and epithets) do not suit her for the business of war; cf. XX 40 (p. 474).

121–122 **There, child, patience:** the speech is interesting both for structure and argument. Diônê's "patience" (line 382) is repeated three times, at the beginning of each anecdote: so "Arês had patience," "Hêra had patience," and "Aïdês had patience." Cf. Hektor's speech p. 169 and the note there. The last paragraph, however, is used as a bridge back to narrative, as if Diônê were offering Diomêdês a warning: great as Hêraklês was (greater certainly than Diomêdês) he went too far in wounding Aïdês. So don't you, even with Athêna's help, fight the gods. The remarkable transposition carries Diônê so far that she imagines the effect on his wife and children. Cf. the list of examples Zeus offers Hêra at XIV 316ff. (p. 340).

122 **Otos and Ephiáltês:** these Giants are better-known for their attack on the Olympians, when they piled Mount Ossa and Mount Pêlion on Mount Olympos to make a way to the gods. Apollo killed them for their trouble (see the *Odyssey*, XI 305ff.).

Eëríboia: stepmothers are no more popular in Greek mythology than in Germanic. Hêra is also a step-mother of sorts, since "Amphitrýôn's mighty son" (Hêraklês) is actually the son of Zeus.

Aïdês: Hades. The allusion here is unclear, but Pylos was probably not, at least originally, the city, but rather the common noun meaning "gate." Hence "at the gate of the dead," a reference to Hêraklês' harrowing of the underworld to fetch the dog Cerberos. If it is the Pylos of Nestor, cf. his account on p. 272.

Paiêôn: the god of healing, who attends the wounded Arês p. 137f.

Aigiáleia, Adrêstos' daughter: Adrêstos was one of the Seven against Thebes; since Tydeus also married one of his daughters (p. 333), father and son were brothers-in-law. Diônê is in fact mistaken, for Diomêdês survived the war to settle in Italy and praise his old foe Aineías (see Vergil's *Aeneid*, XI 243ff.).

For the motif of man attacking the gods cf. the story of Lykourgos p. 145f.

123 **Three times:** cf. Patróklos' battle with Apollo (pp. 398 and 401) and Akhilleus' attack p. 487; see the note to p. 398.

a figure of illusion: Apollo uses a similar trick to fool Akhilleus at the end of XXI (p. 512).

124 **Princes,/heirs of Priam in the line of Zeus:** the gods frequently admonish mortals to recall their fighting spirit. Cf. Athêna's speech at V 787 (p. 134) and Poseidon at XIII 95ff. (p. 302). On the form and typical elements in these speeches see Fenik, p. 48f.

He made them burn at this: the typical result of admonition or rebuke (the line occurs ten times). So after Athêna's (Stentor's) rebuke (p. 134) the line is rendered "This shout put anger into them." Nestor's encouragement at

VI 67–71 (p. 143) differs in tone and content, but the line (VI 72) is used there to indicate the effect of his speech ("Shouting, he urged them on"; p. 143).

What of you,/Hektor, where has your courage gone: Fenik (p. 49ff.) analyzes the typical pattern of rebuke and action: "Hector or Aeneas is rebuked for withholding himself from combat. Most often the speaker is a Lycian ally or Apollo in human guise. The words have their effect, the Trojan advances, either charging or, as here, stiffening his ranks. The fight then either comes to a standstill or, more often, the Trojans are repulsed. Aias always appears in the counter action." (p. 49) Cf. Glaukos p. 393 and p. 412, Apollo p. 417.

125 **though I have no least stake in Troy:** i.e., there is nothing here of mine which the Akhaians want; I have no quarrel with them. Cf. Akhilleus at I 152ff. (p. 16).

yellow-haired Dêmêter: though mentioned occasionally (pp. 58, 309, 340), the goddess Dêmêtêr has no part in the action of the *Iliad*.

126 **that river . . . Alpheíos:** this is the famous river of the western Peloponnesus. All rivers are personified as gods, and several are used as ancestors of warriors. See, e.g., Asteropaíos p. 498.

127 **Pylaiménês:** mentioned in the catalogue (p. 63), and still alive in XIII (p. 319) to mourn the death of his son.

128 **so Diomêdês/backed away:** another indication of restraint during the *aristeia* of Diomêdês. By giving Aineías and Hektor limited success during the *aristeia* the poet maintains the credibility of the Trojan power.

129 **Tlêpólemos:** the speech of challenge and insult often precedes a duel, and the topics in this one are typical: a) charge of cowardice; b) lineage (Sarpêdôn is no true son of Zeus); c) glory of my family (Hêraklês was a son of Zeus); then the charge of cowardice is repeated, and its consequence asserted, i.e., the death of Sarpêdôn. See Fenik, p. 66f.

Laomédôn's chariot horses: see the note on p. 118. The story of Hêraklês and Laomédôn is alluded to in several passages of the *Iliad*. The king of Troy had exposed his daughter Hesionê as an offering to a sea monster which was ravishing his land. Hêraklês killed the monster and claimed

the reward, but Laomédôn cheated him and drove him off.
Subsequently Hêraklês returned, sacked the city, and killed
the king. See pp. 337 and 350. For Laomédôn's earlier trou-
bles with Apollo and Poseidon see pp. 176 and 507. For the
story see Apollodorus II.5.9 and II.6.4.

130   **You'll give up glory/to me:** numerous passages
offer parallels to this sentiment (cf. Odysseus p. 265;
Meríonês p. 396); the "glory" is immediately represented by
the victor's boast over the body, forestalled in this case by the
fact that Sarpêdôn is wounded, and, secondly, by the fame he
will win in the eyes of peers and posterity (see Sarpêdôn's
frequently cited statement p. 291: "Let us attack—whether to
give some fellow/glory or to win it from him"). For other
battlefield challenges see pp. 145, 479, 498, and 523.

      Sarpêdôn's father saved him: the Lykian hero is
the only Trojan warrior descended from Zeus, and the only
son of Zeus on the field. His death in XVI (p. 392) is alluded
to here again on p. 293.

      Alastor, Khromíos: on p. 98 these were the names
of Akhaians (Pylians) under the command of Nestor; a
Khromíos (a son of Priam) is killed by Diomêdês on p. 114;
another is killed by Teukros on p. 190 (in a list of eight) but
reappears in a later list (p. 414; cf. 422 and 424), where he is
trying to assist Hektor and Aineías. The fellow is never
significant, and the name was obviously a handy one which
the poet used for filler.

131   **Not for me/to see my home:** a motif so common
it hardly requires comment, but still it is well to note that
more than horses, booty, and glory is at stake. Meneláos'
threat, "as for their wives and children,/we'll enslave them
when we take the town" (IV 238f.; p. 96), is echoed repeatedly. Hektor, looking for his wife and child, wonders if he
will ever see them again (VI 364ff.; p. 153); see also his
charge to the Trojans at XV 486–99 (p. 365).

      Zeus's oak: the oak was sacred to Zeus. This one,
near the Skaian Gates (p. 214), was a familiar landmark (p.
256 and, probably, p. 510).

      Lake Képhisos: in Boiotia, better-known as Lake
Kopais, but here named for the Képhisos River, which emp-
ties into it.

Hêra . . . Athêna: a similar conversation and decision to prepare the chariot for battle is followed in VIII by a reprimand from Zeus (p. 192ff.). It is not clear why Zeus permits them to check Arês and help the Akhaians here.

132   **fitted upon her chariot:** descriptions in Homer tend to focus on the parts rather than an impression of the whole. Cf., e.g., the arming of Paris, p. 79.

     As for Athêna: these four lines (733–37)=VIII 384–88 (p. 193).

     the stormcloud shield: the *aigis* (see note p. 40); for the personifications see notes on p. 103 and p. 120. Medusa, the only mortal Gorgon, had such a fearful aspect that merely seeing her turned the unlucky prospector to stone. She was slain by Perseus, who used a mirror to avoid his own petrification. She is "reptilian" because her hair was traditionally represented as a mass of seething serpents. Cf. "blazing-eyed as a Gorgon" (p. 192) and the description of Agamémnon's shield at XI 32–40 (p. 252).

133   **child of Power:** the phrase represents an adjective found only here and VIII 391 in the *Iliad*.

     the Hours: the goddesses of the Seasons (cf. p. 507). Here and in VIII (p. 193) they are represented as servants of the Olympians.

134   **ambrosial grass:** "ambrosia" is the food of the gods; the adjective suggests immortality. See the note to p. 458.

     Stentor: the name means "Groaner" or "Roarer"; this is the only reference to him in the epics.

     Shame, shame, Argives: "And the strongest moral force which Homeric man knows is not the fear of god, but respect for public opinion, *aidos* [shame]." Thus Dodds (p. 18), who goes on to compare Hektor's use of the verb from the same stem: "I am ashamed to face townsmen and women" (XXII 105; p. 519).

135   **I simply bear in mind your own commands:** No speech better illustrates the discretion for which Diomêdês is often cited. Cf. his silent acceptance of Agamémnon's rebuke (p. 101) and remonstrance with Sthénelos (p. 102). He can, however, speak up (see p. 204ff.). Perhaps an intentional contrast with other warriors who forget divine commands, to their regret, is designed. Hektor, e.g., "forgets," the time limit set by Zeus (p. 257) and refuses Poulýdamas' advice to retire into the city (p. 443f.); Patróklos "forgets" Akhilleus' warning (p. 380 and p. 398: "By keeping Akhilleus' mandate,/he might have . . .") and ignores, after a time, Apollo's threat on the field (p. 398f.); even Akhilleus is overwhelmed by the river god when he refuses to check his slaughter of Trojans (p. 500ff.).

136   **the helm of the Lord of Undergloom:** Hades ("Aïdês" p. 122) literally means "Unseen" or "Invisible" in Greek.

        as roaring from ten thousand: cf. the shout of Poseidon p. 334 (XIV 148–49=V 860–61).

137   **still be there in pain among the dead:** although he cannot die, Arês can imagine himself suffering "among the dead," which carries anthropomorphism about as far as it can go.

        most hateful to me: the first half of line 890 and 891 entire ("Combat and . . . element") were used by Agamémnon of Akhilleus at I 176–77 (p. 17: "No officer/ is hateful . . .").

138   **Athêna and Hêra retire without summons from Zeus;** apparently it is to be understood that they only had leave to check Arês. Such restraint is unlike them.

BOOK SIX

░░░░░░░░░░░░░

INTERLUDES IN
FIELD AND CITY

Diomêdês' *aristeia* continues and prompts Hélenos to suggest that the Trojans try to appease Athêna with sacrifice. Hektor carries this message to the woman of the city, and has an opportunity to visit his mother. Then he goes on to his brother's house, where he rebukes Paris and urges him to return to battle. Finally he goes in search of his wife and on the way back to the field meets her and his son at the city gates. Hektor is missing from only one scene in this book, the exchange between Diomêdês and Glaukos.

We see him with his brother Hélenos, with his mother, with Paris and Helen, with wife and son. While the poet often uses domestic motifs in his biographical anecdotes (see notes pp. 103 and 104), Hektor is the only character on either side who is seen with all members of his family. Book VI dramatizes the family's love and concern for him and their dependence upon him. Perhaps this theme of dependence, which figures so prominently in Andrómakhê's speeches, explains Priam's

absence. In this book Troy is represented by women and children, and the craven Paris; Troy's defense rests on a solitary
warrior. Had Homer introduced Priam or other Trojan
leaders, the rhythm of this episode might have been complicated by political issues, such as we find in Book VII, which
could only have detracted from the portrait of Hektor. In so
far as issues are raised, they are a matter of defensive tactics
and, more significantly, personal responsibility. Virtually
everything said of Hektor or by him in this book seems to
bear on his sense of responsibility to his family and people.

Modern readers may find Hektor the most sympathetic of
Homer's characters (see Bassett's comparison of Akhilleus
and Hektor, pp. 185–95). While the Akhaians say they fear
him and call him a madman (see notes to pp. 144 and 301),
we are still more likely to think of him as the underdog, citi-
zen soldier, family man, and victim. The Akhaians do not
hear his rebuke of Paris, nor Hékabê's concern for her weary
son, nor Andrómakhê's plea that he be more careful. His enemies know nothing of his self-doubt, pessimism, and frustration. On the last day his values and theirs prove to be the
same, and Hektor dies because he is a typical warrior for
whom shame and honor take precedence over family and
city. But that is a long way off, and in the meantime we shall
think of him as the husband of Andrómakhê and the man
who thinks

One
and only one portent is best: defend
our fatherland!

                                                          XII 243 (p. 288)

Book VI shapes and crystallizes our conception of Hektor, not
simply because of what he says and does but especially because of the attitudes of the other characters toward him.
Even Paris finds his rebuke just, and Helen thinks herself a
bitch to have caused this man such affliction.

141   **between the rivers:** the Skamánder and the
Simóeis (p. 133).

142   **Euryalos:** he is mentioned only three times in the
Iliad and not again until the boxing match in XXIII (p. 556).
After II 740 and this passage Polypoitês appears in two

scenes (pp. 285ff. and 561f.). Lêïtos appears in the catalogue (II 494; p. 51) and then again on pp. 302 and 426, where he is wounded. Consistency in reference and widely scattered appearances of such minor figures imply a remarkable degree of control over the material. By contrast we find Pylaiménês resurrected (note to p. 127) and the indifferent use of Khromíos (p. 130).

Adrêstos threw his arms around his knees: this is the first of several battlefield supplications. His speech occurs again at XI 131–35 (p. 255). Cf. Dolôn's speech (p. 241), which utilizes three of these lines.

143   **hard-wrought iron:** see note to p. 92. This passage reflects a period when iron was rare and valuable.

recalled his brother's mind to duty: the Greek is euphemistic and probably ambiguous: he said what was fitting (fatal). Cf. the context of VII 121 (p. 165), where a "just sense of duty" means a sense of what is fitting and practical. Agamémnon is a mercurial character, now given to pessimism and willing to quit, then again determined and ready to hear counsel (see Diomêdês p. 204f.). As a fighter he is brutal, offering no quarter, but hardly a bulwark for the Akhaians.

144   **Hélenos:** his first appearance. His advice to Hektor in Book VII (p. 163) is equally influential in determining the course of the episode. This scene shares some structural elements with other scenes involving Hektor: Hélenos 1) gives advice, then 2) Hektor vaults from his chariot and 3) rallies the Trojans; earlier Sarpêdôn 1) rebukes Hektor, who 2) vaults from his chariot and 3) rallies the Trojans (p. 124f.); later Iris brings a message from Zeus to Hektor, and 2) and 3) follow (XI 211ff.; p. 257f.). Hektor's exhortation (VI 111ff.; p. 145) is also typical (see the note to p. 260).

the shrine/of grey-eyed Athêna on our citadel: Lorimer (p. 442) observes: "There is no justification for the presence of the goddess in the city of which she is a bitter and consistent enemy and where she never again appears." On the contrary, there is an implicit assumption throughout the poem that the gods are shared by both peoples, despite the animosity of Hêra and Athêna. On several occasions Zeus speaks of the Trojans as favorites of his (see Hêra p. 28) and the

Akhaian leaders wonder that the god who oversees hospitality seems so indifferent to the culpable Paris.

    this fellow fights like one possessed: a warrior at the height of his prowess is "possessed," "mad," or "raging." Cf. Odysseus' observation that "Hektor in his ecstasy of power/is mad for battle" (p. 211; cf. p. 213); Patróklos attacks "on the fourth demonic foray" (p. 401); Akhilleus "wrought to a frenzy" presses the Trojans (p. 510). Dio-mêdês *aristeia* begins (V 1ff.) with Athêna making him "bold"; the "fury" Hélenos notices is the same energy (*menos:* see the note to p. 113). This is a quality in the warrior both necessary and dangerous: cf. Andrómakhê's "your bravery [*menos*] will be/your own undoing" (VI 407; p. 154). See the note to p. 301. Recognition of such fury, since it indicates the favor of the gods, often motivates a defensive reaction, as it does here. See Fränkel, pp. 69–70.

145   **be men, remember courage:** this line occurs seven times in the *Iliad,* only once (XVI 270) addressed to the Akhaians.

    nape and ankle/both were brushed: apparently a reminiscence of the body shield known from Mycenaean times and responsible for the death of Períphêtês (XV 645ff.; p. 370). Generally the warriors fight with round shields, smaller and more easily handled than Hektor's cumbersome piece; cf. the shield of Aías, p. 168. See Kirk, *SH,* pp. 110–12 and plate 2c.

    Meanwhile, driving into an open space: the following scene serves the same function as the teichoscopia in III (see note to p. 71). While Hektor makes his way to town Glaukos and Diomêdês meet. When their exchange is over, Hektor has arrived ("Now, when Hektor reached . . ." VI 237; p. 149). Besides being an exemplary study in chivalry and a unique conclusion to an *aristeia,* the scene indicates the obligations of guest-friendship through successive generations.

    Diomêdês . . . spoke up: the speech offers an example of ring composition: a) who are you?; b) I would not fight with the gods; c) example from myth; b′) I would not fight with the gods; a′) who are you (a mortal or a god)? Lykourgos, king of Thrace, like King Pentheus in Euripides' *Bacchae,* violently rejected the god Dionysos and his worshipers (the maenads).

For the question of birth and lineage cf. Akhilleus p. 498, where Asteropaíos responds with the same line that Glaukos uses on p. 146.

146   **Very like leaves:** cf. the imagery on p. 50 ("countless as the leaves . . .") and at II 800 (p. 61).

      Ephýra: one of the lost cities of the *Iliad*. It was identified by some ancients as the oldest name of Corinth, which Homer's phrasing here hardly verifies.

      Sísyphos/Aiólidês: the famous trickster Sísyphos is seen by Odysseus in Hades (*Odyssey*, Book XI 593ff.). Aiolos, from whom one of the three branches of the Greek people was descended, is mentioned only here in the *Iliad*.

      Bellérophontês: later simply Bellerophon. Proitos ruled Tiryns, according to Apollodorus II.3.1, and Bellérophontês appealed to him for purification after he had killed his own brother. Perhaps Proitos was "scrupulous" because he had received the hero as a suppliant. Ánteia's (called Stheneboia in later accounts) attempt to seduce Bellérophontês is a common pattern, best-known from the tale of Potiphar's wife, who attempts to seduce Joseph, in Genesis 39. Akhilleus' father Pêleus was also the victim in such a story (see Apollodorus III.13.3).

147   **a deadly cipher:** this is the only reference to writing in Homer. Apollodorus identifies the "father-in-law" and Lykian lord as Iobates, and also tells us that Bellérophontês attacked the Khimaira on his winged horse Pegasos.

      Solýmoi: a non-Greek people native to Asia Minor; for the Amazons see p. 74.

148   **Zeus the Profound:** the epithet occurs sixteen times and is used exclusively of Zeus. Fitzgerald has translated it variously: "who views the wide world" (p. 17), "inscrutable" (p. 46), and "profound mind of Olympos" (p. 28).

      Alêïon plain: Herodotus (VI 95) mentions a plain by this name in Kilikia; the name, however, is connected by the poet with a verb meaning to "wander" or "mope." Bellérophontês later attempted to fly on Pegasos to the halls of Olympos itself, but he was thrown and apparently driven mad ("the gods' wrath"). See Pindar, *Isthmian* VII 44–47. Other sources give no reason for Artemis being "angry," but she and Apollo are normally made responsible for the deaths of mortals. Some divine resentment, such as we find in the story of Niobê (p. 587), may be latent.

commanding me to act always with valor: cf. Odysseus' account of Pêleus' injunction to Akhilleus (p. 211) and Nestor's report of the same parting (p. 275).

you are my friend: hospitality descended from father to son. The exchange of gifts was usual.

149   **Zeus/had stolen Glaukos' wits away:** see the note to p. 461 (XIX 137). Since there is no explicit statement of Zeus's interest in these matters other than this formulaic phrase, we may perhaps assume it is a figurative expression.

his gentle mother: Hékabê; she appears again in XXII (p. 518) to plead with Hektor to avoid the duel with Akhilleus, and then to lament his death (p. 529). See also p. 574ff. Redfield's account (pp. 119–27) of Hektor and the women of Troy aptly summarizes the dilemmas Hektor faces.

150   **with hands unwashed:** Hektor's piety is also affirmed by Zeus and Apollo (pp. 520, 568f.).

What an affliction: cf. Hektor's earlier abuse p. 58f., Helen's reference to his "madness" (*atê*: VI 356; p. 153), and Idaíos' aside at VII 390 (p. 174). The decision to rouse Paris, like the later visit to his wife, is an afterthought for Hektor.

women of Sidonia: according to one version of the story, Paris sailed to the south (Sidon is on the coast of Phoenicia) before returning to Troy. In another version, used by Euripides in his *Helen*, the wife of Meneláos never came to Troy.

151   **During the supplication:** with the sacrifice completed the poet begins a new scene, which, however, does not take place at the same time as the supplication but begins immediately upon its conclusion. Thus Homer fills the time during which Hektor moves to the house of Paris; cf. the notes to pp. 71 and 145.

Hektor dear to Zeus: the epithet is used of Hektor four times (Books VI–XIII), of Akhilleus five times (Books I and XVI–XXIV), and also of several other characters. Sometimes these formulaic phrases strike us as odd, given the particular context; e.g., at XIII 674 (p. 320): "Hektor [dear to Zeus] had not learned . . ." The hero "dearest to Zeus" was Hêraklês (XVIII 118; p. 439).

152   **why we aggrieved in private:** the line suggests Paris is nursing a specific anger, but it is not clear what occasion for "resentment" Paris might have, and in his reply Paris denies any ill will toward the Trojans, who after all have far more reason to resent his behavior. There are also problems in his excuse and the next line:

> my desire, on being routed,
> to taste grief to the full.
>
>   In her sweet way
> my lady rouses me to fight again—

"On being routed" is a common explanation of his grief, though the phrase has no counterpart in the Greek. "In her sweet way" can hardly refer to the last scene between Helen and Paris (in Book III), and it is unlike the poet to refer so casually and allusively to a scene between them which he has not described. Helen's words for Paris in the next lines are certainly not sweet. Some scholars have thought this scene a rather unsatisfactory adaptation from a story in which Paris, like Akhilleus and Meléagros (p. 220ff.), retired from battle because of a justified anger. These topics and others are discussed by J. Th. Kakridis, *Homeric Researches* (Lund, 1949), pp. 43–49.

153   **Who knows/if I shall be reprieved again to see them:** perhaps the sight of Helen serves to recall his own wife, but Hektor seems more fatalistic than most warriors, and Homer has clearly developed this tone in the following scene:

> In Hektor's home they mourned him, living still
> but not, they feared, again to leave the war
> or be delivered from Akhaian fury.
>
>   VI 500–2 (p. 157)

In fact, Hektor does return to the city at least once (VII 310; p. 171) before his death, but this is the last dramatized scene beween husband and wife.

The poet avoids excessive pathos by keeping this scene at

some distance from Hektor's death. Though Homer will let
Priam and Hékabê appeal to Hektor to save himself (pp.
516–18), Andrómakhê does not reappear until he is dead.
There are many petitions and supplications in the *Iliad*, but
this one between husband and wife is unique. Usually one
party is angry with the other or resents the request because it
impinges upon his honor or self-esteem. Andrómakhê's plea
fails despite their mutual affection.

154   **whereby/before long he would issue on the field:**
Hektor does not follow her to the tower but plans to return to
battle. Thus their meeting is a matter of chance, which is a
rare thing in the poem.

     Andrómakhê: for the wife of Hektor see also pp.
529ff. and 591f. The sack of Thêbê is mentioned several
times in the poem (pp. 23, 209, 382; see also the references
to Eëtíôn pp. 425 and 561).

     Skamándrios: the boy, like many children, is
named for the local river. His significant nickname, Astýanax,
suggests how Paris may have gotten his second name.

155   **He killed him,/but, reverent at least in this:** unob-
trusively Homer establishes for Akhilleus a norm of conduct
in the past which he will not adhere to again until Book
XXIV. Cf. the fate of Lykáôn (pp. 494–97), who, like
Andrómakhê's mother, was once saved by a large ransom.

     the wild figtree: like the Skaian Gates and the oak,
a familiar feature of the landscape (pp. 256 and 520).

     But I should die of shame: this line (VI 442) oc-
curs verbatim in Hektor's monologue before he faces Akhilleus (XXII 105; p. 519): "I am ashamed to face townsmen
and women." The line occurs in only these two passages, fits
both contexts perfectly, and cuts to the heart of Hektor's ethical dilemma. In both speeches the next line turns to the topic
of cowardice. It seems obvious that such a line can hardly be
termed formulaic in the same sense as transitional lines denoting "answering" or noun-epithet phrases such as "dear to
Zeus." There are a great number of these single repetitions in
the *Iliad* and *Odyssey*, and very often they carry an extraordinary weight in terms of theme or characterization.

     for in my heart and soul I know: lines 447–49
were used at IV 163–65 by Agamémnon. They suit each
context remarkably well, even though the tone of the two pas-

sages differs considerably. Ironic echoes are inherent in a formulaic style. Such passages, because their content is greater than a single line, and so they are more independent of context, look like memorized set pieces. As in the case of the line mentioned in the preceding note, such a repetition inevitably brings up the question of the relation of our text to the performance of the poem. Neither of these examples looks like the chance product of an extemporizing poet, but it is also hard to see how a theory of a text dictated by an oral poet would, in itself, explain the complexly appropriate echo of VI 442 and XXII 105. Most explanations of these significant repetitions, if they do not appeal to the literate revisions of a poet intimately acquainted with the ways of traditional verse, lead to the implicit assertion of staggering feats of memory.

156　　　**at Messêis/or Hypereiê fountain:** these fountains were in Laconia and Thessaly; hence "Argos" would seem to be used loosely for "Greece." For literary treatments of her lot after the war see Euripides' *Andromache* and Vergil's *Aeneid* III 294ff.

157　　　**You know no man dispatches me:** after the gloomy reply to her and the more optimistic prayer for his son, this speech takes an even course between the two. Hektor seems revived by Skamándrios and even has a kind word for Paris as they return to the field.

　　　Think how a stallion: these lines (VI 506–11) are found again at XV 263–68 (p. 358), where the simile describes Hektor. The line below ("his gear/ablaze like the great sun") is used at XIX 398 (p. 469) of Akhilleus.

BOOK SEVEN

⌐⌐⌐⌐⌐⌐⌐⌐⌐⌐⌐⌐⌐⌐⌐⌐⌐

A COMBAT AND A RAMPART

Hektor returns to the field and challenges the Akhaians to select a champion for a duel. The lot falls to Aías Telamônios,
who has the better of the match, though it is formally called a
draw. Conferences in both camps decide that a truce for burial of the dead is desirable. At the same time Nestor advocates the erection of a defensive rampart, while Antênor urges
the Trojans to return Helen and the treasure. The book concludes with a notice of the burials, the building of the rampart, and Poseidon's indignant protest that the Akhaians have
not sacrificed before raising the new fortification.

The book falls into two sections, each of which presents a
problem. The duel seems weakly motivated and redundant
after the duel of Book III. Why are the Akhaians willing to
honor the challenge after the broken oaths that bound Paris
to return Helen? Why are they "afraid" (VII 93; p. 164) to
respond after Diomêdês has proven so strong? Since the

earlier events are not ignored (Hektor explicitly refers to
the "the peace we swore to"), it would appear that the brief
Trojan success of lines 8–16 and respect for Hektor—

> Even Akhilleus
> shivered when for glory he met this man
> in combat
>
> VII 113f. (p. 165)

—must account for Akhaian pusillanimity. In the event, Aías
strikes the better blows, and this leads to the second problem,
much like that discussed in the preface to Book V.

Unexpectedly Nestor proposes that the Akhaians build a
defensive rampart. After the *aristeia* of Diomêdês and Aías'
advantage in the duel, this must be a surprising counsel. But
the Akhaian chiefs agree. Meanwhile Antênor urges the
Trojans to honor the oaths of Book III by returning Helen;
Paris is willing to return the treasure but not Helen. The
problem is this: the Trojans do not feel they have carried the
day, but the Akhaians apparently think the Trojans have. To
explain Akhaian pessimism we should perhaps notice the allusions to Akhilleus (pp. 165 and 169). His absence preys on
their courage. Secondly, Hektor's challenge is prompted by
Apollo and Hélenos' confident encouragement. Implicit in this
motivation is the expectation that Hektor will do well. As we
shall see again in Book IX (note to p. 213), Homer sometimes depends upon the audience's knowledge to make plausible an otherwise inexplicable reaction on the part of one of
his characters. Here, then, the poet plays on the audience's
expectations, using our knowledge of divine favor to make intelligible Akhaian timidity and pessimism.

To the charge that the duel is redundant we should reply
that it continues the focus on Hektor begun in Book VI and
contrasts his character and behavior with that of Paris. Hektor's position in the poem is ambiguous in that he must be
depicted as a worthy foe who is also clearly doomed, for no
one realistically expects him to be a match for Akhilleus. The
duel epitomizes this ambiguous role: he reaches beyond himself and is lucky to survive. Later in the poem he comes to
believe, at least in a qualified way, in his own star; such self-

confidence necessarily precedes his ultimate willingness to face Akhilleus.

161   **Arêithoös:** the name means "swift in war"; Phylomedousa means "she who rules the tribe"; on p. 162 Iphínoös Dexíadês is "strong-mind son of Righthand." The language here would seem to identify this "Arêithoös the macewielder" with the character in Nestor's story (p. 166). But Arnê is in Boiotia (p. 52) and the later Arêithoös is an Arcadian; chronology is also against the identification.

162   **The grey-eyed goddess:** the epithet is applied to Athêna thirty-six times in the *Iliad* and seems to have meant, originally, "owl-faced." So Hêra's epithet "wide-eyed" meant "cow-eyed" or "cow-faced." See Guthrie, p. 70.

Hektor, breaker of wild horses: the first time this epithet is used of Hektor; cf. the last line of the poem. It is also applied, however, to all the Trojans (as a group), and on occasion to the Akhaians.

163   **gifted as you are with foresight/worthy of Zeus himself:** the line occurs at XI 200 (p. 257: Iris addresses Hektor). Otherwise (four times) the phrase characterizes Odysseus.

They halted/and sank down in their tracks: lines 54–56=III 76–78 (p. 70), where they fit better because the two armies have not yet engaged one another.

hunting birds . . . royal oak: they appear in the form of eagles. Both the oak and the eagle were associated with Zeus, whose most famous oracle was in an oak grove at Dôdôna. See p. 189 for the eagle sent as an omen by Zeus; cf. the portent, p. 287.

Hektor addressed them: the speech is marked by its moderation and decorum. In part this comes from Hektor's use of disjunctives: "until you take high Troy, or are defeated"; "if with his whetted bronze . . ."; "And if I kill this man . . ." Within these conditional clauses Hektor provides terms for disposition of the body and armor, stipulating reciprocal and civilized obligations. Still he manages to express his confidence by the imagined future report.

164   **my pride demands:** cf. "Hektor in his pride" (p. 163). These free translations do not violate the spirit of the passage. Pride, far from being a vice in the Homeric warriors,

is a necessary virtue which motivates them to great deeds as
well as great risks.

      Oh god, you brave noisemakers: the poet has al-
ready used five lines (54–56=III 76–78: "At this, great
Hektor's . . ."; 66f.=III 85f.: "Hektor addressed them
. . .") from the scene in Book III and has referred to the
broken "peace we swore to." In III Paris saw Meneláos, was
afraid of him and retired into the crowd (p. 68), and was
then rebuked by Hektor (p. 69). Here Meneláos rebukes the
army, which then provides a champion. When Aías advances,
Hektor sees him and is afraid, but holds his ground (VII
216ff.; p. 168). In III the challenge, delivered by Hektor for
Paris, follows the rebuke; in VII Hektor challenges and the
Akhaians respond after the rebuke by Meneláos and Nestor.
Such transpositions are vital to the oral poet's art. The same
components in a different order and elaboration secure an entirely new tone and tempo. In III, e.g., the formalities of the
sacrifice and prayers (p. 77) enhance the issue, i.e., the possibility of peace, whereas in VII the drawing of lots focuses on
the risk. Again, while the actual duels share some lines (e.g.,
VII 250–54=III 356–60: "Now in his turn great Aías made
his cast . . ." p. 169), a comparison will show that in III
Meneláos' actions dominate the description, while in VII (p.
169f.) the poet shifts back and forth between Aías and Hektor, thus suggesting a more balanced struggle than we find in
III.

165   **Even Akhilleus/shivered when . . . he met this
man:** Meneláos is frustrated and embarrassed. Agamémnon's
protective remonstrance seems at first to belittle his brother,
but his assertion that even Akhilleus feared Hektor serves to
excuse Meneláos (cf. Akhilleus, p. 214).

      Pêleus, the old master of horse: for their visit prior
to the expedition see pp. 211 and 275. The point of the prologue is that the Akhaians do not meet the expectations of
their fathers. Then a ring: a) would I were young again; b)
when I fought Ereuthalíôn; c) the story of Arêithoös and his
armor; b′) Ereuthalíôn; a′) would I were young again. In the
central panel the genealogy of the armor is traced: the last
owner (Ereuthalíôn) is mentioned first, the first owner
(Arês) last. Note the habit of beginning at the end of a story
and moving back into it, but not in strictly chronological

manner. The descent is Arês: Arêithoös: Lykoörgos: Ereuthalíôn; the story runs Ereuthalíôn: Arêithoös: Lykoörgos: Arês: Lykoörgos: Ereuthalíôn. Cf. Nestor's speech p. 271ff. and the notes there.

167   **Eurýpylos:** one of those warriors whose chief function is to fill out lists; cf. pp. 111, 142, and 189 (VII 164–67=VIII 262–65). He is wounded and given a brief speech on p. 269.

    A thrill of joy ran through him: he did not volunteer, but now he is ready. The entire passage implies ambivalence: he tells them to pray silently or openly; they pray for victory or a draw; when he addresses Hektor he praises Akhilleus more than the boasts of his own valor (contrast, e.g., Tlêpólemos, p. 129). The commentators suppose that the silent prayer would prevent the Trojans from countering with their own prayers. Aías' next lines clearly indicate he thinks silent prayer may argue timidity. Some ancient scholars condemned these lines because they are "not in the manner of Aías."

168   **Now the Trojans/felt a painful trembling:** no one feared for Paris in III. The next lines not only contrast him with Paris but show that mixture of fear and integrity which inspires Hektor on his last day (p. 518ff.).

    carrying like a tower his body shield: see the note on p. 145.

    Hylê: in Boiotia (pp. 51 and 131). Tykhios means "Maker."

169   **the lionhearted breaker of men:** such allusions underline the magnitude of the Akhaian loss *as they see it.* "Lionhearted" occurs only twice, of Akhilleus and of Hêraklês. "Breaker of men," four times, all of Akhilleus.

    I know/and know well: Aías began "you'll realize" (226) and Hektor responds using the same verb six times in six lines, a curiously rhetorical retort.

    Rifling his spear: they throw them, then retrieve them to use the spears as thrusting weapons (see the note to p. 252). As this duel illustrates, the sword is secondary to the spear or lance in sequence of usage and in actual effectiveness.

170   **Aías, a powerful great frame:** Hektor's reply is in keeping with the chivalry of his challenge, as is the exchange of gifts. There are few examples of such magnanimous behavior in Homeric battles.

172   you should suspend all action: Homer has compressed a great deal into the following narrative (pp. 172–75). Nestor proposes a truce and the building of ramparts. Antênor proposes a return of Helen and the treasure. Paris rejects half (Helen) of Antênor's proposal. Priam accepts Paris' offer and suggests a truce (echoing Nestor). Idaíos conveys this proposal (next day) and condemns Paris (echoing Antênor). Diomêdês rejects the return of the treasure, even if Helen is added. Agamémnon accepts the truce. They collect and burn the dead. Next day the Akhaians raise the mound and rampart.

Nestor's counsel is surprising on two counts: burning the dead in order to transport the charred bones home is a custom otherwise unknown until the fifth century (Kirk, *SH,* p. 180); secondly, this defensive strategy comes immediately after another Akhaian success (so Diomêdês: "Even a child can see the Trojans/live already on the edge of doom" [VII 401f.; p. 174]).

By the end of Book VIII Hektor is so emboldened that he determines to camp overnight on the plain, the better to observe the Akhaians and to press the Trojan advantage the next day. Nestor's proposal for defensive works would have come more plausibly at that point.

173   What you propose, Antênor, I do not like: Paris, as despised in his own camp as Akhilleus is admired in his, yet has the power to veto proposals touching his person, reputation, and pleasure. The extraordinary willfulness of the epic heroes, society's acceptance of their manner, and the harm which ensues are not so much themes as the data of the poem.

until inscrutable power/decides between us: cf. "the unseen power" p. 171; both phrases translate the Greek *daimon,* and extensive theological or cosmological implications should not be read into the translation. This is simply a way of saying that the gods, though they cannot be named at the moment, will certainly have a hand in the future course of this business. See Nilsson, *HGR,* p. 165ff.

174   would god he had foundered on the way: an ancient commentator suggests Idaíos may be trying to win sympathy for the Trojans (!), or that he offers this wish as an aside. Neither view seems necessary, though possibly the dramatic renderings of these scenes by rhapsodes makes the second a possibility. Helen uses the line (in the first person) at XXIV 764 (p. 593).

176 **Father Zeus:** Poseidon is of course Zeus's brother; the title is formulaic and honorific. Note his jealous concern that the glory he has earned not be superseded by mortal effort. A slightly different version of the indenture of the two gods to Laomédôn is given by Poseidon in XXI (p. 507). The scholiast explains that the two gods were forced to serve Laomédôn because they had rebelled against the rule of Zeus.

Lemnos . . . Iêson's son: Iêson (Jason) led the Argonauts in the quest of the golden fleece (the subject of Apollonius of Rhodes' *Argonautica*, written in the third century B.C.). At the time they landed in Lemnos, which is off the coast west of Troy, the island was ruled by Queen Hypsipylê. The Lemnian women, Hypsipylê excepted, had killed their fathers and husbands because of their infidelity with women of Thrace. Thoas, her father, is mentioned on p. 337.

BOOK EIGHT

rcrcrcrcrcrcrcrcrcrcrcrcr

THE BATTLE SWAYED
BY ZEUS

Zeus gives notice to the other divinities that they may not intervene in the battle. Then from Mount Ida he presides over
a day marked by Trojan success. Diomêdês and Nestor are
persuaded by the thunder and lightning of Zeus that they
must retire; meanwhile Hektor pursues the fleeing Akhaians
to their rampart. Athêna and Hêra start to come to the aid of
the Akhaians, but a second warning from Zeus stops them.
Zeus foretells the death of Patrôklos and Akhilleus' return to
battle. The book concludes with Hektor urging the victorious
Trojans to camp in the plain before the city

that not by night shall the unshorn Akhaians
get away on the broad back of the sea.

VIII 510–11 (p. 197)

The gods, and particularly Zeus, dominate this book. What
Zeus could not accomplish by guile he now achieves in a

more direct manner. His thunder and lightning from Ida intimidate the Akhaians and encourage Hektor and the Trojans. Though there is relatively little fighting, the Trojans are justified in thinking they have carried the day, and the pessimism that led the Akhaians to build a rampart is belatedly given a motivation. The events of VIII thus begin to fulfill Zeus's promise to Thetis, as Athêna recognizes (p. 193). Zeus's forecast (p. 196) is another indication that the action of the poem has assumed a more specific focus on the honor of Akhilleus. Consequently, while in some respects the book is a self-contained episode, it clearly anticipates and motivates the embassy to Akhilleus that follows in IX.

181   Dawn: line 1=XXIV 695 (p. 590); cf. XIX 1 and XXIII 227 (p. 542).

182   Tartaros: other descriptive passages referring to the underworld will be found on pages 196 and 336. In the later tradition Tartaros was often distinguished as a locality within Hadês; here the earth is conceived as equidistant from Tartaros and the sky. See Hesiod, *Theogony* 720ff. Later in (p. 196), where Hêra is the speaker.

earth and sea," which is its situation in the *Odyssey,* Book XI.

     a golden line: Zeus's line was to gain a significance in the European imagination which he could hardly anticipate: see E. R. Curtius, *European Literature and the Latin Middle Ages,* translated by W. R. Trask (New York, 1953), p. 110.

     we are well aware: lines 32–37=VIII 463–68 (p. 196), where Hêra is the speaker.

183   the peak of Gárgaron: the crest of Mount Ida (see p. 339).

     the Father cleared his golden scales: cf. XXII 209ff. (p. 522), which shares three lines with this passage. Though these two passages, the only ones in which Zeus uses the scales, are much disputed, they seem related to other figurative expressions by which Zeus is described as the steward and dispenser of fate. Cf., e.g., IV 84, p. 90 (=XIX 224; p. 464), where Zeus "holds the keys/and rationing of war." At XVI 658 Hektor "perceived/the dipping scales of Zeus" (p. 397). Scholars have offered two views: 1) Zeus consults the scales to determine what is fated; 2) the passage is a figurative depiction of Zeus's power to weigh out portions which he himself selects, and so controls. Does Zeus control fate, or is he subject to fate? The question is not one that Homer himself addresses, and since the evidence remains to some degree ambiguous and contradictory, whatever position we choose to attribute to the poet should be recognized as implicit, and not an aspect of a didactic scheme such as we find in Hesiod's poems. It would appear that Homer, like Hesiod, thinks of Zeus as the most powerful dynamic force in the world. Both here and in XXII Zeus has just indicated his will, and the action of the scales follows his decision. In XXII Zeus first of all shows a personal inclination to "deliver [Hektor] from death" (p. 521). At this Athêna protests that Hektor's "doom is fixed, long ago" (XXII 179; p. 521). Her speech implies that it is Hektor's mortal nature, not the edict of a higher order, that Zeus should consider (note, however, that one may argue that "mortality" is exactly that aspect of fate which here overrides Zeus's personal wish). Zeus acquiesces in her argument, the "two shapes of death" (XXII 210; p. 522) are put in the scales, and "Down/sank Hektor's fatal day" (XXII 212). The motif and scene were undoubtedly traditional, as we see from the similar exchange between Zeus and Hêra at XVI 433ff. (p. 390f.). Hêra uses the same lines that Athêna uses in XXII to deflect Zeus from saving his son Sarpêdôn (XVI 441–43=XXII 179–81; pp. 391 and 521). In both passages Zeus acts (either with lightning or through Athêna) to implement the verdict of the scales. Clearly Zeus and the other divinities have the power to alter at least temporarily the length of man's mortal tenure. It is just as clear that the poet is more interested in realizing the potential dramatic values of such conflicts than he is in developing a coherent metaphysics.

184   **Odysseus did not hear him:** possibly, "paid no attention to him." The scholiast thought the line ambiguous. In the Greek Odysseus is styled "brilliant, much enduring."

185   **Sthénelos and the noble Eurýmedôn:** the latter is Nestor's charioteer. Despite Diomêdês' explanation of the new arrangement ("your groom is wobbly and your beasts are spent"), it seems strange that Nestor should take the risky post of charioteer. Hektor will lose two charioteers in this book and a third at the end of XVI.

          there might soon have been/a ruin of Trojans: the

poet has not forgotten Diomêdês' recent *aristeia*. This ligh
ning that terrifies the team is the most direct intervention
Zeus in the *Iliad*.

186   **That's the way he'll put it:** Diomêdês is sensiti
to his reputation even though he realizes Zeus favors t
Trojans. Nestor reminds him of past triumphs, but a he
must continue to prove himself, as Diomêdês knows, or l
subjected to just the kind of taunt Hektor makes.

O Diomêdês, once: for the motif of feasting as re
ognition of honor due see pp. 96, 188, and 290.

187   **Tawny and Whitefoot:** Hektor drives a four-hors
chariot, whereas most chariots are pulled by two horse
sometimes, as in the case of Nestor's team, with a third in th
traces. There is some ancient evidence for feeding hors
wine, but that Andrómakhê should have served them befo
Hektor seems whimsical.

Nestor's shield . . . enameled cuirass: neither
celebrated elsewhere.

188   **at Hélikê and Aigai:** for the first see p. 54; Aig
is also on the north coast of Peloponnesus. Both were sites o
famous cults of Poseidon.

189   **peer of Enyálios:** elsewhere this word (meanin
"warlike") is a title of Arês, but it is used most often as
proper name; the line occurs four times.

191   **But that mad dog I cannot hit:** even the best o
bowmen are not valued so highly as spearmen. Cf. "You Ar
give arrow boys" (XIV 479; p. 344) and the frustration o
Pándaros p. 116, who is killed when he engages Diomêdê
with a spear. The archer is unarmed and unable to clain
booty, as Idómeneus rather untactfully notes when offering
spear to the archer Meríonês:

I win weapons from the dead.
I do not hold with fighting at long range.

XIII 262f. (p. 307,

It is probably significant that Odysseus, who in the *Odyssey* i
famed for his archery and kills most of the suitors with hi
bow, makes very little use of that weapon in the *Iliad*, and
does not enter the archery contest in XXIII.

193   **Eurýstheus:** king of Mykênai, for whom Hêraklê erformed his twelve labors. At his command Hêraklês ought Cerberus, "the watchdog of the Lord of Un- rgloom," back from Érebos ("gloom" or "darkness," and 10ther name for the underworld).

Hêra whose arms are white as ivory: the clause anslates a single compound adjective used twenty-four times Hêra, three times of Andrómakhê, and once of Helen. êra's epithets ("with wide eyes," "Goddess of the Golden 1rone," "Queen," and "Daughter of old Krónos") hardly ggest the impatient belligerence of her role in the *Iliad*.

Meanwhile Athêna: lines 384–88=V 733–37). 132); she exchanges a long robe for a shorter garment ore suitable for battle.

stepped in the fiery car: lines 389–96=V 745– 2 (p. 132).

Iris of Golden Wings: Iris' epithets (she "who runs 1 the rainy wind," "running on the wind," and "swift") cor- spond closely to her limited function.

95 **the illustrious one who makes the islands tremble:** 1e line represents two words in the Homeric text. This title or Poseidon may refer to the pounding of waves on the 1ore, or to earthquakes. Cf. "girdler of the islands" p. 209.

Alone, apart: these two lines are used of the her- lds to Akhilleus (I 332–33; p. 22: "they stood without a ord"). Because the Greek verb expresses number and per- 1n (e.g., the third person dual, "those two") without re- eating the subject ("Hêra and Athêna"; "the (two) her- lds"), lines are readily repeated with a change of subject.

In war, where men win glory: the clause (translat- 1g a single compound epithet) occurs eight times in the *Iliad*. .lthough the epithet represented here is the most common ingle adjective describing "war" in the poem, a number of ss frequently used adjectives ("tearful," "grievous," "sear- 1g") suggest a less exalting view of war's consequences. Hêra nd Athêna look to their own "glory," but such formulae are ot so flexible that modifications to suit the particular person nd situation are practical for the poet.

95–196 **Zeus fell silent . . . with goddesses, my lord:** these ix lines (457–62)=IV 20–25 (p. 88); and 463–68 ("We are vell . . . your displeasure")=VIII 32–37 (p. 182). The oddesses are described as having the same general reaction

(rebellious plotting and sullen anger) here and in IV, despi
the fact that there Zeus, certainly in a teasing tone, h
made a positive proposal, and no threat of lightning, as I
does here. Hêra's reply suits both contexts in VIII becau
Zeus has initiated each exchange with a threat.

196 The entire episode (from line 350, p. 192) is r
dundant of the first scene in the book—until Zeus offers h
prediction of tomorrow's events. Zeus asserted his authori
and intimidated the ladies; now they have conspired ar
armed for battle, with elaborate preparations, only to I
reminded of his power again. It is not the way of Homer sin
ply to say that Zeus will now turn the course of battle, for I
prefers to show the will of Zeus in action. There are usual
surprises: the limited *aristeia* of Teukros would appear to t
frustrating Zeus's design until Hektor with a single blo
removes him from the field; the machinations of tl
goddesses seem dramatically pointless until Zeus uses the o
casion to announce the circumstances of Akhilleus' return t
battle ("for Hektor shall not . . . until . . . Patróklos dead"

Iápetos and Krónos: Titans, sons of Uranos, wh
were overthrown by Zeus and condemned to prison in the ur
derworld (see Hesiod, *Theogony* 665ff.).

197 **He held/his lance erect:** lines 494f.=VI 319f. (
151). A hero is known by his weapons: "Nestor's shield" an
Diomêdês' "enameled cuirass" (p. 187), the shield of Aíz
"like a tower" (p. 168), and the "Pêlian ash" spear c
Akhilleus (p. 381f.).

198 **Would I were sure:** Leaf describes this form c
wish: "a thing is vividly depicted as certain by opposing it t
an imaginary event which is obviously impossible, or *vic
versa*" (his note to VIII 538). In three of the four passage
Leaf mentions, the thing "obviously impossible" is the immo
tality of a mortal (pp. 324 and 450). The limitations an
conditions imposed by mortality appear in a number c
paradigms and arguments, e.g., Diomêdês' reference to th
fate of Lykourgos (p. 145f.) and Sarpêdôn's exhortation o
Glaukos (p. 291).

and all the lookout points: cf. the simile at XV
297ff. (p. 386), which includes two lines used here.

BOOK NINE

𐎧𐎧𐎧𐎧𐎧𐎧𐎧𐎧𐎧𐎧

A VISIT OF EMISSARIES

The poem returns to Akhilleus. In Book VIII Zeus has taken more direct measures to help the Trojans; Akhaian pessimism now is justified. Once again Agamémnon proposes retreat. Diomêdês rejects this defeatism and Nestor advocates an attempt to placate Akhilleus, to which the king readily assents. An embassy of three warriors is sent to Akhilleus' tent. To their promises of gifts and their pleas in the name of friendship Akhilleus shows an anger and resentment undiminished from Book I. By the end of the book he has tempered his anger a little, but not enough for Odysseus to offer Agamémnon much encouragement.

The book is the most rhetorical of all the episodes in the *Iliad*. The first public assembly (speeches by Agamémnon, Diomêdês, and Nestor) is immediately followed by a private council of the chiefs (speeches by Nestor, Agamémnon, and Nestor). The next scene takes us to Akhilleus' tent: a minimum of narrative introduces long speeches by each of

the three emissaries, to which Akhilleus replies in turn.
Akhilleus' response to Odysseus is a turbulent, chaotic reflection of his angry resentment. His response to Aías' appeal
tersely sets terms that will be crucial for subsequent decisions
in the poem. The emissaries return to Agamémnon's tent
where Odysseus reports, <u>rather misleadingly</u>, Akhilleus' decision, and Diomêdês comments on their effort to win him by
persuasion. As is usually the case, there is little dialogue
though the conferences before and after the embassy approach realistic debate. But the long speeches of Odysseus
of Akhilleus in reply, and of Phoinix, while differing in style
and content, extend Homeric rhetoric to its most studied and
intense forms.

By an odd fate this marvelous book has been reckoned by
some scholars a late addition to the *Iliad*, which on this view
originally did not have an embassy. Readers interested in a
full, vigorous, and dogmatic exposition of this view should see
Page's appendix, "Multiple Authorship in the *Iliad*," pp.
297–315. While I have not taken this excision as seriously
as Page would have it, some reasons for isolating IX from all
or a part of the *Iliad* will be considered in the notes on
Phoinix's appearance in this book and elsewhere in notes to
Books XI (p. 270) and XVI (p. 379f.). Mere lack of reference, as distinct from a lack of relevance, to other scenes in
the poem does not seem to warrant excision. Phoinix's entry
is more difficult, but a clumsy piece of work is not necessarily
unauthentic.

One final note on this episode: from beginning to end the
Iliad presents a series of petitions which prove crucial to the
agents. Khrysês begs Agamémnon for his daughter. Akhilleus
asks Thetis for intercession with Zeus; when Zeus honors
her petition, the plot is set in motion. Later Andrómakhê
fails to secure a more defensive strategy from Hektor (VI).
In XVI Patróklos, after the appeal of Nestor (in XI), is
permitted to aid the Akhaians. Priam and Hékabê cannot
persuade Hektor to leave the battlefield and avoid Akhilleus
(XXII). Finally, in XXIV, Priam carries ransom and successfully petitions Akhilleus for the body of his son. There
are countless other examples, and even the supplications in
battle have a place in this theme. Through scenes of petition,
supplication, entreaty, and persuasion Homer dramatizes
decision making and definition of character. It is instructive

to compare the practice of Sophocles, who often introduces scenes in which one character attempts to mollify the inflexible resolve of hero or heroine. In Sophocles persuasion regularly fails or is too late.

204 **Friends, leaders of Argives:** this speech is composed of two passages used in Book II (lines 18–25=II 111–18 [p. 39]; 26–28=II 139–41). Diomêdês' response would seem to be the one Agamémnon hoped for in Book II, when the entire assembly broke for the ships.

Before this you have held me up to scorn: see Agamémnon's rebuke of Diomêdês in Book IV (p. 100).

205 **Sthénelos and I will fight alone:** cf. the conclusion of Akhilleus' speech p. 380 (XVI 97ff.).

Alien to clan and custom: Leaf suggests that these two lines (63–64) "should naturally introduce the conclusive proposal which Nestor has promised—viz. the reparation to Achilles" (i.e., they more aptly apply to Akhilleus and might be expected at the end of Nestor's next speech [p. 206f.]).

206 **Thrasymêdês:** his first appearance (later pp. 237, 329, 387, 419); **Askálaphos/and Iálmenos:** p. 52; Aphareus, Dêipyros, Meríonês and Askálaphos are together again on p. 314 (the first two are then killed in battle). Lykomêdês is mentioned again on pp. 292, 418, and 464.

the same view that I've held: see pp. 20–21.

207 **you dishonored a great prince:** Nestor's line (110f.) repeats Akhilleus' charge (I 356 [p. 23]: "Agamémnon humiliated me"). The Greek word order indicates the intimate relation between "dishonored" and "taking his prize." Such repetitions, whether we call them formulae or not, have the effect of validating statements which might otherwise be viewed merely as claims or assertions of personal opinion. Thus Nestor, although he advised Akhilleus in Book I "not to vye in honor/with him who hold authority from Zeus," now recognizes the propriety of Akhilleus' claims and action. For another discussion of "borrowed" lines see the notes to Patróklos' speech p. 378.

my blind errors: this translates the same noun (*atê*) Agamémnon used at II 111 (p. 39: "cruel folly"). "I lost my head" (below) translates a verb from the same stem. The idea is that a kind of infatuation or delusion comes upon a man and causes him to act contrary to good sense and his

own best interest (see the example Agamémnon gives on p.
460f.). The noun may be personified, as in XIX, or be used
of a subjective state, as here in IX, or more objectively, as
when Akhilleus says to Thetis:

> All the troops
> may savor what their king has won for them,
> and he may know his madness, what he lost
> when he dishonored me, peerless among Akhaians."
>
>   I 410–12 (p. 25)

"his madness" (*atê*) is defined by "dishonored me."

208   Orestés . . . Iphiánassa: the number of Agamémnon's daughters varied in the ancient tradition. Homer
may have identified Iphiánassa and Iphigeneia, whose sacrifice at Aulis he does not mention.

Seven flourishing strongholds: these are not listed
in the catalogue in Book II. Phêrai would seem to be the
Phêrê of V 543 (p. 126). How it is that Agamémnon controls cities so far from the Argolid, and nearer if not within
the territory of Meneláos and Nestor, is a mystery. Such apparent inconsistencies may reflect historical dispositions of
territory which we cannot reconstruct, or perhaps, as some
critics have argued, they merely represent the poet's desire to
augment the power of Agamémnon, even at the expense of
his own narrative. Yet it would not be unreasonable to suppose that Agamémnon might have tributary states, such as he
proposes to give to Akhilleus, in territory not contiguous with
his own.

the gifts . . . are not to be despised: Nestor called
for "friendly gifts and . . . affectionate words" (IX 113; p.
207). He and the others (cf. Phoinix p. 219) apparently find
the king's compensation sufficient, but they say nothing of
Agamémnon's reassertion of authority ("Let him be subdued . . .": Odysseus will not report these last four lines
when he addresses Akhilleus). Cf. the king's words when he
threatens Akhilleus at I 187ff. (p. 17):

> to show you here and now who is the stronger
> and make the next man sick at heart—if any
> think of claiming equal place with me."

IX 158–61, which conclude his speech, are in the same vein. This is important if, as I think, Akhilleus' violent reaction to Odysseus' speech is predicated on the audience's perception that Agamémnon is not repentant. He certainly has not reached the despair Akhilleus swore he would:

> You will eat your heart out,
raging with remorse for this dishonor

> I 243f. (p. 19)

209   Phoinix, dear to Zeus, may lead the way: this is the first time he is mentioned in the poem, and as a retainer of Akhilleus and a minor figure it is difficult to say why he is in the council at all (he does not return from Akhilleus' tent). More disturbing is the following journey in which (in the Greek) he is not mentioned, and apparently explicitly excluded. Homer uses the dual form of the verb—that grammatical form which explicitly limits the number to two—for "walked together" (the heralds may be discounted, or rather must be) and continues to use the dual in his own narrative and in Akhilleus' address to them (lines 182–98). Aías nods to Phoinix (IX 223; p. 210), as if to signal him to begin, but Odysseus takes the first speech. Between Nestor's recommendation and Phoinix's speech this reference at IX 223 is the only recognition, by poet or characters, of his presence. These considerations, and especially the use of the dual, have convinced many scholars that Phoinix is a late addition to the scene. For more on this topic see D. L. Page, p. 297ff.

Labeling a character or an episode "late" means "post-Homeric" for some, while others, thinking Homer the latest of those poets who worked and reworked the same material, have only the problem of the verb form in the dual to worry about. Various subtle explanations have been offered for the dual, perhaps the best of which sees the scene as an adaptation of other scenes where two emissaries appear, e.g., the two heralds going to Akhilleus' tent in Book I. Such adaptations are natural to oral composition, but the explanation cannot hide the fact that we have a very awkward execution in a poem that often shows extraordinary dexterity and mnemonic capacity in handling a vast narrative (see, e.g., the notes to p.

155, or consider Odysseus' subtle omission of what is better left unreported [notes to p. 208]).

If we look at Phoinix's speech (pp. 217–22), which is after all the reason for introducing him, two rather different, and perhaps even contradictory, points merit notice. The speech itself is the most elaborately developed and thematically pertinent of the three delivered to Akhilleus. The paradigm of Meléagros, which recalls the style of Nestor, the effective admonition through allegory, and the subtle and repeated insistence on the personal relations of Akhilleus, Phoinix, and Pêleus, all of these mark the speech as a high point of Homeric rhetoric, and, it must be added, all have been marked as evidence for the rhetorical lateness of the speech. But consider Akhilleus' reaction to this speech, which is sometimes said to be the most effective in the embassy. His reaction is terse, pointed ("I am honored by Zeus, and that will do"), and in no way attempts to engage the varied cogency of Phoinix's appeal. His brevity in reply does not contradict Homer's manner elsewhere (cf., e.g., Patróklos' response to Nestor's appeal in XI, p. 276), but it is a far cry from his long and vehement rejection of Odysseus' proposal, and it lacks the direct, humane feeling and precise terms found in the reply to Aías. So the speech of Phoinix may seem an unused gem, brilliant in itself but somehow lacking resonance in its context.

We have not solved the problem of the late Phoinix. My own conclusion is that Phoinix may well have come to the party after the initial idea of an embassy was developed in a party of two. If you read the scene without his speech, how much the episode is improved by the addition will be obvious. We cannot know whether Homer or a later ghost writer brought Phoinix into IX, but we can say that whoever brought him on was more interested in the talk than the staging. Only detectives who value the game more than its substance will want to banish Phoinix because he did not leave his footprints on the beach.

Hódios: "Traveler," an appropriate name for a herald. All texts read Odios, but Fitzgerald has accepted the aspirated form found in an ancient commentator. Eurýbatês is the herald of Odysseus; so Hódios must be the herald of Aías.

Following Phoinix: this phrase and "Phoinix had come in unremarked" (below) are Fitzgerald's way of dealing with the dual problem. They have no counterpart in the Greek text, which uses the dual number for the verbal suffix and explicitly mentions Odysseus at IX 192 ("Odysseus leading").

Peace! My two great friends: this and "dearest friends" (p. 210) anticipate a reception very different from that given Odysseus' speech (p. 213). All three visitors, and especially Phoinix and Aías, appeal frankly to his friendship.

210 **Automédôn:** he is the charioteer for Akhilleus and Patróklos, mentioned for the first time here but frequently in Book XVI and XXIV.

Health, Akhilleus: Fitzgerald has paragraphed this speech into three sections. These mark three phases of the argument, and a fourth may be found in the enumeration of the gifts:

a) save your friends who are now threatened by Hektor.

b) Pêleus warned you of "insidious quarrels."

c) if you relent, Agamémnon will give these gifts (264–99=122–57).

d) relent, even if you still hate Agamémnon (pity your friends: thus you win their respect and glory by killing Hektor).

The first section dwells on the danger; the final section returns to the danger (Hektor's "frenzy": 239 and 305;) see the note on p. 510 and adds the motif glory. Pêleus' advice [b] is made to anticipate the present quarrel, and b) is linked to d) by the motif of respect (honor) from friends; c) is framed by the phrase Agamémnon used at 157 ("if he/desists from anger").

211 **your father, Pêleus:** this recollection may not be altogether "historical." Cf. Nestor's account at XI 783 (p. 275) and the comments of Phoinix p. 217.

213 **Even if you abhor/the son of Atreus:** Odysseus omits the concluding imperious lines of Agamémnon's speech (p. 208: "Let him be subdued . . ."), preferring to return to the pitiable condition of the army and Hektor's recklessness.

Akhilleus the great runner answered him: this is a difficult speech which most critics have considered central to the understanding of Akhilleus and his rebellion. Unlike the

preceding speech of Odysseus, this reply lacks large, firmly
defined arguments. It changes topics rapidly and allusively,
and because of its use of argumentative questions an open-
ness and ambiguity pervade language that is passionate and
often more subjective than usual in Homeric speech.

Akhilleus' attitude toward the gifts has been interpreted
variously, but two poles of criticism are clear enough. Some
critics argue that in Akhilleus' view the gifts are merely symbolic of honor, and that true honor for him is an intangible
quality in which loyalty and integrity are paramount. As
David Claus has put it: ". . . while he regards them [the
gifts] as a necessary condition for his participation in battle
he can never regard them as sufficient condition without
abandoning his aristocratic belief that heroic behavior is ultimately something self-imposed and gratuitous, taking place
between men who treat each other as equals. By depriving
Achilles of his *geras* [prize] in *Iliad* I Agamemnon has not
only removed a necessary condition of fighting and publicly
insulted him, but he has transformed the gifts from their
proper status as a mere symbol of Achilles' *arete* ["excellence" or "valor"] into a practical measure of it." (*"Aidôs* in
the Language of Achilles," *TAPA* 105 [1975], p. 23.) On
Akhilleus' *aretê* see the note p. 278.

A more legalistic view has contended that Akhilleus rejects
the offer because of the submission he perceives it demands
and because he swore in Book I to see Agamémnon suffer a
humiliation comparable to Akhilleus' own dishonor. On this
view Akhilleus values the prizes as a legitimate and definitive
expression of honor, trophies awarded whose "higher" value
consists solely in their expressions of status granted by society
to the hero. In cheating Akhilleus of his prize Agamémnon
himself violated the "heroic code"; the angered prince will
not relent

> till he pays me back
> full measure, pain for pain, dishonor for dishonor.
>
> IX 387 (p. 215)

So Akhilleus dismisses the gifts here because he is set on retri-
bution. If we compare IX 387 with XIX 208 (see the note p.
463), we may infer that Akhilleus is concerned for an out-

rage or affront to his honor of a purely personal sort ("codes" have little to do with it). Agamémnon has treated him contemptibly and must be made to pay by suffering an indignity himself. In short, *quid pro quo:* humiliation for humiliation.

Looking more directly to this speech the questions to be answered are: 1) why does Akhilleus reply so violently? 2) what objections does he have to Odysseus' speech as such? 3) to Agamémnon's offer? 4) to the character and behavior of Agamémnon? Two, not altogether exclusive, approaches have been offered to 3) and 4) above. As for the first, Whitman (p. 192) suggests that Akhilleus intuitively perceives that Agamémnon is so far from humbling himself that he has actually set conditions on Akhilleus' return (these are the omitted lines 158–61 noted above). This would be another example (see the introduction to VII and the note on Eurýpylos p. 271) of using the audience's (previous) perception to ground a character's speech or action. We have just seen Agamémnon conclude with "So let Akhilleus bow to me . . ." (IX 160f.), so that we know he is not contrite. The poet tacitly lets Akhilleus speak as if he knows that final arrogant stipulation.

If this reading is correct, whether we call it intuition or technique, then Akhilleus has good reason for resentment. Odysseus makes a show of fair dealing and supplication ("pity us"), but he has spoken less than the truth. Hence the lines "I hate/as I hate Hell's own gate . . ." may have a triple reference: 1) to Akhilleus himself (I hate a liar and won't be one); 2) to Odysseus, who has lied by omission; 3) to Agamémnon, who lies in that he offers the appearance of an apology (the gifts) but not the substance. It may be doubted whether Agamémnon could satisfy Akhilleus and still maintain his own honor.

This speech prompted Adam Parry's provocative essay "The Language of Achilles," *TAPA* 87 (1956), 1–7. For other views see the bibliographical note on Akhilleus.

    I hate/as I hate Hell's own gate: the line (IX 312) also appears at *Odyssey* XIV 156, where Odysseus swears to the veracity of his story and denies that he has made a tale to serve his own purposes. It is tempting to think this line might have been traditionally associated with the speech of the wily Odysseus; if so, Akhilleus would be turning the oath against its proprietor. Cf. "the man [Paris] being abhorred like death itself" (III 454; p. 83).

Give in to Agamémnon: Agamémnon has tried to persuade Akhilleus to submit to the king's authority in return for gifts. But persuasion can mediate only between friends.

I had/small thanks: this sentence appears in a speech of Glaukos (XVII 147f.; p. 412: "What have we gained . . ."), who is charging Hektor with failing to save the body of Sarpêdôn. Hektor has an obligation to the allies and has not kept it. The entire speech repays comparison with the present passage.

The portion's equal: a pun on the Greek *moira*, which means both "fate" and "lot": we shall die in any case and gifts will not change that. Either Akhilleus exaggerates because of his anger, or this is the first, tentative, and partial step in a line of reasoning carried to its conclusion at the end of the speech ("Now I think/no riches can compare . . ." IX 401ff.; p. 216).

What least thing have I: to the end of the paragraph Akhilleus argues that he, and he alone, has not had fair recompense. Those who think Akhilleus is not at all concerned for things must account for a great deal of talk in this speech about things. He does not simply dismiss the prizes once, and for all, as if in his mind they were not worth a penny.

214   **He holds my bride . . . enjoys her:** the word here translated "bride" regularly means "wedded wife," and however it is rendered, Akhilleus stretches the facts a bit in applying it to Brisêis. (Leaf suggests a punctuation which would give "why should he take my share [Brisêis]? He has a wife of his own, let him be content with her.") As the lines stand in most texts, including Fitzgerald's version, they epitomize the contradictory position in which he finds himself: he asserts the personal value of Brisêis while rejecting her return. But there is little romantic love in Homer, and Akhilleus probably sensed less contradiction than we do in talking of his "love" and "prize" in the same breath (cf. p. 216, where he says he will take a bride in Phthía).

Why must Argives/fight the Trojans: these are neither new questions (cf. Akhilleus at I 152ff.; p. 16) nor objections unique to him (as we see from Glaukos' rebuke of Hektor, p. 412).

tricked and defrauded me: the "temptation" here is to be found in the attempt to lure Akhilleus back before Agamémnon has paid in kind. Consequently he turns with scorn to their defensive efforts.

the killer's charge: this recalls his threat on p. 19. For the epithet see p. 583.

Tomorrow at dawn: but at 386f. (p. 215) he talks of being "paid back," which makes no sense unless he stays. After Phoinix's appeal he says "at first light/we can decide whether to sail or stay" (p. 223); after Aías' speech he makes a definite stipulation about the limits of Hektor's carnage (p. 224).

215   **he who gave her took her outrageously back:** "outrageously," i.e., in a hubristic manner, another echo from Book I (p. 18 and note). Cf. "Zeus took his brains away!" (line 377) with I 412 ("his madness"), p. 25.

Okhómenos' town gate/or Thebes of Egypt: the Boiotian city of the Minyans (p. 52) was legendary for its wealth, but in historical times it was eclipsed by Boiotian Thebes. This is the only reference to Egypt in the *Iliad*, whereas the *Odyssey* refers to that country on several occasions.

not till he pays me back: the rhetorical point of the preceding list is that the dishonor he has suffered cannot be compensated by gifts but only by a dishonor suffered by Agamémnon (see note p. 463).

216   **the Archer's shrine . . . at rocky Pytho:** Apollo's oracle at Delphi was called Pytho after the dragon slain there by Apollo. Rich offerings were brought to Delphi by those seeking information and the good will of the god.

Now I think/no riches can compare with being alive: "a completely unheroic evaluation" and "The heroic code has lost its grip on him" (Sale, p. 94). Another way of putting the problem of this speech is to ask if we may properly speak of "the blow to his faith in the heroic system," as Sale does, or if we should rather speak of a blow to his pride which demands extreme satisfaction.

two possible destinies: such a choice is nowhere else explicitly mentioned, but I 352 (p. 23) and I 416f. (p.

25) may allude to a decision already made to elect the short, glorious life. Cf. also Patróklos' comment at XVI 36ff. (p. 378) and Akhilleus' reply (XVI 50f.; p. 379).

      but gain unfading glory: the Greek word *kleos* ("glory") has been translated variously, according to the sense of the context. It is the "fame" that goes out into the world to be reported by heroes and bards. Cf. II 486 (p. 51) "we/can only hear the tales [*kleos*]" and Akhilleus singing "old tales" (IX 189; p. 209). At IV 197 (=207) it is very like "success": "a feat for the enemy/worry and pain for us" (p. 94). So Hektor, using the same word, says: "And the honor/won by me here will never pass away" (VII 91; p. 164). Prizes and spoils of battle are testimonials to glory (see Hektor XVII 232; p. 414). When Akhilleus has determined to re-enter battle, he desires not only revenge but "perfect glory" (XVIII 121, p. 439). A comparison of these and many other passages on this subject will demonstrate how far from the heroic norm Akhilleus' present attitude has taken him.

217   **while my anger holds:** this participial construction (which may also be rendered "because") is used by Akhilleus at XIX 62 (p. 459: "while I abstained in anger") and by the poet at II 772 (p. 60: "raged at Agamémnon"). This verb echoes the "anger" (Greek *mênis*) of I 1. At this moment he seems peculiarly self-conscious. When we assess Akhilleus' "reasoning," it is well to remember that he speaks in anger, not rationally, and any surmises about the implications of his language, especially when they lead to the transvaluation of all values, ought to be made cautiously. If, as Adam Parry argued in "The Language of Achilles," he has rejected the entire basis of heroic life, that rejection ought to be evident in word and deed in Books XVI through XXIV.

      Lord Phoinix,/answered at last: a) personal relationships, b) anecdote and paradigm, and c) admonition are interwoven to organize this speech:

  a)   Phoinix, Pêleus, and Akhilleus.
  b)   the youth of Phoinix (anger and revenge the themes).
  a′)   Phoinix and Akhilleus (Phoinix is like a father).
  c)   admonition ("Quell your anger" p. 219).
  b′)   allegory of the prayers and Folly.
  c′)   admonition ("Relent,/be courteous . . ." p. 219).

b") paradigm of Meléagros.

c") admonition ("Oh, do not let your mind . . ." p. 222). The anecdotes [b)] become increasingly germane to Akhilleus' case: the first chiefly serves to reinforce a) and a'); the second is brief and much like a bridge between the two admonitions (these vary: the first relies on Phoinix's image as father, the second reflects on Agamémnon's gifts and petition); the last anecdote, the paradigm of Meléagros, is drawn as a parallel to Akhilleus' present situation. c") draws the moral, and is admonitory in a strict sense, for it warns Akhilleus to beware of Meléagros' fate.

nothing of war . . . nothing of assembly: a familiar polarity: words and deeds. Cf. Nestor to Diomêdês p. 205; the poet on Hektor and Poulýdamas p. 443; Akhilleus on himself p. 439; Patróklos to Merionês p. 396.

Hellas: elsewhere, e.g., p. 57, this is thought a part of Pêleus' realm, but here Phoinix emigrates from Hellas. There are further difficulties in Amyntor Orménidês, who appears again at X 266 (p. 237) but has been transposed to a different locality. Migrations within Greece are often used to explain such discrepancies, but unfortunately our evidence is usually scanty and uncertain.

ghostly Furies: spirits often associated with revenge, especially within the family or social group, they are described by E. R. Dodds (*The Greeks and the Irrational*, p. 7) as "the personal agent who insures the fulfillment of a *moira* [lot]"; cf. Agamémnon's speech p. 460 (XIX 87). Usually they are the agents of fate and Zeus, but here the relationship is reversed and "Zeus of undergloom" (i.e., Zeus who also takes an interest in the dead) and "cold Perséphonê" (daughter of Dêmêtêr and queen of the underworld) are their agents (contrast XV 204; p. 356). (This description, unique in Homer, of Zeus as lord of the underworld may imply a view in which Zeus ruled all the world, whereas in Book XV Poseidon claims all the world was divided into three portions between himself, Zeus, and Hadês.)

218   **Dolopês:** they are a northern Greek tribe, connected with the Thessalians (Herodotus, VII 132).

Now, it was I/who formed your manhood: Phoinix's claim is not necessarily incompatible with the story

that the centaur Kheirôn was Akhilleus' teacher (see p. 277).
He describes himself in the role of a father, but does not say
"you owe me this"; instead he assumes the father's place and
advises: "Quell your anger . . ."

**219   And are they not still greater in bravery/in honor
and in strength:** these human standards and values are
equally applicable to the gods, who excel mortals in degree,
not in kind.

      prayers are daughters of almighty Zeus: allegory is
very rare in Homer and this is certainly the most developed
example. Folly (*atê:* see p. 39) will cause a man to act
foolishly and to injure another man; if the injured party lis-
tens to prayers (the repentance of the victim of Folly), "he
is rewarded," but if he refuses the petition, he himself will be
visited by Folly (cf. Agamémnon's apology p. 460).

      till suffering/has taken arrogance out of him: al-
ternatively, "till having suffered he makes payment (for his
failure)."

220   The Kourêtês . . . Aitolians: what follows is the
best-known exemplary myth in Homer; it tells the story of the
Kalydonian hero Meléagros in whom mercy prevailed too
late. Involuted and allusive in style, the story presents numerous difficulties.

The tribes mentioned here belong to northwestern Greece
(see p. 56). Typically the poet begins his story *in medias res*
and then reverts to earlier stages (cf. Nestor's story p. 165).
King Oineus of the Aitolians had failed in sacrifice to Artemis, who rouses a boar to ravage the countryside. After-
ward she causes the victorious huntsmen to fall to quarreling
("set on a clash") over the spoils. This clash is insensibly
transferred from its probable rural setting to the walls of
Kálydôn.

      swollen with rage/at his own mother: the reason
for his rage is given after the digression concerning the
genealogy of his wife, Kleopátrê. Apollodorus (I.7.8–9)
tells us that Idês and Apollo contended for Marpessê, who,
given the choice by Zeus, preferred the mortal Idês. Her nickname Alkýonê is the Greek for kingfisher, a bird said to
mourn plaintively when separated from its spouse.

221   in her anguish over a brother slain: Althaiê has
kin among the Kourêtês and curses her son for killing her

brother. The more familiar version to later readers makes Althaiê the controller of her son's fate through possession of a piece of charred wood destined at his birth to be coexistent with his life (see Apollodorus, I.8.2).

222   His folk no longer/cared to award him gifts: one of the problems in this speech is that Phoinix begins this paradigm by saying "great men . . . were still amenable to gifts and to persuasion" (p. 220), but then his story portrays a hero who waited too long. From "act on the example of the men of old" we move to "be warned by the example of the men of old," a shift which suggests adaptation for the sake of foreshadowing Akhilleus' actual course of action.

Honored . . . by Zeus's justice: this means "according to the dispensation of Zeus," an abstract and rather oblique allusion to the promise to Thetis. Since Akhilleus now says a decision on departure can be postponed till dawn (p. 223), it may be argued Phoinix has swayed him. His reaction, however, is minimal, limited to the last topic ("honor"), and more a simple rejection than a counterargument such as he offered Odysseus.

223   There is no pity in him: cf. Patróklos' charge at XVI 33 (p. 378) and Akhilleus' recollection, XVI 204 (p. 383).

for a brother slain: Aías takes the extreme case of moral responsibility and argues that even the provocation of a slain brother or son can be laid to rest by sufficient compensation. Yet Akhilleus cannot be appeased "for one girl alone." Aías reduces the contention to a mere girl, an argument Akhilleus ignores in his reply. It is generally assumed that the argument from friendship is the one which has touched Akhilleus most effectively. Cf. Patróklos' "A friend's persuasion . . ." (p. 362 and note).

224   I will not think . . . until: implicit is a decision to remain. Since the Myrmidons hold one end of the line, Akhilleus is in effect saying, "Hektor may burn your ships, but not mine," a concession of sorts, but not enough to give Agamémnon much hope.

Diomêdê: she is mentioned only here, and in the Greek text her name is modified by the same adjective used of Brisêis and Khrysêis in Book I (see pp. 15 and 22).

Skyros: this is probably not the island associated in

later stories with Akhilleus' youth (cf. p. 467); neither the place nor its king, Enyéus, can be identified.

     Prince Odysseus, made reply: he ignores the apparent modification in Akhilleus' position to report the reply to his own speech.

225   **When he had finished . . . in silence:** this line (IX 693) occurs ten times in the *Iliad;* the phrase beginning the next line (here "in perturbation") occurs six times in similar contexts.

     he is a proud man: etymologically the word translated "proud" means "very manly"; in the next book Diomêdês uses this same adjective twice ($220^b=244^b$) of himself ("pride and excitement" p. 236) and of his chosen comrade, Odysseus ("cool and brave" p. 237). So "vanity and pride" translates an abstract noun made from the same adjective (hence "manliness"); it is translated "courage" in the simile on p. 282 (XII 46) and "pride" when used to describe the attribute which always keeps Hektor in the forefront of the battle, XXII 457 (p. 530). Naturally connotations vary, and perhaps Diomêdês pronounces these otherwise commendatory words with a sneer, but also note that real virtues, much valued by his peers, have brought Akhilleus to this personal and social crisis.

226   **When they had spilt their wine:** this is the libation (p. 224), the offering of wine poured out for the gods.

BOOK TEN

🔁🔁🔁🔁🔁🔁🔁🔁🔁🔁🔁

NIGHT IN THE CAMP:
A FORAY

No book in the *Iliad* is more generally regarded as "late" than X, which is called the "Doloneia" after the Trojan spy captured by Diomêdês and Odysseus. Though stylistic and linguistic arguments have some force in the censure of this episode as "post-Homeric," it is the lack of thematic or structural connection with the rest of the poem which will be most evident to readers in translation. We have already noticed the tendency to incorporate integral scenes and episodes into the poem. Such a procedure is natural, perhaps necessary, in oral poetry. What distinguishes the Doloneia from scenes such as Hektor's visit with Andrómakhê is the absence of any thematic point for Book X. Some readers, too, will find the night raid a morally sordid business, one hardly suited to the character of the gallant Diomêdês. The results of this scouting have no effect on subsequent events; in fact

Books XI–XXIV do not contain a single allusion or reference to Book X.

If we look from Book X outward, however, signs of attempts to create ties with the rest of the poem appear. The first lines, e.g., recall the transition used at the beginning of Book II, and Agamémnon's view of "the plain/where fires burned, a myriad," recalls the scene concluding Book VIII. Such details, together with now familiar allusions to Akhilleus' anger and the achievements of Tydeus, show an effort at integrating the episode into the poem. Any number of theories have been offered concerning its composition. In antiquity some scholars thought that Homer himself had composed the episode, but that it was only included in the *Iliad* at the time of the Athenian tyrant Peisistratos. Such reports are just as likely to reflect aesthetic judgments ("worthy of Homer, but not in place in the *Iliad*") as actual knowledge of the history of the text.

230   **Will you call for a volunteer:** Menelaos gains some credit in the first pages of the book, and this inquiry anticipates Nestor's advice (p. 235).

231   **what Hektor did to the Akhaian army:** the reference would apparently be to the events of Book VIII, e.g., the wounding of Teukros (p. 191).

           his own son heads a company: a reference to Thrasymêdês (p. 206).

232   **the son of Phyleus:** Megês, II 627ff. (p. 55).

234   **on a razor's edge:** this familiar proverb is found only here in Homer.

236   **his feat would be/renowned:** here are the typical rewards of success, i.e., fame, prizes, and celebration at the feast. Nestor does not emphasize the usefulness of the exploit, nor even the gratitude earned, so much as the honor and personal distinction to be gained by the individual. Cf. Hektor's offer to the Trojans p. 239.

237   **a helmet that was first a cap of hide:** the description is famous because it reports a type of helmet known from archaeological evidence to have belonged to the Mycenaean era, but which was not used in later times. Hence the description must have survived from an earlier period than the actual composition of the poem, ironically enough appear-

ing in a book generally thought late. For a discussion see Lorimer, p. 211ff., or *A Companion to Homer*, p. 516.

Autólykos: he is the grandfather of Odysseus (see *Odyssey* XIX 394ff.), a notorious thief and trickster. He steals the cap from its Boiotian owner (Amyntor has migrated [!] from Hellas, neighboring Thessaly, southward since Book IX [p. 217]) and gives it to a resident of Kýthêra, an island off the Peloponnesus, whose main city was Skandeia; from there it traveled to Krete, the home of Mólos. This is assumed to be the route of travel in Mycenaean times between the continent and Krete.

238 **Tydeus . . . messenger to Thebes:** this is the same adventure told at greater length on p. 100f.

239 **Hektor, pride and excitement urge me on:** Dolôn and Diomêdês use the same line (220=319) in response to the calls of Hektor and Agamémnon. The scene in the Trojan camp parallels that in the Akhaian camp. Cf. in VII (p. 172f.) the paired conferences in which both sides are concerned for a truce to bury the dead. So in XVIII (pp. 438–45) Akhilleus' decision to accept death as the price of revenge is followed almost immediately by a Trojan council in which Hektor declares he is willing to meet Akhilleus in combat.

241 **against my own good sense:** like Agamémnon (see note to p. 207), Dolôn blames *atê* ("folly") for a decision he now sees was a mistake.

242 **beside the funeral mound of the patriarch / Ilos:** Ilos was the great-grandfather of Priam (see p. 480) and his tomb is a landmark on the plain (p. 579).

Karians . . . Mêionians: all these tribes save the Lélegês and Kaukônês are mentioned in the catalogue (p. 63), but casual references to these two occur elsewhere (pp. 476 and 483).

243 **Rhêsos Eïónidês:** the scholiast tells us Rhêsos was the son of the river Strymon and the Muse Euterpe. The father named here, Eïóneus, is not otherwise known, but *eion* means "shore" or "beach" so that the patronymic may indirectly reflect the river god's paternity. A tragedy concerning this story and attributed to Euripides survives.

Dolôn no doubt thought Odysseus had accepted his supplication. By a nice technicality Diomêdês, who said nothing, now kills him, a <u>trick</u> worthy of the grandson of Autólykos but perhaps not expected from the gallant Diomêdês.

246–247 The horses, rather than any pertinent information, are all the subject upon their return. <u>A good haul of spoil provided more than enough reason for their raid;</u> intelligence has turned out to be an incidental purpose.

BOOK ELEVEN

ꙮꙮꙮꙮꙮꙮꙮꙮꙮꙮꙮꙮꙮꙮꙮꙮꙮꙮ

PROWESS AND WOUNDS
OF AKHAIANS

Once again the poet approaches his goal by an indirect route. After the failed embassy in IX and Zeus's active intervention in VIII, we may expect the Akhaian fortunes to take a rapid turn for the worse, but Book XI begins with an *aristeia* of Agamémnon. Hektor is warned by Zeus that he must not oppose Agamémnon, though he is promised glory "till the sun dips"—after the king retires. When Agamémnon's *aristeia* is cut short by a wound in the arm (p. 259), we begin to see the poet's plan; shortly thereafter Diomêdês and Odysseus are wounded, and Aías retreats, harassed by Hektor and the swarming Trojans. At this point (p. 269) Akhilleus sees Nestor taking the wounded Makháôn from the field, and he sends Patróklos for a report.

Thus the day's fighting dramatizes, first, a significant reversal for the Akhaians, and secondly, a gesture of sympathy from Akhilleus. Zeus's promise to Hektor foreshadows that

hero's *aristeia,* which may even be said to begin in XI. Ultimately, Hektor's success will cause Akhilleus to return to battle. At the same time Akhilleus' return is foreshadowed and
Patróklos' role as a surrogate for his friend is established.
This last section of the book is devoted to Patróklos' inter-
views with Nestor and Eurýpylos. Patróklos' sympathy for the
battered Akhaians is drawn, and for the first time he assumes a dramatic importance in the poem; from Nestor's argument that he should help the Akhaians, even if Akhilleus
will not, we begin to see the fatal rhythm of his career.

**251   Dawn came up . . . leaving her lord Tithonos'
brilliant side:** these two lines begin *Odyssey* Book V. Books
VIII and XIX also open with the appearance of Dawn. Her
special epithets in Homer are translated "in her saffron
robes," and "with finger tips of rose." Tithonos is mentioned
elsewhere only at XX 237 (p. 480); he is the brother of
Priam, beloved by the goddess Dawn, who gave him the gift
of immortality but forgot to ask Zeus for agelessness for him
(see the Homeric *Hymn to Aphrodite,* 218ff.).

           Strife gave tongue: see the note on p. 103.
252   The son of Atreus . . . clothed himself in armor:
a comparison of the arming scenes on pages 79 (III 328ff.),
381 (XVI 130ff.), and 468 (XIX 364ff.) will show a number
of repeated lines, the same sequence in the arming (greaves,
cuirass, sword, shield, helmet, spear[s]), and the addition of
descriptive details. Curiously, Paris, Agamémnon, and Patróklos all wear a cuirass obtained from a friend or relation,
and Akhilleus' armor is newly made by Hêphaistos. For a
comparison of these scenes see J. I. Armstrong, "The Arming
Motif in the *Iliad,*" *AJP* 79 (1958), 337–54.

           Lord Kinyrês: he is mentioned only here in
Homer, but later he was famous as king of Kypros and
founder of a cult to Aphrodítê.

           Next he took his shield: Agamémnon carries a
round, hoplite shield, with terrible representations (cf. the
aigis, p. 132) on the central boss and adjacent to it. The entire description emphasizes the richness and brilliance of a
great king's armor, rather than its weight and potential for
war (cf. the description of Akhilleus arming p. 468f.). He
carries two spears, like Patróklos, but kills Koôn with a thrust
(XI 260; p. 259), i.e., apparently using a heavier weapon.

Paris first appears with two spears (III 18), then selects a single spear when he arms (III 338). Patróklos takes two (XVI 139), but carries one heavy weapon when he is killed (XVI 801). The weight and length of Akhilleus' spear (p. 469) suggest a weapon for thrusting (which seems to have been their use in Mycenaean times), although in the actual fighting Akhilleus and Hektor cast their spears. Homeric usage, then, implies a mixture of historical practices dating back to a large, thrusting spear of the second millennium. Casting the spear, however, is the norm in all duels, whether the warrior carries one or two into battle.

Athêna/thundered . . . Hêra thundered: thundering is otherwise reserved to Zeus.

253   Zeus . . . sprinkled bloody dew: cf. "showered bloody drops," XVI 459 (p. 391).

noble Poulýdamas: almost casually the poet introduces this adviser to Hektor, yet he will play a crucial role in the plot. See XII 60ff. (p. 283), XII 210ff. (p. 287), XIII 725ff. (p. 321), XVIII 249ff. (p. 443), and XXII 100 (p. 518).

Antênor's three sons: at least nine sons of Antênor are mentioned, and most of them die shortly thereafter. Agênor will survive to face Akhilleus (XXI 545; p. 511). Akámas is not forgotten (pp. 344 and 388); cf. the fates of Iphídamas (p. 258) and Koôn (p. 259).

a baleful summer star: cf. Priam's vision of Akhilleus "bright as that star/in autumn rising" (XXII 26ff.; p. 516) and "conspicuous as the evening star" (XXII 317; p. 525). The gleam of armor is regularly likened to fire or a star (see the helmet of Diomêdês, V 5 [p. 109]).

254   withdrawn from all, he gloried, looking down: for the battlefield as spectacle for the gods compare VII 58ff. (p. 163), XX 23 (p. 474), and VIII 51 (p. 183). When Zeus is not attentive, the play may go awry (XIII 1ff.).

First Agamémnon/charged: the typical elements in Agamémnon's *aristeia* are the following: 1) he arms; 2) the bronze of his shield gleams brightly; 3) a brief, indecisive period follows; 4) he kills three pairs of opponents; 5) he rages like fire among the enemy (p. 256); 6) he drives the Trojans back to the gates of the city; 7) the wounding of the hero cuts short his *aristeia* (p. 259). If Diomêdês' *aristeia* in

Book V is compared (p. 109ff.), we notice 1) Diomêdês is already armed (p. 109); 2) Athêna "on his shield and helm . . . kindled fire . . ." (p. 109); 3) the focus changes to the success of individual Danáän chiefs (pp. 110–12); 4) Diomêdês kills three pairs of brothers (p. 114); 5) he breaks the enemy ranks like a spring storm (p. 112); 6) the Trojans do not actually flee to the city, but cf. Sarpêdôn's "They will be pillaging your city soon!" (p. 125) and the fact that Hélenos recommends to Hektor that he go to the city to order sacrifice to Athêna (p. 112f.). Every heroic *aristeia* does not share all the elements that may be reckoned typical, nor are they always in the same order, but despite omissions, additions, and significant modifications, there does appear to be a typical scenario for these events within which the poet exercises a good deal of freedom. (Source: Tilman Krischer, *Formale Konventionen der homerischen Epik*, München, 1971.)

    Akhilleus took and bound . . . for ransom: no suppliant's plea for his life in exchange for ransom is accepted in the *Iliad*, but the poet indicates on several occasions that in earlier days ransom has been accepted (see on p. 155 and the introduction to Book XXIV).

    A lion, discovering a forest bed: Agamémnon is compared to a lion three times during his *aristeia* (also pp. 255 and 256). So Diomêdês is likened to a lion prior to his slaughter of Trojans (p. 113, and again p. 114). Hektor and Patróklos are compared to lions and to winds contending in a storm (p. 400).

255   **Antímakhos:** his motivation recalls the arguments used by the disguised Athêna to persuade Pándaros (p. 91). Antímakhos means "opposed to battle." For the occasion alluded to here see Antênor's speech, p. 74f. Other indications of dissension within the city may be found in Hektor's speech (p. 68f.) and Idaíos' speech (p. 174).

    heard a voice beyond appeal: Agamémnon is regularly characterized as merciless in battle (cf. p. 143).

256   **Past the old tomb of Ilos . . . past the wild figtree:** a few familiar markers and the clouds of dust are virtually all the scenic description Homer offers of the plain before Troy. See Andersson, *Early Epic Scenery*.

257   **till the sun dips and starry darkness comes:** lines

193f.=XVII 454f. (p. 421), where Zeus remembers this stipulation. Hektor will forget, or ignore, this crucial limitation on the "power of massacre" granted by Zeus (see p. 444f.).

258   **these he duly beached at Perkôtê:** on the Hellespont (see p. 62).

259   **He moved in to behead him:** decapitation is rare but does occur elsewhere, p. 305, e.g. and p. 345 (a particularly gruesome example). Agamémnon has already cut off the hands and severed the neck of Hippólokhos (top of p. 256). Cf. the threat of Euphórbos (XVII 39f.; p. 408), Hektor's intentions (XVII 125; p. 411), and Iris' report of this to Akhilleus (XVIII 176f.; p. 441).

     goddesses of Travail, Hêra's/daughters, Twisters: Homer uses the plural of Eileithyía, goddess of childbirth, here and at XIX 119. She appears in anecdotes concerning the birth of heroes on pp. 383 and 460.

260   **Trojans, Lykians, and Dardan spears:** cf. the exhortations with the same opening line(s) at VIII 173f. (p. 187), XIII 150 (p. 304), XV 486 (p. 365), and XVII 184 (p. 413). The lines are always Hektor's, and in the first three of the five he claims Zeus favors the Trojans. Here and in VIII he is the typical warrior looking for "victory and glory" (p. 187); in XV he adds praise for the man who dies defending his country.

     when Zeus accorded him this rush of glory: Zeus has promised success, and the wounding of Agamémnon signals the beginning of Hektor's *aristeia,* which is stipulated to last through the third day of battle. The comparison to a "high screaming squall" and the list of "Danáäns he destroyed" are typical elements of the *aristeia,* but Hektor's success is intermittent and at the same time so prolonged—it includes the *aristeia* of Patróklos—that its formal cohesion is less strict than those of Diomêdês and Akhilleus.

     Asaios first . . . these leaders of Danáäns: these "leaders" have not been mentioned previously.

261   **a Trojan pair . . . sons of Mérops Perkôsios:** lines 329–32=II 831–34, where they are named. For the motif of the clairvoyant father see also V 148 (p. 114) and XIII 663 (p. 319).

263   **you bow-and-arrow boy:** these notes emphasize repetitions of various kinds, but here Diomêdês' abuse (line 385) is composed of rare or unique words particularly suited to Paris, or at least to mocking him as an effeminate, cowardly womanizer.

Here is trouble: "genuine personal decisions" have been denied to Homeric agents by Bruno Snell (p. 20), but this passage and others (cf., e.g., XVII 91ff.; p. 410) evince a weighing of alternatives and decisions reached on the basis of values and circumstances.

264   As when around a wild boar: Hektor is like a hunter (p. 260), Odysseus and Diomêdês are like two boars charging the hounds (p. 261), Odysseus is compared to a wounded deer (p. 266). In this last simile the addition of the lion might be thought to anticipate the arrival of Aías, but the comparison cannot be pressed inasmuch as the wounded deer will become carrion for the lion.

Odysseus, great in all men's eyes, unwearied/ master of guile and toil: this is the only appearance of Sôkos. The formality, and praise, of his address may seem odd, especially from a totally unknown warrior. Sôkos and Agamémnon (IX 673; p. 224) and Nestor (X 544; p. 246) all use the first half of this line in addressing Odysseus. In part such formality is the result of the economy of oral poetry; in part it may be traced to the conventions of aristocratic, courtly speech. Cf. Hektor's address to Aías on p. 169 (VII 234=IX 644 [Akhilleus]=XI 465 [Meneláos]).

265   your soul to that strong driver, Death: Death (Aïdês) is associated with horses (this line occurs three times), perhaps because of the power usually attributed to both. Properly, he is the god who rules the underworld, not a god of Death. Four horses are sacrificed on the funeral pyre of Patróklos (p. 541). See Guthrie, pp. 95–98.

Now he gave ground, backing away: after the monologue Odysseus kills five Trojans, is wounded, but kills and vaunts over his enemy, and then decides he had better retreat. Even the wounded Akhaians are able to avenge themselves, and those individuals surrounded by swarms of the enemy fight their way clear. Such episodes clearly demonstrate the general superiority of the Akhaians, as does Zeus's admonition of caution to Hektor. Scholars often speak of the poet's "nationalism," which is not quite the word to describe martial superiority.

266   But Hektor/had no report of it: Hektor and Paris have suddenly moved to another sector, though minutes before Paris wounded Diomêdês, who had just stunned Hektor (p. 262f.). Odysseus accompanied Diomêdês, and is now hurt, apparently not far from the same engagement. The poet shows little regard for such logistics; once a warrior is off-stage he may reappear anywhere without explanation of his activity in the meantime.

267   Makháon: see on pp. 59 and 94. Kebríonês first appeared in VIII (p. 191).

268   and shunning only Aías in the combat: this is a surprising comment after the preceding lines. Perhaps Hektor remembers the duel in VII, but if that were the case, we would expect this poet to tell us. The next line ("Zeus took it ill . . . betters") is not found in the manuscripts, but comes from a quotation found in Aristotle and Plutarch. It should be deleted.

        like a dun lion: the adjacent similes of lion and ass, by complementing one another, aim at a single portrait. The spirited and formidable lion and the stubborn ass, one denied his victim, the other successful in spite of assailants, combine to portray the grudging retreat of the great-shielded warrior. See parataxis in the index.

269   Eurýpylos: see pp. 59 and 111.

        And/Akhilleus the great runner saw Makháon: since Akhilleus holds the right wing, we must assume the reference on p. 266 to Hektor "on the left wing" takes, for the moment, a Trojan perspective on the field.

270   though his doom/was fixed that instant: cf. the prediction of Zeus at VIII 470ff. (p. 196) and especially "they fight over Patróklos dead" (VIII 476). For another prophecy by Zeus see XV 65 (p. 351) and for another mode of foreshadowing see XVI 252 (p. 385).

        the Akhaians now will come/to beg and pray: scholars who doubt that the *Iliad* was composed by a single poet have frequently cited these lines as evidence that Book IX is a late addition, for Akhilleus seems to ignore, or be ignorant of, the petition in that book. D. L. Page puts the objection in his usual forceful manner: "Now it seems very ob-

vious that these words were not spoken by an Achilles about
whose knees the Achaeans were in fact standing in supplication on the previous evening; an Achilles who had rejected
their prayers, who had made it clear that he would never accept apology or compensation, but would wait until Hector
was killing the Greeks in their tents and burning their ships"
(*History and the Homeric Iliad*, p. 305). The most satisfactory response to this argument has been to take Akhilleus
literally at his word: the embassy did not "beg and pray"; on
the contrary, it offered, for Agamémnon, gifts and restitution,
"if you/desist from anger" (p. 213). The Akhaians make conditions, offer opportunities, and try to buy his return, but they
certainly are not desperate (despite Diomêdês' "pled" at IX
698; p. 225). His impassioned response to Odysseus in IX
demonstrates how inadequately the offer would compensate
for the insult, so far as he is concerned. In Book I he wanted
to see Agamémnon humiliated and the army desperate for his
help; now the army is pressed, three of its leaders wounded,
and an appeal from "inexorable need" rather than from expe-
diency may appear imminent. By the end of Book IX, moreover, his wrath has moderated considerably, as the reply to
Aías implies, and his concern for Makháôn here is of a piece
with his susceptibility to Aías' arguments from friendship.
Further notes on this problem will be found among those on
the opening pages of Book XVI. See Eichholz, "The Propitiation of Achilles."

      sweat-soaked khitons: the khiton is the cloth shirt
or tunic worn beneath the armor.

      Akhilleus' plundering of Ténedos: cf. Akhilleus'
reference (p. 214) to a "dozen towns" plundered in sea raids.
This was probably the same raid that brought Brisêis and
Khrysêis to the camp (p. 12).

      a cup of wondrous beauty: the description has
been thought to date the cup to the Bronze Age, "for doves,
frequent in the Bronze Age in Crete and Cyprus as attributes
of a goddess, as dedications to her or symbols of her presence, are but rarely found in Greece" (Lorimer, p. 328f.).

271   **Pramnian wine:** whether Pramnian refers to a
place or a quality is not known.

      No time to take a chair: Patróklos' response,
though different in its diction, may recall Diomêdês' opinion

of Akhilleus at IX 697ff. (p. 225). He has the same reputation in the Trojan camp: "There are no bounds to the passion of that man" (Poulýdamas at XVIII 262; p. 443). With "accuse me without cause" cf. "Hektor, since you are moved to blame the blameless" (XIII 775[b] [p. 323]=XI 654[b]).

How is this, that Akhilleus cares for any/Akhaians: this rambling discourse (lines 656–803) falls into three sections. The first begins with an abuse of Akhilleus and quickly turns to a long story which contrasts Nestor's behavior as a young man with that of Akhilleus now (XI 656–764; pp. 272–74: "so was I then . . . not so/Akhilleus"). The second section (lines 765–90) exhorts Patróklos by recalling the injunction of his father Menoitios, and concludes: "These were your father's words" (p. 275). The third section urges action and proposes alternatives: either Akhilleus should return himself or send the battle-aid of Patróklos (lines 791–803). The first section's paradigm is difficult to follow because of its circular style: rather than proceeding chronologically through the story of the Epeian and Pylian dispute, Nestor begins in the middle, drops back to give the antecedents and explanations, and finally picks up the initial thread to its conclusion (cf. especially Phoinix's tale of Meléagros in IX, p. 220ff.).

272   Eurýpylos, hit by an arrow: this line is omitted by some editors for want of full manuscript support and because Eurýpylos was wounded (p. 269) after Nestor left the field (p. 267). It may also be noted that Nestor would seem, from "until the ships/on the sea verge are fanned by billowing fire," to know of Akhilleus' reply to Aías (p. 224).

Elians: elsewhere, and below, called Epeioi. Nestor begins by recounting the Pylian raid against the Epeioi, which retaliated for Augeías' refusal (p. 273) to reward a Pylian victory in games in Elis. Before describing Augeías' bad faith, however, he digresses briefly to explain why the Pylians were "a scanty people" and liable to the depredations of the neighboring Epeioi. Hêraklês had sought purgation for the murder of Iphitus at the house of Nêleus, king of the Pylians. When Nêleus refused his supplication, Hêraklês led an expedition against Pylos (see also the notes to p. 122).

273   Augeías,/lord of Elians: he is famous for his stables, which Hêraklês cleaned as one of his labors. Augeías has

taken a four-horse chariot (a rare sort: see Hektor's call to
his team p. 187 [VIII 185]) from a Pylian, which occasioned
the "cattle-raiding" Nestor used by way of introduction. In
turn the Epeioi made a raid "on the third day" led by
"Molionês' two boys" (Ktéatos and Eurýtos, II 621; p. 55).
This pair is of uncertain, or excessive, parentage, since they
are now called the sons of Molionês, again the sons of Aktor,
or of both, and at 751ff. (p. 274) their true father is
Poseidon. Leaf considered them a set of divine twins like the
Dioskouroi (see on p. 75). Cf. Webster p. 174f. and figure
25a and b and Bernhard Schweitzer, *Greek Geometric Art*
(New York and London, 1971), pp. 44 and 209, figure 13
and plate 232. According to tradition they were killed by
Hêraklês during his expedition against Augeías.

       Thryoessa: this is apparently the Thryon of II 592
(p. 54), where Arênê and the Alpheíos River are also mentioned.

274   **Agamêdê:** this may be the Homeric form for the
name Medea, who "knew all medicinal herbs" and was also a
granddaughter of the sun.

       Bouprasíon,/Olênie Rock . . . Aleisíos: cf. II
615ff. (p. 55).

       Not so/Akhilleus: the point is that Akhilleus
would use his valor for his own gain, unlike Nestor, who
helped his people; but Akhilleus will find grief from this
selfishness. See on p. 378. "Valor" (XI 763) translates the
Greek *aretê*, a generic term used for the peculiar excellence
or innate virtue of anything. For the warrior, fighting skill
and valor are the natual realizations of his *aretê*. *Aretê* may
be used of the gods (at IX 498 Phoinix speaks of the *aretê*
["bravery"] of the gods), of horses (at XXIII 276 Akhilleus
speaks of his team surpassing other horses in *aretê* ["in form
and breeding"]), and of the feet (at XX 411 "showing his
speed" translates the *"aretê* of his feet"). Some scholars
describe *aretê* as an object to be achieved or attained, but
Homeric usage often suggests a more dynamic view in which
aretê is the realizable potential of anything capable of active
and passive states. This view makes better sense of passages
like the present one and Patróklos' allusion to it at XVI 31
(p. 378).

275   **Menoitios made your duty doubly clear:** cf. Odysseus' recollection of this meeting (IX 252ff.; p. 211). Glaukos (VI 208=XI 784) had an exhortation from his father like that Pêleus gave Akhilleus ("commanding me to act always with valor . . ." p. 148).

Akhilleus is a higher being/by his immortal blood: i.e., he is the great-grandson of Zeus and son of the goddess Thetis. Menoitios' counsel plays on the familiar division in the *Iliad* between speech (reason) and action. Cf. Odysseus, XIX 216ff. (p. 464) and the note to p. 217.

If in his own mind he is keeping clear: XI 794–97=XVI 36–39 (p. 378). In XVI Akhilleus denies any such motivation as is suggested here, but commentators generally assume Nestor alludes to the "two possible destinies" (p. 216).

276 **At this, Patróklos' heart bounded within him:** this formulaic line (Patróklos' name is actually represented only by a pronoun) occurs five times. "He made their hearts leap in their breasts" (II 142; p. 39); "Helen's heart beat faster in her breast" (III 395; p. 81); "The message stirred him" (IV 208; p. 95); "The appeal roused Aineías" (XIII 468; p. 314). Frequently there is no verbal response to speeches of appeal, command, exhortation and the like, and the stock formulaic description of the speech's effect makes precise definition of intellectual and psychological reaction difficult. In most cases subsequent action indicates the tenor of the response; in this particular case we have Patróklos' appeal to Akhilleus (p. 378f.), as well as the more immediate expression of sympathy for Eurýpylos.

277 **How can this be:** this brief speech offers a good example of the way Homer portrays ambivalence in a character: first Patróklos expresses the impossibility of helping Eurýpylos because of his commission, and then in the last clause he reserves himself to act on the contrary feeling. See the note to p. 72.

BOOK TWELVE

ᕤᕦᕤᕦᕤᕦᕤᕦᕤᕦᕤᕦᕤᕦᕤᕦᕤᕦᕤ

THE RAMPART BREACHED

At the conclusion of this book Hektor has broken through the
Akhaian rampart, and that success is the primary narrative
goal of the episode. Prior to this breach in the wall the book
features a number of consultations and appeals. Two exchanges between Hektor and Poulýdamas deserve particular
attention: in the first Poulýdamas' prudent tactical advice is
accepted by Hektor (p. 283f.); in the second Hektor rejects
the same counselor's advice to retreat (p. 287f.). Between
these exchanges the Trojan Ásïos is introduced (his career
will be continued in Book XIII) and the defense of the Lapith
twins is described. With the wounding of the chieftains in XI,
Aías the Tall, Aías the Short, and Teukros become the leading defenders for the Akhaians (p. 289ff.). Sarpêdôn attacks
and encourages his comrade Glaukos (p. 290f.). Menéstheus
appeals to Aías and Aías, who have some success before the

Lykians counterattack. Finally, Hektor breaks through the rampart.

If Book XII lacks the dramatic rhythm and focus of the preceding episode, it is still important to the poet's plan in at least two respects: Hektor's relationship with Poulýdamas is now firmly secured and can be used plausibly in later scenes; secondly, the impending threat of Book XI is realized in the actual breakdown of the Akhaian defense.

281   the rampart they had built to save the ships: the poet's archaeological interest explains why the wall can no longer be seen in the Troad. The failure to sacrifice, i.e., to recognize the prerogatives of the gods, is the usual explanation of trouble; cf. in the Meléagros tale the negligence of Oineus, who "made/no harvest offering from his vineyard slope" (p. 220). In Book XV (p. 361) Apollo kicks in the embankment and levels the rampart, making way for the Trojan attack. Since this later passage is attendant on Hektor's advance, the poet probably did not think it contradicted the present explanation, if he thought of the matter at all.

282   then/Poseidon and Apollo joined: cf. (below) "Thus before long Poseidon and Apollo/settled this earthwork." For Poseidon's vexation see VII 442ff. (p. 176). See ring composition in the index.

rivers . . . all that flow/seaward: only three of these, the Aisêpos, Skamánder, and Simóeis, are mentioned elsewhere in the poem.

boarlike, or like a lion: Homer's frequent use of such disjunction within a simile indicates their generic character. This kind of animal epitomizes a furious valor. The extent to which the similes are organically related to the action of the narrative has been much debated. Here the death of the animal—"his own courage kills him"—goes well beyond any obvious relevance to the narrative, and it seems unlikely that this development is intended, even obliquely, to foreshadow Hektor's death ten books later.

283   Poulýdamas' counsel to avoid the risk: his advice is usually defensive. As a foil Poulýdamas highlights the more confident, rash, and aggressive character of Hektor.

284   They formed/five companies: the division and leadership do not conform to that in the catalogue. Here the role of allies is diminished. The names and organization may be chosen for the immediate situation, however, without any reference to the entire army.

Alkáthoös: he is killed by Idómeneus in XIII, where we are told something of him (p. 312f.).

Asteropaíos: he is not mentioned in the catalogue, but is identified as a prince of the Paionians (XVII 350ff.; p. 418). In XXI he challenges Akhilleus (p. 497ff.).

all except Ásïos/Hyrtákidês: lines 96–97=II 838–39 (p. 62f.). The apparent intention of describing some exploit, or more probably his death ("the idiot," "all a delusion"), gives way to the description of the Lapith spearmen, whose success and an omen prompt an exchange between Hektor and Poulýdamas. Not until XIII 384 (p. 311) does Ásïos return, when he is killed by Idómeneus, as announced at XII 115f. (p. 285).

285   **two Lapith spearmen:** Polypoitês (II 738ff.; p. 59) is the son of Peiríthoös, who led the Lapiths against the centaurs and accompanied the Athenian hero Theseus to the underworld (see Nestor's story p. 20).

like oaks: cf. below, like "savage boars": complementary views of defensive and offensive prowess are presented in separate similes, like the two describing the retreating Aías (p. 268). Here "some hunter makes the kill" pertains only to the simile, since the Lapiths are not killed (see above, p. 282).

Adámas Asíadês, Thoôn, and Oinómaos: they appear only here (XII 140) in this book, and all three die in XIII (p. 315f.).

286   **O Father Zeus,/you, even you, turn out to be a liar:** Ameis-Hentze suggest Ásïos has Hektor's assurance at XI 288 (p. 260) in mind, and perhaps the following comment by the narrator supports this, even though the exhortation there is distant from present events and general in content.

like agile-waisted hornets: a swarm of hornets or bees reduced to two is a little awkward. Cf. the simile at XVI 259ff. (p. 385), where the Myrmidons are like hornets.

286–287   **Damásos' . . . Down went the man:** the poet puns on the name and the verb *damasse:* "Downer went down" or the like.

287   **Hektor, you always manage to rebuke me:** Pou-

lýdamas' most recent advice was approved by Hektor (p.
283f.). From XIII 726ff. (p. 321) we gather they were usually at odds in council, though <u>their talents should complement one another</u> (XVIII 251ff.; p. 443). In this last passage
we learn they were born on the same night. Poulýdamas is,
then, Hektor's alter ego and brother, with symbolic and
thematic associations similar to those which Patróklos shares
with Akhilleus.

288   **One/and only one portent is best:** defend/our fatherland: Cf. his encouragement to the troops in XV, "defending his own land" (XV 496; p. 365), and Priam's "fighting for his land" (XXIV 500; p. 584). Such explicit references to Hektor as a defender of his country are relatively
rare, perhaps because the poet does not want to make a
martyr of Hektor. The phrases translated here are formulaic.

289   **Imagine/flakes of snow:** for other similes from a
snow storm see pages 286, 468 (XIX 357), 355 (XV 170).

290   **had not/Lord Zeus impelled Sarpêdôn:** this introduction of Sarpêdôn, with its brief notice of his shield and a
lion simile, might be expected to signal more than actually
comes about. After Sarpêdôn's exhortation the poet switches
to Telamônian Aías, who immediately kills a comrade of
Sarpêdôn's (p. 292). Then Teukros wounds Glaukos (p.
293), and, having killed but one man, Sarpêdôn makes a
breach in the parapet (397ff.; p. 293), which anticipates an
honor seemingly reserved for Hektor (459ff.; p. 295). As
though he had let Sarpêdôn steal a bit more of the show than
he intended, Homer tells us that Sarpêdôn "fell back a little"
(p. 293) as soon as he had broken the wall.

        What is the point of being honored so: this famous
speech is often cited a epitomizing the "heroic code." The
argument runs: we are honored by the Lykians; now we must
fight among the foremost; then they can say we are justly
honored and famed; if, however, ageless immortality were
possible, I would not fight; but we are all mortal, and to win
glory is the supreme lot of a mortal. The second movement
of the argument hardly follows from the first, but it is well
chosen to lead to the last line, and the sentiment of that line
is common; cf. the following lines which conclude speeches:
XIII 327 (p. 309); XIII 486 (p. 314)=XVIII 308 (p. 445);
XXII 130 (p. 519).

291   **But now a thousand shapes of death:** this is not merely a figurative expression. Numerous references in Homer and in archaic Greek literature as well as representations on vases testify to the belief in a demonic agency attendant on man's life and death. In Homer these spirits (in Greek *kêr* in the singular, *kêres* in the plural) are at times synonymous with fate, as, e.g., when Akhilleus speaks of "two possible destinies" (IX 411; p. 216). They are weighed in the scales of Zeus (p. 183, where they are used in a collective sense; p. 522, of Akhilleus and Hektor). So they have some substance, weight which can press down on the scales or on a man's existence. Patróklos speaks of the *kêr* ("day of wrath") which became his lot at birth, and in the same passage he uses this noun synonymously with the word normally translated as fate (*moira*, XXII 78–80, p. 538). Onians considers them binding agents that put the thread of fate upon man, thus fixing or yoking him to a specific day of reckoning. Homer's use of this noun often makes "death" an appropriate translation:

Retiring now to bleed among his men
and shun black death,

                    XI 585; p. 269 (the line occurs six times)

The fundamental Greek feeling, however, points to an active demonic presence, personalized, dread ("heavy"), and ultimately ineluctable. Onians, pp. 395–410; Schweitzer, *Greek Geometric Art,* p. 92f.

          Menéstheus: see p. 53.

          In haste he sent Thoötês off to Aías: Thoötês means "Swifty."

292   **Lykomêdês:** one of the young captains of the guard in Book IX (p. 206).

294   **Think of an honest cottage spinner:** T. B. L. Webster takes this simile as an example of the long simile used to "provide a whole picture to explain a whole event." He goes on: "The two battle lines are taut and straining, just as the two strings holding the scale pans are taut and straining, but they quiver this way and that, just as the two pans quiver when the woman adds a little more wool; the military operation is desperately important, just as the woman's weighing is desperately important because it is her only means of getting food for her children." (*From Mycenae to Homer,* pp. 225–26). Other critics have found such readings too subjective, since there is little to indicate Aías is feeling desperate. The last three similes of this book are more homely and commonplace (a boundary dispute, weighing wool, a ram's fleece in weight) than those drawn from the lion hunt. Webster contends the lion similes date from Mycenaean poetry, elaborated from the original short comparison, "like a lion" (op. cit., p. 223ff.).

Of the simile above which begins "Think of two men contending . . ." G. S. Kirk, who is comparing it with XIII 795ff. (p. 323f.), observes that "in both examples there is a certain looseness which is not so much due to carelessness as to the exploration of extreme possibilities in a medium which is completely mastered. The similes have a double purpose: to crystallize, in a sphere close to the listener's own understanding, a sight or a sound or a state of mind; and to give relief from the harshness and potential monotony of warfare by suddenly actualizing a quite different and often peaceful, even domestic, scene . . ." (*SH,* p. 346f.). This is traditional criticism, but it appears rather rationalistic. One may doubt that most of the situations exemplified by the similies actually required intellectual clarification; and there is far too much narrative of battle in the *Iliad* for us to believe that Homer's auditors found it monotonous.

Lord Zeus conferred on Hektor . . . the glory of bursting through: 438=XVI 558 (p. 394). In XVI the honor of breaching the wall is attributed to Sarpêdôn by Patróklos. Either Patróklos thinks of Sarpêdôn's success in this episode (p. 293), which he does not personally witness, or perhaps he would claim more glory for himself by praising the warrior he has just killed. The greater glory is Hektor's for breaking through the gate and leading the Trojans within the defensive works.

BOOK THIRTEEN

𝍖𝍖𝍖𝍖𝍖𝍖𝍖𝍖𝍖𝍖𝍖𝍖𝍖𝍖𝍖𝍖𝍖𝍖𝍖𝍖

ASSAULT ON THE SHIPS

This is one of the most varied and chaotic books in the *Iliad*. Together with Book XIV it is sometimes classified as a retardation, but to read the book is not so much to be impressed by Trojan reverses as by the energy of battle dissipated into innumerable discrete encounters. Lacking the organizing rhythm of an *aristeia*, Book XIII offers some of the most realistic moments of Homeric battle narrative, isolating again and again individual confrontations, incomplete engagements, chance encounters, narrow escapes, and sudden death. It is also a book of gossip, battlefield talk of veteran soldiers, a book which more than any other focuses on the work of warriors in the second rank.

At first XIII would seem to be an episode devoted to Poseidon, for, having refused Hêra's invitation in VIII to aid the Argives (p. 188), he takes the opportunity, offered by Zeus's negligence, to encourage both warriors named Aías,

Idómeneus, and others who now replace the wounded chieftains. The description of the god's approach is in a style both
grand and lyric, but after three scenes of exhortation (pp.
300–6) his presence is less felt in the subsequent scenes.
The poet is certainly not unaware that Poseidon's role will
surprise his auditor, and in the middle of the book (p. 310)
he comments parenthetically on his covert aid in spite of
Zeus. His partisanship continues through XIV until he is
checked by Zeus in XV (p. 355). He returns to participate in
the theomachy of XX and XXI, and at a crucial moment re-
assures Akhilleus of divine support (p. 502).

299   he left them/to cruel toil of battle: the beginning
lines of Books XI, XII, XIII, and XIV clearly mark transitions and changes in theme. The poet is usually careful to
look back explicitly to the preceding episode (especially here
and XII) before taking up his new subject. Since the oral poet
did not often perform the entire epic, and was regularly called
upon for one or another episode—as much, perhaps, as would
fill an evening's recitation after dinner—these junctures in the
narrative probably mark the limits of such songs. They are a
part of the *Iliad,* but they also have a certain autonomy which
made them very useful to the rhapsode. XIII is a good example of such autonomy: though there are references here and
later to the breach in the wall (Poseidon, p. 303), the
fighting is not apparently restricted by a lack of space or the
restricted access that might realistically be expected after the
conclusion of XII. The poet's references to "left," "right,"
and "center" seem more appropriate, moreover, to combat in
the open field than to restricted fighting within the walls. Yet
so brisk is the pace of action and so sharp is the focus on the
foreground that most readers, will not quibble over any supposed lack of
verisimilitude.

           Mysoi . . . Hippêmolgoi . . . Ábioi: the second
noun means "milkers of horses." Like the "Sunburned" (Ethiopians, p. 25), these tribes of the north, Thracian and
Scythian, have an excellent reputation with the curious
Greeks.

299–300   Samos . . . off Thrace: i.e., Samothrace, to be distinguished from the large island farther south off the coast of

Turkey. The Trojan plain is in fact visible from the high peak on this island.

300   **Aigai:** this is the name of at least two cult centers of Poseidon, neither nearer Troy than Samothrace. It is probably a generic name for a center of the god's worship.

   Here he entered . . . stepped up into his car: lines 23–26=VIII 41–44 (p. 182f.), where the lines are used of the chariot of Zeus.

   Kalkhas he seemed: there have been no references to Kalkhas since Book II, and he will not appear again. See Introduction, p. 72f. (p. 56).

301   **Here this madman,/Hektor, like a conflagration:** Hektor's reputation outruns his prowess: cf. Odysseus' "crazed" (p. 213) and "mad for battle" (p. 211) and Teukros' "mad dog" (VIII 299; p. 191). See the note to p. 144. The comparison is used several times of Hektor: "like a flame" (XIII 688; p. 320); "his helmet/flashing, and his shout rose like a flame" (XVII 88; p. 410); "strong as fire" (XVIII 154; p. 440); "like a wild flame" (XX 423; p. 486). See Whitman's Chapter VII, "Fire and Other Elements."

   instilling fury: this access of energy (cf. Aías' "Power is rising in me" p. 302) is the usual gift of the gods: "Athêna filled Diomêdês' heart/with fury" (X 482; p. 244); "The Olympian/again at this put heart into the Trojans" (VIII 335; p. 192); "This inspired a surge of fighting spirit" (XV 262; p. 358). See the note to pp. 113 and 144.

   like a hawk he soared: since he reappears in human form on the next page, we may assume this gesture is intended to give a sign to the warriors.

302   **Teukros first . . . Antílokhos:** of this group only Teukros and Meríonês have any significant role in the present book.

   by our commander's fault: Poseidon's censure, like the references to Akhilleus on p. 309f. and the allusion on p. 322, keeps the central theme before us even during Akhilleus' absence. But Agamémnon later refers twice to the Akhaian "grudge" against him (XIV 49f. [p. 331] and XIX 85f. [p. 460]); little or nothing is made of this motif in the action of the poem. Much of Poseidon's argument would seem applicable to Akhilleus (e.g., "good men's hearts/respond to remedies" and "a fresh grip on his pride/and look to his standing"), but the arguments also recall the Meléagros paradigm in Book IX and have a general applicability to all the heroes.

303   **Hektor . . . like a rolling boulder:** this simile develops a more detailed analogy to the narrative events than most of the longer similes.

304   **Déíphobos:** he was first mentioned at XII 94 (p. 284) and will be a leader now until he is wounded (p. 315). Later Athêna impersonates him when Akhilleus and Hektor meet in Book XXII (p. 522ff.).

        Imbrios . . . had a young wife: for similar anecdotes see Iphídamas XI 221ff. (p. 258), Othrýoneus XIII 363ff. (p. 310), and Alkáthoös XIII 428ff. (p. 312).

        an ash hewn by an ax: cf. "falling like lofty pines" (V 560; p. 127), the simile of the poplar (IV 482ff.; p. 104), the "oak or poplar" (XIII 389ff.; p. 311: a simile used again at XVI 482ff. [p. 392]), and Hektor's fall at XIV 414ff. (no ax this time, but the bolt of Zeus [p. 342]).

305   **Then from his tender neck:** see the note to p. 259.

306   **As Thoas:** see on p. 56.

        the pleasure / of arrogant Zeus: cf. the sentiment of Agamémnon at XIV 69 (p. 331). Zeus is "arrogant" because he can capriciously, as it seems to the speaker, overwhelm a man when he wants to (cf. also Agamémnon's blame pp. 39 and 204).

307   **how is it that you left the battle:** his spear broke (p. 304), and he has returned for another. The warriors usually recover their spears and use them again. But this conversation may allude obliquely to the fact that Meríonês is also a bowman (see p. 319). If this is true, Idómeneus' compliment on the next page is also an apology.

308   **against Ephyroi / or gallant Phlegyai:** little is known of these tribes. One might expect a mythological allusion in such references, but that is apparently not the case here.

310   **At cross-purposes, / the sons of Krónos:** some editors have considered this paragraph an interpolation. Its self-conscious interest in offering an explanation of Poseidon's intervention recalls the lines concerning the disappearance of the wall which begin Book XII.

        but Zeus had been first-born and knew far more: Zeus was both youngest and oldest son of Krónos, for Krónos swallowed all of his children until Rhea saved Zeus, the youngest, who became the oldest when Krónos vomited up the children born to Rhea before Zeus. See Hesiod, *Theogony* 492ff. That Zeus "knows more" is a major theme of the *Theogony*.

> **Othrýoneus . . . Kassandra:** the bridegroom is mentioned only here and in Hektor's roll call on p. 323. Kassandra, famous in later legend and art for her prophetic powers (e.g., in Aeschylus' *Agamemnon* and Euripides' *Trojan Women*), appears briefly in Book XXIV (p. 590f.).

311   **Othrýoneus, I'll sing your praise:** this sort of sarcasm is not uncommon in vaunts over the dead or dying. Cf. Hektor's address to Patróklos (p. 402) and Akhilleus to Lykáôn (p. 497).

> **Ásïos, now dismounted:** he was introduced on p. 284. His appearance in the two episodes has led to speculation about the order of composition of XII and XIII. Mazon in his *Introduction a l'Iliade* (p. 190), considers the fact that here in XIII there is no allusion to the events of XII, a "proof that XIII is prior to XII." Others would say the poet of XIII has simply fulfilled the promise made in XII.

312   **Enraged at Ásïos' fall:** grief for a fallen comrade is a recurrent motivation. Below Antílokhos "whose heart was stirred" moves to protect his fallen comrade; cf. XVII 459 (p. 421): "Automédôn . . . though grieving for his friend." Frequently the construction is adversative: "They could not help him,/bitterly as they grieved for him" (XV 651; p. 370); cf. Hektor's loss of charioteers VIII 125=317; pp. 185 and 191.

> **Hypsênor:** the Greek indicates he dies of the blow ("tumbling down") and that he is "groaning deeply" as his friends carry him off. These last lines (420–23: "On the run he reached him . . . to the sheltering ships") appear verbatim at VIII 331–34 (p. 191), where the victim is clearly only wounded.

> **Dêíphobos gave a great shout and exulted:** this line introducing the vaunt is used four times (with a change of the proper name): XIII 413=445 (p. 313: "Idomeneus yelled and exulted savagely")=XIV 453=XIV 478 (both p. 344). In XIV the same pair of lines occur after each vaunt (458–59=486–87).

Alkáthoös: introduced p. 284.

313   Aineías . . . resentful against Priam: this resentment and the slight by Priam are unexplained. There may be
another allusion to this at XX 306ff. (p. 482).

314   But to his friends he called out: of the five names
here, all save Antílokhos were captains of the guard in Book
IX (p. 206).

            Both masses came together . . . around Al-
káthoös: this theme, i.e., striving to claim the body of the
slain, may be elaborated; cf. the fight over Sarpêdôn (p.
394ff.) and that over the fallen Patróklos (p. 407ff.).

315   Oinómaos: another tie with Book XII: Oinómaos,
Thoôn, and Adámas (next page) figured in a list on p. 285.

            Askálaphos: Hêra will incite Arês by the an-
nouncement of his death in Book XV (p. 353).

            Dêíphobos took the dead man's/helm, but
Meríonês: this incident renews, and reverses, their abortive
engagement on p. 304.

            Polítês: he is impersonated on p. 61 and men-
tioned again p. 360. Polítês survived the battles before Troy
to die at the hands of Akhilleus' son Pyrrhus (Neoptólemos)
on the night the Akhaians sacked Troy. His death in the presence of his father is vividly described by Vergil in the *Aeneid*,
Book II, 526ff.

316   because Poseidon/protected him: cf. below "who
grudged him this man's life." Homer expects us to remember
that Poseidon is the father of Nêleus, hence the great-grandfather of Antílokhos.

317   On a threshing floor: cf. the simile based on win-
nowing, but with a different point of comparison, p. 125.

318   Then in a lower tone/he said: by this comment
and the paragraphing Fitzgerald marks the shift in attitude
and tone within the speech. In the first half indignation,
anger, and a determination to have revenge characterize the
tone; in the second half pessimism and a sense of futility
predominate. Each part is developed independently, but neither is complete without the qualifying attitude in the other
half of the speech. See parataxis in the index.

319   Harpálíôn, King Pylaiménês' son: the father is
mentioned in the catalogue (p. 63) and is killed by Meneláos
(p. 127), only to be revived here ("his father, weep-

ing/walked behind"). With all the killing, the wonder is that such lapses are not more frequent than they are.

Polyïdos: cf. Polýeidos p. 114 and the note on p. 261. We may compare the destiny of Akhilleus (Thetis, p. 25) and the oracle concerning the first to land at Troy (see on Prôtesílaos, p. 58).

320 **the heavy fine/men paid who stayed at home:** so Ekhepôlos gave a mare to Agamémnon "to avoid the toil/of serving under him at windy Troy" (p. 544).

And the rest fought on like fire's/body leaping: XIII 673=XI 596=XVIII 1, and cf. XVII 366 (p. 418). See the note to p. 301.

the ships of Aías and Prôtesílaos: they are on the Akhaian left; Hektor is at the opposite end of the field from Akhilleus. For the dead hero Prôtesílaos see p. 58. Later his ship is the focus of Hektor's attack (p. 371ff.).

Ionians in long khitons: the only reference to the Ionians by name in Homer. The line has been suspected because they are wearing the long shirt (khiton) peculiar to those tribes but inappropriate to war. The epithet, however, may be ornamental.

the Epeian leaders: these are not the same men listed as captains in the catalogue (p. 55), where Mégês leads the islanders of the northwest. Medôn (p. 59) and Podárkês (p. 58), too, have changed commands. Medôn dies on page 360, where the four lines, "Aye, this Medôn . . . Eriôpis," occur again. The lines seem more fitting in the later passage.

321 **No Lokrians/backed up the other Aías:** cf. the lack of distinction between the troops of Telamônian and Oïlean Aías on p. 97. The catalogue does not attribute any distinctive armor to them (p. 52), though Aías himself wears a "corselet all of linen." Such apparent discrepancies may point to accretions within the tradition, but condemnation as un-Homeric is arbitrary.

322 **I fear/the Akhaians may still pay the debt they owe/for yesterday:** this is usually taken as a reference to the Akhaian defeat in VIII, for which, he fears, the Trojans must now suffer a defeat in turn (perhaps the metaphor of the scales of battle is latent here).

This wariness won Hektor's nod: cf. pp. 287–88, where Hektor rejects defensive advice. The poet does not

want a mere foil to Hektor, one whose advice is always rejected, for then Hektor's recollection in XXII of his counsel
would have less cogency.

323   Paris, you bad-luck charm . . . seducer: line
769=III 39 (p. 68). See Introduction, p. 28.

          since you are moved to blame the blameless: this is
the same charge Patróklos makes against Akhilleus at XI 654
(p. 271).

          Phálkês . . . Mórys: only Askánios has been men-
tioned previously (p. 63). Phálkês and Mórys reappear and
die at XIV 513f. (p. 346).

324   on the right/an eagle soared: the army reacts happily to the eagle because it is the bird of Zeus, but Zeus is not
said to have sent this flight, and for him to have done so
would contradict the opening lines of this book and his expressed intention to aid, at least temporarily, the Trojans.

          Iakhê: this is the sound of their shout.

          I wish/I were as surely all my days/a son of Zeus:
cf. the last words of Hektor's speech VIII 538ff. (p. 198).
Akhilleus, of course, is a descendant of Zeus.

     Aías' challenge and Hektor's reply would seem to announce
another duel rather than a general engagement; in fact they
do fight in Book XIV (p. 342f.) without benefit of these preliminaries.

BOOK FOURTEEN

🞑🞑🞑🞑🞑🞑🞑🞑🞑🞑🞑🞑🞑🞑🞑🞑🞑🞑🞑🞑🞑🞑🞑🞑🞑🞑🞑

BEGUILEMENT ON MOUNT IDA

Book XIV falls into three sections, the first and last of which continue the fighting while the middle section, for which the book has been named since antiquity, offers an extraordinary episode of Olympian guile and sexual duplicity. Demódokos' song of the cuckolding of Hêphaistos by Arês (*Odyssey* VIII 266ff.) is thematically similar. In the first section the wounded chieftains reappear and, after a conference with Nestor, determine to re-enter battle. Poseidon is still present rallying the Akhaians (p. 334), and Hêra decides to help him by distracting the attention of Zeus. Her efforts, which involve seduction and a heavy sleep, enable Poseidon to continue his work. In the last section the Akhaian success is highlighted by the wounding of Hektor.

329   **Now Nestor heard that tumult:** the word translated "tumult" is a noun formed from the same stem as *iakhê* and so provides an explicit verbal reference to the preceding episode. See the note on p. 299. In the subsequent reference ("while he drank," Makháôn, Hékamêdê) the poet connects this episode with the scene in Nestor's tent in Book XI (p. 270f.).

330   the princes came/along the shipways: the following passage has occasioned much debate because of a vagueness and ambiguity in its phrasing. Fitzgerald's translation accepts the view that some ships had been hauled inland so that those nearest the sea might be said to be "distant from the fighting." The wall referred to, on this view, might be the wall constructed in Book VII, though others have taken it to be a wall built at the time the Akhaians first landed. Nothing in the passage is made easier by the fact, offered by Leaf, that the actual distance "between the two promontories" is about five miles.

331   Hektor, will make good his word: possibly a reference to Hektor's speech at VIII 173–83 (p. 187), where firing the ships is explicitly his design. Agamémnon is not said to have heard that speech, although he rallies the troops at VIII 217ff. (p. 188). The poet tacitly gives Agamémnon the reader's knowledge of Hektor's intentions.

          the rest of the Akhaians,/like Akhilleus, hold a grudge: see Poseidon's comment p. 302. Although the theme remains undeveloped, it may be used here to motivate Agamémnon's suggestion (for the third time: see p. 204) that they prepare to abandon the field. In fact, after Book IX the Akhaians do not again fault Agamémnon for his treatment of Akhilleus.

332   to wind upon the spindle of our years: the Fates are represented as old women spinning wool (see note to p. 477). Odysseus' figure implies that Zeus controls fate.

          Contempt, no less, is what I feel for you: XIV 95=XVII 173 (p. 412), where Hektor rejects Glaukos' imputation of cowardice.

333   Tydeus: see on p. 100. This speech is a particularly striking example of the habit of validating an argument by prefacing it with an extensive description of the speaker's ancestry, experience, or knowledge. Here the ring composition ("noble father . . . My lineage/therefore is noble") precedes the simple exhortation to fight. Diomêdês' rhetoric reflects that of Sarpêdôn in XII: I am of noble birth; it is the duty of nobles to fight; therefore let us fight.

334   **the god . . . who now appeared as an old man:** Poseidon's anonymity here is unique in the *Iliad;* in all other cases of the impersonation of a mortal the divinity takes a particular person's form and name.

     Compassion is not in him: the expression in Greek (line 141) is vague. The line could also mean, as the scholiast takes it, that Akhilleus lacks good sense.

     Now Lady Hêra of the Golden Chair: the ancients called the following episode "the deception of Zeus." The transition between the two sections is abrupt. Homer might, e.g., have had Zeus notice the roar of Poseidon or the rally of the Akhaians, and then introduced Hêra's stratagem as a way of distracting him. On the other hand, the poet devotes much of the episode to Hêra's preparations, and had Zeus noticed the present turn of events before Hêra's toilet, the transition might seem more crude than it does at present. It is not apparent why Hêra's intervention was not placed a book earlier, i.e., before Poseidon's aid in XIII.

336   **Lend me longing, lend me desire:** on the preceding page the extraordinary craftsmanship of Hêphaistos and Athêna is noticed; so here, as in Book III, Aphrodítê presides over the powers of love, and she puts aside momentarily her loyalty to the Trojans, which is in any case more a matter of partiality to Paris and Aineías than to the Trojan state.

     Okéanos,/from whom the gods arose, and Mother Tethys: in Hesiod's *Theogony* (133ff.) they are said to be the children of Sky (Uranos) and Earth. They are not elsewhere described as primal beings. We do not know the nature or origin of their "quarrel," but M. L. West (in his commentary on the *Theogony,* p. 204) observes: "One would guess the reference to be to a 'separation of the waters', sc. the upper and lower waters, a separation corresponding to that of heaven and earth. Oceanus and Tethys would in this case correspond to Apsu and Tiamat in the Babylonian cosmology, the male and female waters which were originally united (*En. El.* 1. 1ff.)."

     who go to lie in the great arms of Zeus: does Aphrodítê guess Hêra's actual design? An alternative translation would read: "I cannot deny your account; for you are accustomed to lie in the arms of Zeus." The rhapsode's recitation might well indicate that Aphrodítê is winking at Hêra's story, even though Hêphaistos uses the first of these two lines quite seriously at *Odyssey* VIII 358.

    a pieced brocaded girdle: cf. the adornment of Pandora in Hesiod's *Works and Days,* 70ff.

337   **Hêra glided from Olympos:** Zeus, on Mount Ida near Troy, does not observe the plain below him, but Hêra, on Olympos, watches him closely. Piéria is a region in Thessaly bordering Olympos; Emathía is the later Macedonia; Athos is the eastern-most promontory of the Chalcidian peninsula.

    old Thoas: see the note on p. 176.

    Sleep, brother of Death: see Hesiod, *Theogony* 211ff., where Death and Sleep and other progeny of Night are listed. So it is to his mother that Sleep flees when he gets into trouble with Zeus (p. 338). Cf. "Death and sweetest Sleep" p. 391.

    when Hêraklês . . . had plundered Ilion: this adventure is alluded to at the end of Book V (p. 129) and again at the beginning of XV (p. 350).

338   **one of the younger Graces:** according to Hesiod (*Theogony* 907ff.) Eurýnomê, daughter of Okéanos, had three daughters, "fair-cheeked Graces," whose names were Aglaia, Euphrósynê, and Thalía. They were daughters of Zeus. The name of Sleep's beloved, Pásithea, means "goddess for all."

    Styx' corroding water: Hesiod (*Theogony* 775ff.) identifies the Styx as the "eldest daughter of Okéanos" and says the penalty paid by a god who swears falsely by the Styx is to be immobilized for a year and then to spend nine years separated from the company of the gods.

    she called on all the powers of the abyss,/on all the Titans: the Titans belong to the generation of Krónos and were banished to Tartaros in the underworld by Zeus (cf. note to p. 24).

    Lekton promontory: a spur of Mount Ida on the southern coast of the Troad.

339   **called "khalkis" by the gods:** cf. the distinction in speech made to p. 24. The four examples in the *Iliad* of divine and mortal names for the same thing or person do not reveal a reason for the distinction. Explanations which have been advanced are based on distinctions between poetic and colloquial speech, between cultic and secular usage, and between significant and non-significant words. None of these, however, has proven convincing for all examples.

340   **Not for Ixion's bride:** this catalogue of the loves of Zeus was condemned by ancient critics as inappropriate, and "an untimely exemplification of the preceding thought," as one modern commentator puts it. Such criticism hardly reckons with the character of Zeus. Ixion's bride is Dia (for Peiríthoös see the note to p. 59). All the women and sons mentioned here are well-known figures in Greek myth, but with the exception of Hêraklês, son of Alkmênê, they are seldom mentioned in Homer. Dánaë was the daughter of Akrisios. Her father locked her in a chamber, but Zeus found a way by taking the form of a golden shower. Eurôpa was the sister of Kadmos, founder of Thebes. Dêmêtêr (see p. 125) had Perséphonê by Zeus. Lêto's children were Apollo and Artemis.

    it would be so embarrassing: cf. Arês' embarrassment when Hêphaistos catches him seducing Aphrodítê (told in the song of Demódokos in *Odyssey* VIII).

341   **The god of sleep went gliding to the beachhead:** Hêra actually gives no warrant for this message, which effects a transition back to the battleground.

    Any fresh man who bears against his shoulder/a light shield: this advice to exchange armor has stuck many students as unrealistic and impractical.

342   **Hektor/drove at Aías:** now the poet takes up his narrative from the challenge and reply exchanged by these two at the end of Book XIII.

343   **Glaukos:** the passage ignores the fact that Glaukos was wounded earlier (XII 387f.; p. 293), even though the wounding figures in Glaukos' actions later (XVI 509ff.; p. 393).

    the ford of Xánthos: i.e., of the Skamánder, as men call it (XX 74; p. 475). These lines begin Book XXI and appear again in XXIV (692f.; p. 590).

    Sátnios: the river from which this warrior takes his name runs from the slopes of Ida westward.

344   **Prothoênor:** he is a leader of the Boiotians who has not appeared since the catalogue (p. 51).

          Arkhélokhos: he is in fact a son of Antênor (II 823; p. 62).

          Prómakhos: he is not mentioned in the catalogue, but Pênéleos (p. 345), who is apparently his comrade, is another Boiotian (p. 51). Prómakhos "has gone to sleep," with which cf. the "sleep of bronze" p. 258.

345   **drove his spearhead/into the eye-socket:** cf. the detailed description of the beheading p. 305.

346   **By the wound slit, as by a doorway, life/left him:** "life" in his *psyche,* sometimes translated "soul," the breath of life. See the notes to pp. 526 and 537.

BOOK FIFTEEN

THE LORD OF STORM

Books XI and XII showed the Akhaians suffering the reverses we had anticipated since Zeus's promise at the end of Book I. Books XIII and XIV unexpectedly offered aid to the Akhaians in the form of the intervention of Poseidon and Hêra. Now Zeus once again attends to the battle: he rebukes Hêra, orders Poseidon from the field, and sends Apollo to revive Hektor and to encourage the valor of the Trojans. Hektor crosses the rampart again and at the end of the book is threatening the ships with fire. Although Patróklos has already determined to help the Akhaians, the action of Book XV reasserts the necessity of that aid and presents a suitable dramatic prelude to his appeal (p. 362). Thus the scenes of XV comprehensively pick up the themes and events of the last four books while bringing the Akhaians to their most serious crisis thus far. Not only does the rhythm of the action prepare the way for the events of Book XVI, but another, and more particular, prophecy from Zeus (p. 351) foreshad-

ows later scenes in the poem as well as their consequences
for the fate of Troy.

349   **Running among the stakes:** the first three lines of
the book were used at VIII 343–45 (p. 192), where the
metrically equivalent "Trojans" is substituted for "Danääns."

        And now Zeus . . . awoke: another passage of
transition and summary; cf. the note to p. 299.

350   **Fine underhanded work:** for the tone and the
threats of Zeus cf. his speech on p. 182. For the allusion to
Hêraklês' misadventures see p. 337 and note.

        Earth be my witness: these lines preface Calypso's
oath to Odysseus in *Odyssey* V, 184–86. For the Styx see
the note to p. 338.

351   **Then in the time to come:** Zeus moves from a facetious acceptance of Hêra's oath to a prophetic statement of
events likely to appease her. Cf. his prophecy at VIII 473ff.
(p. 196); here the death of Sarpêdôn is added to his forecast.

        as Athêna planned and willed it: an allusion to her
help in capturing the city. In *Odyssey* VIII Odysseus asks
Demódokos to "sing that wooden horse/Epeios built, inspired
by Athêna" (p. 140 of Fitzgerald's translation).

352   **the heart's desire of the son of Pêleus:** this is the
promise made in Book I, p. 28.

        quick as a thought: see the note to p. 521.

        rose-cheeked Themis: the adjective is generic. It is
used of Khrysêis, Brisêis, Theanô (VI 298), and Lêto. For
the association of Themis and Zeus see the note to XX 4 (p.
473).

353   **dearest of men to him: Askálaphos:** this is another
particular link with earlier events; see XIII 518ff. (p. 315),
where the poet specifically notes that Arês was not aware of
his son's death. Contrary to the intentions of Zeus, Hêra
provokes Arês. Like any warrior, Arês desires revenge and
speaks of the "fate" that may be his as a result. Athêna,
here playing the dutiful and intimidated daughter, must quell
Arês' anger.

354   **more powerful by far than he,/and senior to him:**
cf. Agamémnon at IX 160f. (p. 208), who claims "higher
rank" and "precedence of age." For Zeus's seniority see
note to p. 310. The last two lines of this speech are reminiscent in language and thought of Agamémnon's threat at I

185–87 (p. 17). Cf. Poseidon's claim below to be "his peer in honor."

355   **as snow or hail flies:** cf. the similes at XII 278ff. (p. 289) and XII 156ff. (p. 286).

   Sons of Krónos . . . whom Rhea bore: Hesiod (*Theogony* 453ff.) lists the children of this pair of Titans as Hestia, Dêmêtêr, Hêra, Hadês, Poseidon, and Zeus. Hesiod does not mention any division of honor or authority, but rather he consistently celebrates Zeus as the high god and powerful successor of Krónos.

356   **All princely hearts/are capable of changing:** cf. the gnomic wisdom of Poseidon at XIII 115 (p. 303) and of Phoinix at IX 497 (p. 219). Agamémnon turns the motif to his personal ends in his final instructions to Odysseus (IX 157ff.; p. 208). For the Furies see IX 454 (p. 217).

   his peer in destiny: like "peer in honor" (line 186; p. 355), this phrase appeals to Poseidon's possession of an equal portion of the world after the casting of lots. "Destiny" translates a word cognate with the Greek *moira* ("fate"; see the note to p. 40). The gods have their lot, i.e., their portion, which in turn symbolizes the status, or honor, accorded them.

   he incurs our unappeasable anger: the truculent Poseidon gives way before the "towering anger" of Zeus. The quarrels and jealousies of the gods develop a burlesque counterpoint to the anger that divides Akhilleus and Agamémnon.

357   **round fallen Krónos:** see on p. 24 and p. 336. Krónos and the Titans were banished to the underworld after their defeat at the hands of Zeus and his allies (see *Theogony* 713ff.).

   The mind of Zeus . . . reanimated him: a rare expression: usually the intervention of the gods is directly physical, but Zeus never appears on the field of battle. Since the word translated here as "mind" (XV 242) "always implies some long-range plan or decision," "decision" would be another possible translation, with the understanding that Apollo is acting as the immediate agent (Kurt von Fritz, "*Noos* and *noein* in the Homeric Poems," *CP* 38 [1943], p. 82). Cf., however, XVI 688 (p. 398) and the note there.

358   **Apollo of the golden sword:** this unexplained epithet is also used at V 509 (p. 125). Cf. Poseidon's sword (p. 342), which, despite the ample description, plays little part in the subsequent action.

As when a stallion: the same simile appears verbatim on p. 157.

Think of hunting dogs: cf. the similes at III 23ff. (p. 68) and XI 548 (p. 268).

359   **Bad luck . . . this marvel that I see ahead:** the reasoning in this speech is a familiar way of motivating a change of action on the field; cf. Diomêdês' reaction to Hektor's charge on p. 128 and Aineías' reasoning p. 476.

360   **Each man slew his man:** 328=XVI 306, the beginning of another catalogue. Some of these victims have been mentioned in the catalogue in II or elsewhere, but as usual none has any prominence in the poem.

361   **Apollo kicked the embankment of the ditch:** see the poet's story of the fate of the wall on p. 281f. While the gods are often involved in humorous and even ludicrous incidents, it is a mistake not to recognize their power, and the respect poet and auditor alike had for it. There is no reason to assume that actions such as the one Homer describes here were considered metaphorical.

thundered a great peal: such a sign would normally mark the god's acquiescence in the prayer, which would be strange here because Zeus has designed the rout of the Akhaians. So the eagle sent at the end of Book XIII (p. 324) does not discourage the Trojans, although the Akhaians take heart from it. For other omens see pp. 189 and 424.

Like a surging wave: cf. the similes at XV 624ff. (p. 369).

362   **Patróklos stayed/inside the shelter with Eurýpylos:** the poet returns to the scene at the end of Book XI (p. 277); cf. the beginning of Book XIV and the note there. The fortunes of battle have varied a good deal in the meantime, and the poet has saved Patróklos' re-entry for a moment when the Akhaians are badly pressed. The concluding lines of Patróklos' speech ("Who can say/if with god's help . . .") echo Nestor's thought at XI 792f. (p. 275).

363   **Kalêtôr, Klytíos' son:** at XX 238 (p. 480) we learn that Klytíos is the brother of Priam; Kalêtôr, like Kleitos below, appears only here.

for he had killed a Kýthêran: cf. the story of Medôn on p. 360.

364   **Telamônian Teukros:** this patronymic is usually reserved for Aías.

365   **Trojans, Lykians, Dardanoi:** see the note on p. 260. For the motif in "a man defending his own land" see the note to p. 288 and cf. Hékabê's "he stood and fought for the sweet wives of Troy" (XXIV 215f.; p. 574). The present exhortation comes when Hektor is on the attack and hopes to make "the Akhaians sail for home."

Argives, where is your pride: this exhortation has a characteristic structure: a) fight like men; b) what else can we do?; c) Hektor will fire the ships; b′) is there any better plan than to fight?; a′) no, it is better to die proudly in battle. "Pride" means regard for the good opinion of others. This passage and Aías' speech on p. 367 are useful for defining the significance of "shame" (*aidôs*) for the warrior.

mad to fire the ships: cf. Thoas' comment, "wild as he is" (line 298; p. 359) and the poet's description of "Hektor, furious in arms as Arês/raging, his spear flashing, or as fire/that rages . . ." (p. 368). Cf. the note on p. 210 and 301.

366   **Skhedíos, son of Perimêdês:** at II 517 (p. 52) he has a different father.

the Kyllênian, Ótos: the more famous Mount Kyllêne is in Arcadia, but this one is in Elis.

Mégês wounded/Kroismos: note how the poet elaborates this scene: Mégês kills a man; while stripping his gear (524) he is attacked by Dólops; the lineage of Dólops; Mégês is saved by his battle jacket, which is described in respect of material, origin, and the person who gave it; Mégês attacks Dólops, who is struck on the helmet by Mégês and killed by Meneláos; Meneláos and Mégês strip the gear (544) from Dólops. The twenty lines offer a nice example of elaborated ring composition in the narrative.

out of Ephyra, from the Sellêeis river: the line occurred at II 659 (p. 56). This Ephyra was located either in the western Peloponnesus or in Thesprotia (see the note on p. 146).

367   **Hiketáôn:** a brother of Priam's.

"Friends," he cried, "respect yourselves as men: cf. Nestor's exhortation p. 370 (line 561=661) and Agamémnon's p. 126 (XV 561–64=V 529–32).

Antílokhos . . . no one is faster on his feet than you: so he is summoned to bear news to Akhilleus (p. 429) and takes third prize in the quarter mile held in Book XXIII (p. 559).

368–369   and his eyes/were flaming: cf. the description of Akhilleus at XIX 365–67 (p. 468).

369   for he would be diminished soon: cf. I 352 (p. 23), where Akhilleus uses the word translated here "diminished soon" of his own life, "though it is brief."

a day/of wrath for him at Lord Akhilleus' hands: so much we were told by Zeus in the speech at the beginning of this book (p. 351), but now the poet adds another detail, namely that Athêna will have a hand in the death of Hektor (see p. 522ff.).

like a sheer cliff of granite: the torrent of similes on this page suggests the poet felt they more vividly represent the dynamic qualities of Hektor's attack than simple narrative description can. After this imagery the death of only one man is something of an anticlimax.

Períphêtês, a Mykênaian,/son of Kopreus: Leaf observes that "it is noteworthy that Periphetes is the only Mykenaean who appears in the *Iliad;* the town is rarely mentioned except as the realm of Agamémnon." Kopreus means "dung" in Greek, appropriate enough for the mean servant of a mean man.

370   Eurýstheus: see p. 193.

he tripped upon the body shield: see the note on p. 145.

All of you, remember/children and wives, possessions, and your parents: Nestor's exhortation resembles Hektor's (p. 365), who, however, explicitly refers to defense of the native land, while the present context ("respect" [*aidôs*]; see note p. 365) suggests that the Akhaians should remember their honor and fight like men rather than shame their families by retreating.

371   which had brought/Prôtesílaos to Troy: the fight rages over the same ground disputed in Book XIII (see p. 320).

372   through cowardice/of our old counselors who held me back: the speech is far removed from the fatalism Hektor expressed when he talked with Andrómakhê in Book VI (p. 155f.). In the fury of battle and the *aristeia* Homeric warriors "forget themselves" and become men possessed. In the next book Patróklos is the victim of a similar battle fury. Hektor's rejection of the "old counselors" is another foreshadowing of his decision in Book XVIII (p. 444f.).

BOOK SIXTEEN

░░░░░░░░░░░░░░░░░░░░░░░░░░░░░░

A SHIP FIRED,
A TIDE TURNED

Book XVI brings a crucial reversal in the plot of the poem. Responding to the plea of his companion in arms, Akhilleus lets Patróklos have his armor and men to use against the victorious Trojans. This decision, which Nestor has anticipated in Book XI, shows Akhilleus relenting. But it is too late, for Patróklos, carried away by the spirit of battle, attacks the retreating Trojans and is killed. With a fine irony the episode concludes with Hektor boasting over the body of the dying Patróklos, whose death will impel Akhilleus to a new rage, this time against Hektor, and a revenge that costs Hektor his life. Thus Book XVI simultaneously depicts the high point of Hektor's efforts (his *aristeia*) in the defense of Troy and an action certain to bring his own death and the ruin of the city.

Critics have been concerned to explain why Akhilleus relents, why he does so at this moment, and why he sends Patróklos rather than return himself (see Owen, p. 153; Motto/Clark, p. 115; Whitman, p. 196ff.). Answers have varied, but it is apparent that Akhilleus' will is still divided, that his resentment at the slight offered by Agamémnon is at odds with a concern for his companions (see notes to pp. 224 and 270). If there is something contradictory in Akhilleus' speech and decision here, as many critics have felt, that contradiction is consistent with the situation into which he has been forced and which he willfully maintains. For the warrior committed to honor and glory cannot achieve his goals apart from battle, and yet it is in the name of his honor that Akhilleus has retired from battle. Homer prefers to dramatize this dilemma rather than to articulate it explicitly; nevertheless, in the first scene Akhilleus' ambivalence and frustration are made sufficiently clear.

377   **Meanwhile Patróklos . . . streaming/warm tears:** he left the tent of Eurýpylos at XV 405 (p. 362). This comparison was used at IX 14f. (p. 204) of Agamémnon.

378   **Or is this weeping/over the Argives:** after a gentle and familiar mockery Akhilleus recognizes that Patróklos' tears are the result of the errand Akhilleus sent him on in XI (p. 271). On this scene see the analysis of Owen, p. 146ff., who notices that "Nothing has been made so far of Achilles' affection for Patroclus; at most it has been implied. This is the first time we have heard them talking together, and it is the first time we hear Achilles talking friendlily, not at a tension. And so when Patroclus outspokenly condemns his conduct, he shows no resentment, but tries to explain his feelings, not defiantly, but as to himself." (p. 146)

          Patróklos, you replied: the following appeal uses fourteen lines from the speeches of Eurýpylos and Nestor in Book XI. It falls into three sections. 1) From "All who were . . ." to ". . . in his thigh" reports the situation (all these lines appeared in XI). 2) The central section, "But you are . . ." to "a mind so harsh," is a rebuke which draws upon Nestor's argument at XI 763 (p. 274: "Not so/Akhilleus, who alone gains by his valor"). In the Greek Patróklos' phrase "fearsome pride" is for the *Iliad* a unique compound made in part from the word rendered "valor" on p. 274 (see the note there). The argument "What good will come of it . . ." also draws on Nestor's language. We are not, however, talking about formulae here. 3) The last section (from

"If in your heart . . ." to the end of the speech) repeats Nestor's arguments, and much of his actual phrasing, at XI 794–803 (p. 275f.), and proposes that Akhilleus lend Patróklos' aid to the Akhaians.

Such repetitions, and particularly the last nine lines, have to be distinguished from those formulaic phrases and lines which occur numerous times, often in the same sort of context. Nestor's proposal was specifically applicable to Akhilleus, and Patróklos repeats it almost verbatim, excepting a change from third to second person and a few other changes in phrasing. From the perspective of understanding oral poetry, we can say that such a passage implies total mnemonic recall rather than composition from formulaic phrases and lines. From an aesthetic point of view, the repetition validates Nestor's argument, makes Patróklos' appeal in some sense an instrument or extension of Nestor's persuasion, and introduces an irony predicated on our knowledge and Akhilleus' ignorance of the true source of the argument. See the discussion in notes to pp. 155 and 207.

Have you no pity?: cf. Aías' arguments p. 223. Later (p. 383) Akhilleus will say the Myrmidons called him "merciless."

379   **There is no oracle:** it is sometimes suggested that Nestor and Patróklos allude to the "two destinies" Akhilleus himself mentions at IX 410f. (p. 216). His denial of any "oracle" here may be an indirect way of saying, "that business is not relevant to my decision." That his mother has told him of his fate is reaffirmed in Book XXI (p. 502).

I swore/I would not rest from anger till the cries: see his reply to Aías p. 224. If strict logic is demanded of Akhilleus in this speech, he may appear a bit incoherent. Sending relief to the Akhaians will not bring Agamémnon to his knees, and when he speaks of the return of his "lovely girl, with bright new gifts," he may seem to have forgotten the offer of Book IX. His ambivalence, however, is evident in the juxtaposition of hatred of Agamémnon and desire for "great honor for me, and glory/among Danáäns" (p. 380), which leads him to press unrealistic stipulations upon Patróklos.

380   **so that you'll win great honor for me:** some editors have condemned lines 84–86 because Akhilleus seems oblivious to the offer of Agamémnon, through the embassy, in Book IX. In a provocative and controversial interpretation Adam Parry offered another explanation: Akhilleus is disillusioned with the world around him, with the hypocrisy of his peers and the difference between true honor and what men call honor. But lacking any language to express this disillusionment, Akhilleus makes shift to express his feelings in the only way he can: he misuses and abuses traditional language and conventional expressions in order to reject them and the values they imply. For example: "he speaks to Patroclus in Book 16 of a hope of being offered material gifts by the Greeks, when we know that he has been offered these gifts and that they are meaningless to him; or as when he says that he has won great glory by slaying Hector, when we know that he is really fighting to avenge his comrade, and that he sees no value in the glory that society can confer." ("The Language of Achilles," p. 7; Parry's second reference is to XXII 391–94 [p. 528].) Other critics have been content to find in these lines evidence of a confused and agitated sensibility. It is also possible, if we look back to Akhilleus' words in XI (see the note on p. 270), to believe that he still wants the girl and gifts on his terms, i.e., insists that Agamémnon "beg and pray" for his return (see David E. Eichholz, "The Propitiation of Achilles"). And finally we must remember how different the heroic sensibility is from our own, a fact perhaps nowhere better illustrated than at XVIII 114ff. (p. 439), where Akhilleus speaks of revenge, the inevitability of death, and his desire to "win perfect glory." Throughout the drama of revenge Akhilleus seeks a purely personal glory; hence Leaf's allusion to the "selfishness of Achilles" in his note on XVI 85.

 beaten by the mind of Zeus: see the note on p. 357; perhaps this means "by the plan of Zeus." This interlude is obviously inserted to highlight the crisis.

381 **He did not take the great spear of Akhilleus:** the thematic significance of armor, and especially the armor of Akhilleus, becomes increasingly important now. Patróklos assumes Akhilleus' role, but he cannot fully take his place. Cf. XVI 793ff. (p. 401) for the loss of the armor.

382 **It was a Pêlian ash:** the poet plays on Mount Pêlion and Pêleus, Akhilleus' father. For another reference

to Kheirôn, the good centaur who acted as Akhilleus' tutor, see XI 831f. (p. 277).

Automédôn yoked the fast horses: he has been mentioned previously only at IX 209 (p. 210).

Xánthos . . . Balíos . . . Podargê: in a line condemned by ancient critics (VIII 185; p. 187) Hektor calls two of his four horses Xánthos and Podargos (translated as "Tawny and Whitefoot"). Balíos means "Dapple" and Pêdasos "Leaper." For other references to them see pp. 420f., 544, and esp. 469f.

Like wolves: the development of this simile, particularly in its emphasis on the "glutted" pack, illustrates a tendency of many longer similes to move away from an initially relevant comparison to a situation and description independent of—some would say contradictory of—the narrative context.

Five he entrusted with command: despite the attention to the lineage of Menésthios and Eudôros, they, like Peísandros, are mentioned only here; Alkimédôn appears again only in XVII (p. 422f.).

383   **beautiful Polydôrê:** nothing else is known of this sister of Akhilleus.

Hermés,/pure Deliverer: the etymology of this epithet (Argeiphontês, p. 578) is uncertain. Fitzgerald has connected it with Hermês' function as guide for travelers and for souls journeying to the underworld.

Eileithyía: see the note on p. 259.

Myrmidons, let not one man forget: reference or allusion to scenes not directly presented in the poems is infrequent in the *Iliad*. Neither Akhilleus nor the poet has offered a hint that the Myrmidons are disgruntled, or that their reproaches may have affected their chief. Such allusions violate the "rule" for the exclusive priority of the foreground in Homeric narrative.

brought you up on rage: as the scholiast noticed, Akhilleus puns on literal and figurative senses here (cf. our "gall").

384   **and he made offering to no god but Zeus:** cf. "Honored I think I am by Zeus's justice" (IX 608; p. 222). This special standing with Zeus becomes thematically more significant in later books; in XVI later developments of this

theme are foreshadowed in the death of Sarpêdôn (cf. the notes to pp. 390, 520, and 521). See the note to p. 477.

Zeus of Dôdôna, god of Pelasgians: Dôdôna (see p. 60) was the site of an ancient oracle of Zeus. On the Pelasgians see II 681 (p. 57), where Pelasgian Argos is placed in northern Greece and particularly associated with Akhilleus and his people. Pelasgian would seem to be an alternate, and older, name for the Hellenic peoples, and behind Selloi may lurk Helloi, i.e., Hellenic; but in this passage the Selloi are clearly identified with a clan which has jurisdiction over the god's oracle.

My lord, you heard me/praying before this: 236–38=I 453–55 (p. 26: in Khrysês' prayer).

386   **Let King Agamémnon learn his folly:** 273–74=I 411–12 (p. 25). Leaf contends "they [these lines] are hardly appropriate here where Patroclus is going to aid the Greeks, whereas in their original position they are a threat. Patroclus' mission is, so far as it goes, a renunciation on Achilles' part of the severe lesson he wishes to read Agamémnon." But at this point, before he is seized by the battle's fury, Patróklos may still be thinking of the limited aid Akhilleus has stipulated and his role as an extension of Akhilleus' power and glory (p. 380).

had put aside his wrath for friendship's sake: that the Trojans would consider this likely is further indication of the cogency of Aías' arguments in Book IX.

387   **Now veteran/Meneláos:** as usual, many of the Trojans killed are otherwise unknown. The death of Sarpêdôn's companions (cf. p. 390) prepares the way for his duel with Patróklos.

So these two, overcome by the two brothers: cf. the note on p. 109. Thrasymêdês is the brother of Antílokhos.

the fierce Khimaira: the monster of the Bellerophon story (see p. 147).

388   **Akámas:** introduced on p. 253. Another Erýmas is killed by Patróklos on p. 390.

Patróklos . . . with slaughter in his heart: by now he has accomplished his mission, but, as the poet says on p. 398 (XVI 705), "more than human in fury" he pursues the fleeing Trojans. Cf. Whitman: "When he puts on the armor of Achilles, a great change comes over him. The gentlest man in the army becomes a demon-warrior, who drives the Trojans headlong from the ships, slays the redoubtable Sarpedon, utters proud, insulting speeches over his fallen enemies, and sets foot on the ramparts of Troy itself, threatening to take it." (p. 200)

389   As under a great storm black earth is drenched: the identification of Zeus as the agent punishing "crooked judgments" implies a moral function rarely invoked in the *Iliad,* although his interest in guest-friendship and oaths indicates an ethical development the god is not always inclined to fulfill in this story.

He hooked him by the spearhead/over the chariot rail, as a fisherman: this comparison seems a reasonable approximation of the grotesque. Fenik (p. 61f.) comments: "Phantasmata [grotesque descriptions] are, according to Friedrich's definition, those incidents in the battle scenes that are so extraordinary that they contradict both probability and possibility. In [V 580ff.; p. 127f.] Mydon's head sinks so deeply into the sand that his body remains upright until it is knocked down by the horses . . . No two phantasmata in the poem are alike, and yet they clearly form a class of their own by reason of their bizarre details. A headless and armless corpse rolls along the ground like a cylinder [XI 145ff.; p. 256], or marrow spurts out of a severed spinal column [XX 481ff.; p. 488]. All combine a special interest in the horrible and impossible." Cf. XIV 493ff. (p. 345).

390   all in quick succession he brought down: this line occurs three times; cf. the lists on pp. 190 and 287.

and learn what man he is: 424–25=V 175–76 (p. 115), where Aineías speaks of Diomêdês.

Sorrow for me: the gods, as well as men, are dominated by momentary impulse, a habit which further confuses Homeric statements about fate ("the scheme of things"). Zeus forecasts the death of Sarpêdôn at XV 67 (p. 351), but in the event he ponders saving the Lykian hero. Hêra's response (next page) expresses as clearly as any passage in the *Iliad* the clash of conceptions: Sarpêdôn is destined to die, but Zeus can save him. Contrast the interpretation of Lloyd-Jones: *"Moira,* one's 'portion,' is in the last resort identical with the will of Zeus; when Hera reminds him that he cannot save his son Sarpedon, she is only warning him that he cannot sacrifice to a sudden whim his own settled policy" (p. 5).

391   **O fearsome power,/my Lord Zeus:** this is Hêra's regular response (the line occurs six times; cf., e.g., pp. 29 and 196). Hêra does not deny that Zeus has the power to counter "destiny," but she appeals to his sense of what is natural and inevitable for man. Cf. the scene on p. 520ff. and the notes there.

          Death and sweetest Sleep: see the note to p. 337. The subject was taken up by Greek painters who represent Death and Sleep lifting Sarpêdôn or the Trojan ally Memnon, who was killed by Akhilleus.

392   **Sarpêdôn fell/the way an oak or poplar:** the simile (four lines) was used earlier at XIII 389ff. (p. 311).

          Glaukos, old man: only the greatest of Homeric warriors are given speeches as they die; cf. pp. 402f. and 526f.

393   **where Teukros . . . had hit him:** see XII 387 (p. 293).

394   **The man who crossed the rampart of Akhaians/first:** see the note on p. 294.

          and not the least . . . noble Epeigeus: yet he is mentioned only here, and his town, Boudeion, has not been located. His motivation for leaving his native place is a stock motif: cf. the story of Medôn p. 320 and that of Tlêpólemos p. 57.

          Zeus unfurled a deathly gloom of night: an embracing image which anticipates the general slaughter. The association of Night, Sleep, and Death has already been noted (p. 337). "Unfurled" pursues the common image of night as a veil or curtain which covers the eyes at death (e.g., V 310 [p. 119] and XIII 425 [p. 312]). Their mythical personification may account in part for the tangibility of these figures; cf. "Death's cloud/poured round him" and "hateful darkness took him" (p. 395).

396–397 **Zeus . . . watched them all and pondered/long:** though such passages would seem to fix the fate of warriors and the course of events, it should be noticed that on the next page the poet suggests that Patróklos might have kept "Akhilleus' mandate" and survived. A little later Apollo warns Patróklos to retire, a warning the hero temporarily heeds, but

when Hektor attacks, Patróklos returns to the fight. Having
been struck by Apollo and Euphórbos he tries to retire, only
to be killed by Hektor. In effect the poet shows the gods plan-
ning and manipulating while he simultaneously grants his
characters sufficient dramatic freedom to make them more
than puppets of fate. The mediating figure is the demonic
fury that possesses the warrior. Cf. the note on Hektor's fate,
p. 515.

397   **the dipping scales of Zeus:** see the note p. 183.

       anoint him with ambrosia: see the note p. 458 for
the use of ambrosia.

398   **But overpowering is the mind of Zeus:** this line
and the two following (688–90) occur later in Hektor's
speech at XVII 176–78 (p. 413), where the context gives
them a more aphoristic quality than they appear to have here.
Parallels to the language used in the last line of this paragraph ("he stirred Patróklos' heart to fury") do not suggest
that Zeus has driven Patróklos mad, yet in the next paragraph
he is "more than human in fury," i.e., like a god in his power.
Cf. the interpretation of this access of strength offered by Er-
land Ehnmark: "Man is invested with divine power and becomes undoubtedly like the gods. The transmission of the
divine power may be effected in various ways, such as direct
touch, or through a rod or wand, or by breath. Generally the
god is present; but action at a distance also occurs and invariably in the case of Zeus." (*The Idea of God in Homer* [Upp-
sala, 1935], pp. 5–6) Cf. the note to p. 357.

       **a fourth time flung himself against the wall,/more
than human in fury:** the line occurs four times; cf. "But on
the fourth demonic foray" p. 401. The comparison of the
hero to a demonic power ("beside himself," "like a fury")
is used three times of Diomêdês (pp. 123, 124, and 137),
and later of Akhilleus ("beside himself," p. 487).

401   **the Akhaians outfought destiny to prevail:** this is
the only occasion in the *Iliad* where something actually happens "beyond destiny," although the suggestion that something might have happened beyond destiny (but for the intervention of the god or for some other reason) occurs often.

       three times, wild/yells in his throat: on p. 398 in
three lines he kills nine Trojans; twice he attacks the wall

three times before being thrown back on the fourth attempt; in the second attack he kills nine men in each assault.

 Pánthoös' son,/Euphórbos: this brother of Poulýdamas makes his first appearance here and is killed by Meneláos at the beginning of Book XVII (p. 409). That a god and two mortals are required to bring Patróklos down augments the glory of the dead hero. So Athêna aids Akhilleus in his duel with Hektor (p. 522ff.), thus asserting the divine favor shown Akhilleus as well as the prowess of his adversary.

402 **Easy to guess, Patróklos, how you swore:** even the most chivalrous of heroes may become infatuate and arrogant in the vaunt of victory (cf. Patróklos' jeer over Kebríonês, p. 400). Hektor's threat to feed Patróklos' body to the kites anticipates the struggle over the corpse in Book XVII, besides telling us something about the character of the Trojan victor.

403 **They stripped me of my arms:** cf. the note on "good armor," p. 410.

 This day/your death stands near: line 853= XXIV 132 (p. 571), spoken by Thetis to Akhilleus.

BOOK SEVENTEEN

CONTENDING FOR A SOLDIER FALLEN

The armor of a hero, like a slave or a team of horses, represents the prize of battle and a tangible emblem of honor and fame. Although Homer does not actually describe Hektor stripping the arms of Akhilleus from Patróklos, that feat has been accomplished early in Book XVII (p. 411). The balance of this book focuses on the action over the dead hero, the efforts of the Akhaians to save him and of the Trojans to win the body that they might mutilate the corpse (p. 411).

The archaic Greeks believed that only a proper burial would ensure passage of the soul of the dead to the underworld. Consequently, not only friendship and honor but religious piety demanded that the corpse be rescued and given proper rites. Glaukos and Zeus shared this concern for Sarpêdôn. In XXIII the shade of the dead Patróklos appears to Akhilleus to urge him to hasten the funeral (p. 537). In

XXIV Priam risks his own life to reclaim the body of Hektor, which Akhilleus has tried to mutilate.

So in several ways the last third of the poem is concerned with the dead: claiming the body on the field, revenging a dead friend, honoring the fallen, saving a body from sacrilege. Through all this we know that the living have consigned themselves to death, Hektor when he disregards the advice of Poulýdamas (p. 444), and Akhilleus when he willfully chooses to avenge the death of Patróklos (p. 438). But despite the thematic importance of death the poem is neither morbid nor pathetic; the characters remain vigorous and the poet retains his dispassionate objectivity.

408   **Hyperênor:** at his death in XIV (p. 346) no notice is taken of his family ties, nor is the exchange alluded to in "sneered at me" described.

you will give satisfaction for my brother: it is often noted that Homer favors the Akhaians, and there are good reasons for this observation. The sentiment of Pope's note, however, will win the assent of many readers: *"Menelaus* putting him in mind of the Death of his Brother, gives occasion (I think) to one of the finest Answers in all *Homer* in which the Insolence of Menelaus is retorted in a way to draw Pity from every Reader; and I believe there is hardly one, after such a Speech, that would not wish *Euphorbus* had the better of Menelaus: A Writer of Romances would not have fail'd to have giv'n *Euphorbus* the Victory. But however it was fitter to make Menelaus, who had receiv'd the greatest Injury, do the most revengeful Actions."

For the combination of loss to bride and parents see pp 153 (Hektor on his own prospects) and 592. (XVII 37= XXIV 741: "his parents harrowed by the loss"). Phronti is the mother of Hyperênor.

409   **fair as the Graces':** for the Graces see p. 120. A *Odyssey* VI 162f. Odysseus compares Alkínoös' daughte Nausikaa to the beauty of a young tree:

So fair, one time, I thought a young palm tree
at Delos near the altar of Apollo—

                                   Fitzgerald's version, p. 103f

clamping with his great jaws: 63–64=XI 175–76 (p. 256), where in a shorter simile a lion attacks cattle.

Mentês, Lord/of Kikonês: he is mentioned only here; in the Trojan catalogue (p. 63) Euphêmos leads the Kikonês.

410 **What now? If I/abandon this good armor:** according to Fenik (p. 96f.), who is summarizing an article by C. Hentze, this is only the second monologue in the *Iliad*: "A genuine monologue appears for the first time in XI. They are confined to XI, and books XVII through XXII. The loci are XI 404, XVII 91, XVII 201, XVII 443, XVIII 6, XX 425, XXI 54, XXI 553, XXII 99, XXII 297." Of this group the monologues of Odysseus (p. 263), of Agênor (p. 511), and of Hektor (p. 518) are all concerned with whether or not the warrior should take his stand and fight. Meneláos has been consistently represented as a warrior of the second rank. He remains prominent throughout this episode and is finally able to help in the rescue of the body (p. 430). After Book XVII Meneláos will appear again only in Book XXIII.

Whose "good armor" is at issue? The preceding description "bent over/to take his gear"; "He might with ease/have borne Euphórbos' gear away," p. 409) point to Euphórbos'. But "leave Patróklos" and lines 122 and 125 ("his gear in Hektor's hands"; "he had stripped Patróklos of his armor") indicate Patróklos'. His arms, however, were knocked off by Apollo just before he was killed. J. B. Hainsworth (*Homer*, p. 30) follows F. M. Combellack ("Some Formulary Illogicalities in Homer," *TAPA* 96 [1965], 41–56), who offers the following explanation. When Hektor kills Patróklos, he strikes a warrior whose armor has already been stripped from him by Apollo (p. 401). Patróklos falls:

He crashed, and all Akhaian troops turned pale.
XVI 822 (p. 402)

The first half of this is formulaic (eight times), but the line in all other passages concludes:

He thudded down, his gear clanged on his body,
XVII 50 (p. 409)

Homer, conscious that Apollo had left Patróklos "disarmed," changed the second half of XVI 822 to fit the context. When the poet turned to the fight over the body, however, "the usual pressure of the general or normal moves the poet back into the old familiar paths, and again and again, in speaking of the removal of Patroclus' armor, he employs a phraseology that fits the normal situation and is wholly inconsistent with the unique one he has himself so impressively described" (Combellack, p. 47f.). That is, he is able to modify one formulaic line because of the unique circumstance he has created, but the habit of describing fighting over an *armed* warrior betrays the poet's own innovative description in the preceding episode (XVI). Combellack considers this an illustration of the "validity of the 'oral law': the general takes precedence over the particular" (p. 49).

Unless we resort to a theory of multiple authorship or interpolation, this analysis best explains the anomaly. Yet some readers will surely be uneasy with an analysis that attributes a unique and brilliant scene, including a significant adjustment from normal formulaic usage, to the same poet who, only a few lines later, cannot remember, or maintain, his invention. If the book division also indicates the beginning of an episode regularly performed independently of XVI, the lapse is more intelligible. The problem of Phoinix, discussed in the notes to p. 209, is in a way analogous. There, however, the initial "adaptation" (the introduction of Phoinix) is clumsy, while his speech must be considered one of the poem's finest.

Why go on arguing with myself: this line is used in all four of the monologues in which the warrior is faced with the danger of taking a stand and the shame of retreat. See the note to p. 511.

411   now to behead it/and give the trunk to Trojan dogs: both poet and Akhaians (p. 415) consider mutilation to be Hektor's purpose. Cf. Glaukos' fear for Sarpêdôn p. 412.

412   the Argives would return Sarpêdôn's arms,/his body, too: since the body of Sarpêdôn is missing, his comrade assumes the Argives have carried it from the field.

413   taken from Patróklos when I killed him: see the note to p. 410.

without respect: this is unclear: some scholars refer to Zeus's speech about the horses of Akhilleus (p. 421) and assume that it is the divine origin of the armor which makes Hektor's action inappropriate.

414   **Mesthlês, Glaukos, Medôn . . . :** five of these warriors appear in the Trojan catalogue p. 63f.

     Hear me, hosts of neighbors and allies: Hektor's reasoning here has rightly struck one recent critic as "bizarre." He explains the passage in this fashion: "Although Hector plainly has no objection to imposing the simplest standard of 'results' on his allies ('I gave you food, now you must fight') and although he himself by any conceivable measure of such sort has a tangible and calculable obligation to his allies for their aid—indeed it is surely *he* who is obligated and not they—he attempts to transform the relationship into one in which it is his actions that are gratuitous, not theirs. The assertion is bizarre, and the lines in which it is made are, not unsurprisingly, obscure in their meaning. . . . But the impulse on Hector's part to evade the pragmatic subservience and obligation of his position is clear enough." (David B. Claus, "*Aidôs* in the Language of Achilles," *TAPA* 105 [1975], p. 20f.) For further remarks by Claus on the applicability of this view to Akhilleus and other heroes see the notes to p. 213.

415   **Hektor's a battle-cloud, covering everything:** the entire battle over Patróklos is fought in a mist or cloud. To protect Patróklos Zeus "poured thick mist/about their shining helms" (line 268ff.). Cf. Arês at V 506f. (p. 125), who "veiled them everywhere in dusk" to aid the Trojans. Later "all was darkened in the battle-cloud" (XVII 368; p. 419) and "those in the center, though, endured the cloud/with toil of war" (XVII 375f.; p. 419). This imagery culminates in Aías' prayer for light and Zeus's response (XVII 644ff.; p. 427f.). The gods commonly use a cloud, night, or a mist to protect their favorites or to confuse the advance of their enemies: cf. XV 668ff. (p. 370), XVI 567 (p. 394 and the note there), XXI 6f. (p. 493), and XX 444 (p. 487).

416   **nor ever/would be repay his parents:** cf. IV 477ff. (p. 104).

417   **they dragged off/the bodies of Phorkys and Hippóthoös:** although the Argives spend the entire episode defending Patróklos, they have more success than the Trojans in

killing and securing the gear of their enemies (cf. the fate of
Arêtos [p. 424] and Podês [p. 425]). As the following lines
suggest, the battle does not really go with the Trojans, despite
the protracted struggle over the dead Akhaian hero.

418   **Apisáôn Hippásidês:** XVII 348–49=XI 578–
79=XIII 411–12, excepting only a difference of one word
in each set: in XI Apisáôn is the son of Phausios (p. 269),
while in XIII Hypsênor is the son of Híppasos, i.e., Hippásidês (p. 312).

420   **Patróklos would, he thought,/approach the gates
but then turn back:** this has been said to contradict XVI 87ff.
(p. 380), where Akhilleus warns Patróklos not to carry the
fight to Ilion. But in his concern for his companion Akhilleus might have warned him to avoid just that temptation
and danger so natural to battle fury. His prayer for
Patróklos' safe return (p. 385) is another indication of anxiety.

         This time/she gave no word to him: when he sees
the Akhaians "turning tail" at the beginning of Book XVIII
he remembers a prophecy of Thetis that "the most admirable
of the Myrmidons" would fall while he still lived (see the
note to p. 436). Perhaps this forewarning, though it is not
explicitly mentioned, accounts for his concern for Patróklos'
safety. The negative character of the present passage (Akhilleus does *not* know what is happening) has aroused criticism,
but it seems natural enough for the poet to think of the inactive Akhilleus and to account for his ignorance of events by
noting the distance of the battle from Akhilleus' ships.

421   **warm tears flowed:** this "humanizing" of the
horses is extended to the power of speech at the end of Book
XIX (p. 469f.).

         **Is it not enough/that he both has the gear and
brags about it:** Zeus has set a limit on Hektor's glory and the
immortal team is not included in his spoil. The last phrase
might also be translated "boasts in vain," by which Zeus apparently alludes to Hektor's imminent duel with Akhilleus.

         until they reach the ships: two lines (454–55)
are repeated here from his message to Hektor in XI (p. 257).
The fact that the Trojans do not again carry the battle to the
ships seems a trifling criticism of lines that so aptly remind us
of the limitations set upon Hektor, and observed by him in XI

when he waits until the Akhaian leaders are wounded before he presses his attack. Cf. the references in Book XVIII (pp. 435 and 440) to the Akhaians fleeing to their ships, pursued by Hektor, which the poet may well have thought sufficient to satisfy the sense of these lines.

Automédôn gave battle as he rode: when Hektor loses his charioteers in VIII (pp. 185 and 191), he immediately looks for replacements. Automédôn foolishly tries to fight from the chariot while guiding the team.

422   **Alkimédôn:** see p. 383.

423   **upon the gods' great knees:** the origin of this phrase is obscure; it has been connected by Onians (pp. 303–9) with the ancient practice of spinning wool while sitting, i.e., over the knees, and so with the gods as spinners of fate. The knees are also a seat of power (cf. "Power . . . his knees," XVII 569; p. 425).

424   **so, folded in a ragged cloud of stormlight:** cf. the dispatch of Athêna by Zeus and the subsequent simile at IV 73ff. (p. 90). In both passages the goddess' appearance is assimilated to the simile in its concluding line.

425   **and may Athêna give me force:** this kind of dramatic irony is more common in the *Odyssey* than the *Iliad*.

son of Eëtíôn,/Podês: apparently neither the brother of Andrómakhê (p. 154) nor the son of Eëtíôn of Imbros (p. 494).

426   **Then a cloud of pain/darkened the heart of Hektor:** XVII 591=XVIII 22 (of Akhilleus' grief for Patróklos). Ameis-Hentze compare VIII 124 (=VIII 316): "Now a cold gloom of grief passed over Hektor" (p. 185). Cf. also the note on "battle-cloud" p. 415.

Koíranos: two Boiotians wounded (Pênéleôs and Leïtos) and this otherwise unknown charioteer killed seem a minimal motivation for Idómeneus' flight and Aías' desperation (p. 427). But it is the lightning and thunder of Zeus, as well as stones and javelins hitting their mark, which influence the warriors. Although Zeus answers his prayer and disperses the cloud, Aías still feels they must send for Akhilleus.

428   **Antílokhos:** last mentioned on p. 419, and before that he was fighting with his brother. Perhaps he is sought because of his reputation as a runner (see p. 367), but Homer may have been relying upon friendly ties between Akhilleus

and Antílokhos known from other stories in the tradition. Akhilleus is said to have killed Memnon to avenge the death of Antílokhos.

Patróklos . . . his warmth of heart: for this special characterization of Patróklos see the note on p. 543.

429   **Meneláos sent Thrasymêdês:** Antílokhos' brother has accompanied him to hear Meneláos' instructions; now he is sent back to lead his Pylians.

But I doubt/Akhilleus will appear: Meneláos anticipates both the rage Akhilleus will feel and the futility of sending for a warrior who has no armor. These lines thus foreshadow the major themes of the next book.

430   **like a dog pack chasing a wounded boar:** Pope admires "the Heap of Images which Homer throws together at the End of this Book, (which) makes the same Action appear with a very beautiful Variety." Such clusters of similes at high point in the action are very much in Homer's manner: cf. p. 400 (prior to Patróklos' death), p. 369 (Hektor about to reach the ships), and p. 294 (Hektor breaches the gates to the rampart). The concentration and variety here is comparable to that in Book II preceding the catalogue (pp. 50–51).

BOOK EIGHTEEN

〽〽〽〽〽〽〽〽〽〽〽〽〽〽〽〽〽〽〽〽〽〽

THE IMMORTAL SHIELD

This book is best-known for the description of the shield of
Akhilleus, made by Hêphaistos to replace the armor lost to
Hektor. But the varied scenes which precede this famous de-
scription are of extraordinary dramatic interest.

We return to Akhilleus. The battle in XVII not only
signified the importance to both sides of claiming the body,
but it also delayed the announcement to Akhilleus of Patróklos' death. Although Akhilleus, in the first lines of this
book, intuitively guesses that Patróklos has met his fate, when
the news is delivered he is so stunned wih grief that he cannot
speak. Yet his cries rouse Thetis from her chambers in the
sea. In a scene reminiscent of their meeting in Book I (here
again the brevity of Akhilleus' life and his desire for revenge,
this time on Hektor, are major themes) she attempts to dis-
suade him from his resolve to kill Hektor. Failing in that
effort she promises to bring him new armor. Now Iris ap-

pears, prompted by Hêra, to remind Akhilleus of the danger
to the body of his friend. Akhilleus' thrice-repeated war cry at
the moat sends terror through the Trojan ranks, and enables
the Akhaians to save the body of Patróklos. Once again Hektor rejects Poulýdamas' advice of caution and wins the assent
of the Trojans to continue the battle on the field. Immediately
Homer juxtaposes a scene in the camp of the Myrmidons and
a speech of Akhilleus full of regret, guilt, and the promise of
revenge. Both heroes are resolved to battle, and yet, having
portrayed that resolve, Homer will postpone it until Book
XXII.

So the first half of Book XVIII recapitulates themes and
decisions while vividly moving the story to a new stage, the
turning of Akhilleus' wrath against his Trojan enemy. After
the pathos of grief and the grim excitement reflected in the
decisions of the antagonists, the business of Hêphaistos offers
a contrast in tone and content that could hardly be more
marked. Removed from the suffering of men, the gods are
free to pursue their art. The great shield, emblematic of a
world beyond the transient destinies of Akhaian and Trojan,
assumes the exclusive right to our attention. While it may be
an interlude between scenes of more pertinent dramatic interest, it nonetheless recalls, in the manner of the recurrent
formulae, the scenes of ritual sacrifice, and the similes, a
larger, more stable and enduring context in which the poet
views the struggles of mortal men.

435   the curled, high prows: the same epithet is used of
cattle, and the impulse for its transference (from cattle to
ships) may be found in sound and meter:

. . . *neôn orthokrairaôn* (XVIII 3[b] and XIX 344[b])

. . . *boôn orthokrairaôn* (VIII 231[b] and XVIII 573[b])

Both phrases end the line and both have the same scansion.

Ai! why are they turning tail once more: the sight
of the fleeing Akhaians prompts Akhilleus to remember a
"warning" from Thetis. We may wonder why he did not think
of this prophecy when he dispatched Patróklos to battle. The
scholiast, noting that some ancient editors rejected lines
10–11, observes that Patróklos was a Lokrian in origin, so
that the prophecy concerning "the most admirable of Myrmidons" was at least a little ambiguous. But conceivably some
such concern was in the back of Akhilleus' mind when he

warned Patróklos not to fight with Hektor. Cf. his lament on p. 467 and especially XIX 328ff.

436 **A black stormcloud of pain:** see the note to p. 426. The first two and a half lines of this description are used of Laërtês' grief at the thought of his lost son (Fitzgerald's translation of the *Odyssey*, p. 454). For the self-defilement cf. Priam "caked in filth" from "rolling on the ground" (p. 573). In subsequent scenes Homer gives Akhilleus several speeches in which he expresses his grief and sense of guilt, but in this first reaction the poet is restrained, content to let Akhilleus' gestures and "dreadful cry" suggest the depth of his feeling. So in *Odyssey* Book XI, when Odysseus has addressed the shade of Aías, the poet shows the extent of Aías' indignation by describing him turning away without a word to his old comrade (*Odyssey* XI, 563ff.; Fitzgerald's version p. 203).

he feared/the man might use sharp iron: suicide is rarely mentioned in the epics. In the passage from the *Odyssey* cited in the last note Odysseus tells us that Aías died by his own hand (this is the subject of Sophocles' play titled for that hero) and at *Odyssey* X 49ff. Odysseus contemplates, for a moment, taking his own life.

The constant use of brothers and close kin fighting in pairs and the frequency with which one dies trying to save the other or avenge his death indirectly anticipate and explain the depth of Akhilleus' grief. It was not until Book XVI that their mutual affection found any significant dramatic treatment, but now we see Akhilleus virtually dedicating himself to death upon the death of his companion.

all Nêrêïdês/who haunted the green chambers of the sea: this list of the daughters of Nêreus is often stigmatized as an interpolation modeled on Hesiod's list of fifty Nereids (*Theogony* 240ff.). Most of these names are significant (e.g., "Grey," "Swift," "Headland"), but not all of them pertain to qualities of the sea ("True," "Reliable," "Fair-ruler").

437 **like a blossoming orchard tree:** see the note to p. 409 (XVII 53ff.).

Now I shall never see him/entering Pêleus' hall: it has been argued that this line (used in part by Akhilleus at 89f.: "never again . . . will you embrace him!") implies that

Thetis still lives with Pêleus. Oral poets were constantly adapting materials from other versions and different stories, and it is no wonder that this kind of creative process occasionally resulted in phrasing more appropriate to another context. In the *Iliad* Thetis is regularly found at home in the sea.

while he lives, beholding sunlight: Homeric idiom equates "being alive" with "seeing the light"; so the imagery associated with clouds and mist inevitably suggested death to the Greeks. Cf. line 102: "Not the slightest gleam of hope did I / afford Patróklos . . ."

Child, why are you weeping: XVIII 73=I 362 (p. 23), the beginning of their conversation in Book I.

438 **Mother, yes, the master/of high Olympos brought it all about:** note the way Akhilleus' thought moves away from the present to past events, which he wishes undone, and then back to the present.

for the slaughter of Patróklos: the word he uses here refers as much to his friend's being "spoil and prey" (usually "for dogs") as to his "slaughter." Akhilleus is able to think simultaneously of the loss of a friend (for which he feels responsible) and the loss of personal honor (Hektor has his divine armor). If guilt motivates him, as the beginning of the next speech suggests, he is also intent upon winning "perfect glory" (XVIII 121; p. 439) for himself. His sense of honor and his desire for fame are not diminished by remorse, which in the Homeric view evidently makes the remorse no less profound. Cf. Iris' unprompted assertion: "If that body suffers/mutilation, you will be infamous!" (XVIII 180; p. 441). Guilt and shame both operate upon his sensibility. The revenge, i.e., the payment Hektor must make, will make amends for Patróklos' death *and* will repair Akhilleus' tarnished honor and reputation. On shame and guilt see Lloyd-Jones, *The Justice of Zeus*, p. 25f.

May it come quickly: as in the preceding speech, Akhilleus dwells on the past, on his failure to help Patróklos, and on the curse his strife with Agamémnon has become. This last reference ("strife and rancor") recalls the opening lines of the poem (p. 11: "quarrel") and will be taken up by him again in Book XIX (lines 56ff.; p. 459) in his "apology" to Agamémnon.

439 **Not even Hêraklês escaped that terror:** although

the *Odyssey* (Book XI 601ff.) knows of the deified Hêraklês, no passage in the *Iliad* refers to this elevation. If Akhilleus feels that he has erred and been a "useless burden to the earth," yet, as the analogy implies, he has not lost his sense of self-esteem.

440   Go down/into the cool broad body of the sea: another indication that this scene is derivative may be found in the presence of the Nêrêïdês, who have no function in this version.

None had been able to pull Patróklos clear: we might have assumed that the action at the end of Book XVII saved the body, but now that action is taken up again by way of a transition to Akhilleus' appearance at the moat.

441   to sever and impale Patróklos' head: Hektor himself never expresses an intention to mutilate the corpse, but the poet has signified as much (XVII 125f.; p. 411). Cf. Akhilleus' vow "to carry back the gear and head" of Hektor. (XVIII 334f.; p. 446). See the note on p. 259. For the force of "infamous" see the note to p. 463.

442   whom Zeus loved: a generic phrase, also used of Hektor, Apollo, Phyleus (II 628), Phoinix, et al.

Around his shoulders/Athêna hung her shield: the shield (*aigis*) has consistently been used to inspire terror. Cf. p. 359f. So the imagery of cloud and fire in the following description conforms with the *aristeia* of the warrior and also connotes death and devastation (cf. Athêna's enhancement of Diomêdês [V 4ff.; p. 109] and the description of Hektor at XV 605ff. [p. 368f.]).

443   Hêra, made the reluctant sun,/unwearied still, sink: it is not obvious why the sun should be "reluctant," and Leaf supposed the line reflects an older, and shorter, version of the story (this day of battle began in Book XI). Owen (p. 183) perceptively observes that the poet emphasizes the end of the day in order to remind us that Hektor's triumph is now over (XI 194 and 209; p. 257). In this subtle fashion Homer makes a transition to the Trojan conclave.

Clearheaded Poulýdamas: while Poulýdamas has functioned as an adviser since Book XII, this is the first time Homer uses this epithet of him. It anticipates the judgment of XVIII 311 (p. 445: "fools, for Pallas Athêna/took away their wits"). That they were "born on the same night" implies a nearer relationship than is elsewhere suggested; ideally their talents should complement each other, but in this crucial scene they are antagonists. Cf. Akhilleus' admission that "in council/there are wiser" (p. 439). Among the distinguished warriors Odysseus would seem to be the man who most nearly embodies the ideal of excellence in council and in battle. But he is a survivor, and not a tragic figure. (At XIV 449, where phrasing and rhythm exactly parallel XVIII 249, Poulýdamas is characterized by an epithet meaning "shaking his spear." Homer had a choice of adjectives in the present case and exercised it judiciously.)

There are no bounds to the passion of that man: see the note to Patróklos' apology to Nestor p. 271. The adjective used here ("no bounds") occurs elsewhere in the *Iliad* only in the first line of Meneláos' speech on p. 408, where it is used in a pejorative sense. Inevitably the "passion" and pride of the hero are violent and dangerous (cf. Diomêdês' reflection on Akhilleus p. 225 and the note there).

444   Under his shimmering helmet/Hektor glared: this line and the following line (284–85) introduced Hektor's speech at XII 230–31 (p. 288), where Poulýdamas' interpretation of a sign is rejected on the grounds that Zeus has promised Hektor glory. Hektor may be alluding to this promise (first lines p. 445) here, or he may simply have taken confidence from their success; if he is thinking of Zeus's promise, then he has forgotten the stipulation "till sunset."

to Phrygia/and fair Mêîoniê: see notes p. 63f.

445   I might/just win, myself; the battle-god's impartial: this is a familiar sentiment (cf. the note to Sarpêdôn's exhortation p. 290f.).

fools, for Pallas Athêna/took away their wits: so when Glaukos makes a bad trade of armor the poet says "Zeus had stolen Glaukos' wits away" (VI 234; p. 149). Zeus has predicted the death of Hektor (e.g., p. 351), and we are told that Hektor is fated to die (e.g., p. 515), but Homer also dramatizes through speech and decision the human causality that leads to these events. Hektor persuades the army to take an aggressive posture that proves to be foolish, yet the decision is based on recent success and Hektor's willingness to face even the greatest of the Akhaians. While it is tempting to view expressions such as "Athêna took away their wits" as figures of speech, they more likely represent doubled and coordinated concepts of causality, which we also see, e.g., in "beaten by the mind of Zeus/and Trojan shots" (p. 380) and in Agamémnon's elaborate apology in XIX (p. 460f. and notes).

Akhilleus led them in their lamentation: lines 316–17=XXIII 17–18 (p. 536) this is the first of several scenes of mourning over the dead Patróklos.

446 **brought back/to Opoeis:** this is a town in Lokris (p. 52) from which Patróklos was banished with his father (for the story see p. 538).

I'll cut the throats/of twelve resplendent children of the Trojans: see XXI 26ff. (p. 494) and p. 541.

sweet oil for his anointing: perhaps some rudimentary form of embalming was practiced by the Akhaians; see the note on p. 458.

447 **Grace in her shining veil:** as the scholiast explains, Grace is made the wife of Hêphaistos because he needs grace (elegance) in his art. In the *Odyssey* Book VIII Aphrodítê is said to be his wife.

448 **after the long fall:** cf. the story of his fall to Lemnos p. 31. The sea goddess Eurýnomê (mother of the Graces, Apollodorus I.3.1) appears in Homer only here.

maids of gold, like living girls: cf. the automated tripods on the preceding page; such mechanical marvels are comparatively rare in the epics.

449 **Of sea-nymphs I alone was given in thrall:** elsewhere ancient legend tells how Thetis, who was destined to bear a son stronger than his father, struggled to avoid being subdued by the mortal Pêleus (see Apollodorus, III.13.5). Much of the following account repeats earlier matter (437–43=56–62). Thetis gives Akhilleus a romantic motivation ("he pined with burning heart," line 446), which may strengthen the somewhat less than conclusive evidence for this from Akhilleus himself (see note to p. 214).

450 **His first job was a shield:** this famous description is by far the longest of its kind in the *Iliad* but is plainly related, stylistically, to the descriptions of Agamémnon's cuirass and shield in XI (p. 252), the cup of Nestor in XI (p. 270f.), and especially to the similes. Though shields of fine workmanship and elaborate heraldic design are known from Mycenaean times, nothing so comprehensive and detailed as this

could ever have been seen by Homer or his audience. It is, then, a studied literary adaptation of a historical phenomenon, utilizing reference to actual construction ("a shining rim," "welded layers") and techniques of inlay. Hêphaistos uses bronze, tin, gold, and silver to achieve a degree of verisimilitude (cf. the impression made by the plowed field [p. 452], where different metals are used to animate the scene). But while certain obvious devices suggest an ordered depiction, and various scholars have succeeded in illustrating the shield's design, the total effect is cosmic, beginning with the Heavens and concluding with river Ocean, and evidently could never have been achieved on an actual historical shield. The dramatic imagination which shaped the Homeric similes here gives itself full play (e.g., consider the way the pictorial mode proceeds into the dramatic mode in the scene of the city at war [p. 451f.]).

        Plêïadês,/Hyadês, Oríon: cf., in Fitzgerald's translation, the night sky above Odysseus as he travels from the island of Kalypso:

<blockquote>
and his eyes
picked out the Plêïadês, the laggard Ploughman,
and the Great Bear, that some have called the Wain,
pivoting in the sky before Oríon;
of all the night's pure figures, she alone
would never bathe or dip in the Ocean stream.
</blockquote>

Odyssey V 271ff.

The constellations mentioned here are perhaps chosen for their usefulness to the farmer and sailor, though the formulaic character of the list (only the Hyadês are unique to the *Iliad*) suggests a generic rather than special function. Most scholars who have attempted to show how Homer's description might actually be laid out pictorially have placed the heavenly bodies in the middle of the shield, farthest from the stream of Ocean which circles it (p. 454).

451   **two cities:** in both cases the initial descriptions are essentially static and thus admit of easy representation; both soon turn to more dramatic forms.

452   **Strife and Uproar . . . and ghastly Fate:** cf.

"Terror and Rout, and Hate," who incite the battle on p. 103. Fate is here conceived as the spirit of Death.

But it was gold,/all gold: cf. the use of "blue enamel and tin" and "gold and tin" on the next page; the technique of inlay of precious metals on bronze was known in the Mycenaean period.

454   **A dancing floor:** unlike the entire preceding description, which has been a comprehensive and generalized picture of life, this last section contains elements peculiarly Cretan: "royal Knossos" has revealed extensive remains to the modern excavator and was in myth the palace of King Minos. This king retained the legendary artisan Daidalos to build the labyrinth which housed the infamous Minotaur. Minos' daughter Ariadnê helped the Athenian hero Theseus escape from the labyrinth after he had killed the Minotaur. In antiquity Crete was famous as the home of the dance (which perhaps adds some point to Aineías' taunt on p. 396, since Meriônês is from Crete). Cf. W. H. Auden's "The Shield of Achilles."

BOOK NINETEEN

▨▨▨▨▨▨▨▨▨▨▨▨▨▨▨▨▨▨▨▨▨

THE AVENGER
FASTS AND ARMS

Akhilleus' fortunes are marked by paradox: for most of the poem the greatest warrior finds himself in self-imposed exile from battle; though he desires honor and glory, he must remain inactive, depending on others for vindication. This irony is continued, in a different mode, in the later books. The central scene of Book XIX is devoted to the reconciliation of Agamémnon and Akhilleus, yet it is made clear in a variety of ways that, at least so far as Akhilleus is concerned, the reunion is a formality. He cares nothing for Agamémnon, nothing for his gifts, and but little for the other Akhaians. He has rejoined his comrades, but he is committed to revenge and death, and this alienation of spirit remains the dominant tonality until the funeral games of Book XXIII.

The dispute between Odysseus and Akhilleus ought to be seen in this context. Odysseus urges that the army should eat and refresh itself before battle. Akhilleus impetuously rejects "these ceremonies": like the gifts, the feast, symbol of friendship and community, is meaningless and unnecessary. He accepts the form but not the spirit of reconciliation, which can mean little to the avenging death spirit Akhilleus finds in himself ("Slaughter and blood are what I crave, and groans/ of anguished men!" XIX 214f.; p. 463). That he is persuaded to yield to the needs of the others foreshadows the reintegration that takes place in Books XXIII and XXIV. And when Athêna instills "nectar and ambrosia . . . within Akhilleus" (XIX 352ff.; p. 468), we are reminded not only of his standing with the gods, but also of his need as a mortal for the sustenance he has refused. These themes—dedication to revenge and death, divine aid, gift-giving and feasting that effect reconciliation—are interwoven into many of the scenes of these last six books.

Book XIX concludes wth the arming of Akhilleus, accompanied by a brilliant intensification of the light imagery (p. 468f.; see Whitman, p. 138ff.) and a miraculous conversation between Akhilleus and his divine horses in which he thinks of the pain caused his father and mother by his commitment to death. The theme of parental loss has figured repeatedly in the anecdotes associated with death in battle; now it is developed into a major source of pathos as the poet works toward Priam's appeal for the body of Hektor in Book XXIV.

457   **Dawn in her yellow robe:** cf. the beginning of Book XI (p. 251) and Book VIII (p. 181).

458   **Myrmidons/began to tremble:** the appearance of Akhilleus in his armor has the same effect on Hektor (14[b]=XXII 136[b]; p. 519).

                call the Akhaians to assembly: it was Akhilleus who summoned the assembly in Book I. The public wrong done there must be erased by public apologies.

                red nectar and ambrosia: cf. p. 446, where mortals use "sweet oil for his anointing." Onians (pp. 292–99) discusses the Homeric evidence for the nature of these substances. Though ambrosia is thought of as the "food" of the gods (cf. their gift to Akhilleus p. 468), the evidence suggests it is a kind of fluid, which can be "infused" or "instilled" (p. 468), and Onians argues it is the divine counterpart of the unguents and oils used by man, just as nectar is the divine counterpart of wine. As he says, the adjective "ambrosial" is "expressive of immortality"; appropriately, the goddess used these divine substances to protect the body of Patróklos.

459   If only Artemis had shot her down: Akhilleus exhibits some ambivalence about Brisêis (cf. Thetis' report p. 449 and the note to p. 214). Lyrnessos: a famous raid (see p. 476). Akhilleus does not fault himself much in this speech; only the Trojans have gained from this feud, but that can be changed soon enough.

  Akhaians . . . will remember: cf. Helen's words to Hektor (p. 153): "our portion, all of misery, given by Zeus/that we may live in song for men to come." The word Helen uses for "madness" (*atê*) there is the same term Agamémnon will use (p. 460f.) of his own mistake (translated here "Folly").

460   Friends, fighters,/Danáäns: for an analysis of Agamémnon's reasoning see E. R. Dodds, *The Greeks and the Irrational*, Chapter 1: "Agamemnon's Apology." It is essential to notice that while Agamémnon blames Folly (*Atê*) and Zeus, he also assumes personal responsibility. Cf. the note on p. 39.

  Zeus and Fate . . . Fury: see notes p. 217; Zeus is the dispenser; the Fury is agent; Fate is the lot that falls to man; Folly is both the condition that leads to irrational action and the personified agent. Agamémnon's example, another paradigm from the career of Hêraklês, hardly furnishes an exact parallel to his own situation, for no one tricks him, whereas in the story Hêra actively strives to undo Zeus's plans. As in so many other situations in the poem, the point is that man's success and failure can always be attributed to the gods. Alkmênê: XIV 323 (p. 340); Eileithyía: XI 270 (p. 259).

461   the strong wife of Perseus' son,/Sthénelos: for Perseus as son of Zeus see p. 340; the wife of Sthénelos was called Nikippê or Antibia.

  flung her/out of the sky: the motif last appeared p. 448; cf. Zeus's "Any I caught I pitched headfirst/over the rampart . . ." (p. 350).

  Zeus had stolen my wits: the language reminds us of the delusion of Pándaros (p. 91), of Glaukos (p. 149), and of the Trojans who follow Hektor's advice (p. 445). The

language here, as well as the recollection of Odysseus' mission, recalls Agamémnon's speech on p. 207f.
462   make the gifts/if you are keen to—gifts are due; or keep them: Akhilleus recognizes the propriety of Agamémnon's offer, but has no time for these formalities (cf. his next speech, p. 463).

Replied Odysseus: his speech falls into two parts, the first half addressing itself to the last theme of Akhilleus (we need to prepare for battle with food and drink), the second half ("Let the Lord . . . Agamémnon . . .") looking to Akhilleus' first theme and his apparent indifference to the gifts. Odysseus pragmatically emphasizes the need of the average soldier and considers the ceremonies (gifts, the oath, and the feast) necessary for healing the breach between king and warrior. His efforts to mediate and to define what is "just" may recall Nestor's attempt at conciliation in Book I (p. 20f.). The oath concerning Brisêis is the same one offered during the embassy ("never to have made love . . .": 176f.=IX 275f. (p. 212; cf. Agamémnon's offer of an oath p. 207).

463   when our shame has been avenged: the line (208) is interesting because Akhilleus' language, particularly the Greek noun *lôbê*, recalls IX 387 (p. 215):

> not till he pays me back
> full measure, pain for pain, dishonor for dishonor.

Akhilleus finds a shared quality in the "insult" of Agamémnon and the "shame" felt in Hektor's killing of Patróklos. The word is further defined by "infamous" in Iris' speech to him at XVIII 180 (p. 441):

> If that body suffers
> mutilation, you will be infamous!"

Akhilleus returns to the idea at XXIV 531 (p. 585) when he describes to Priam man's uncertain lot:

> But one
> to whom he [Zeus] sends all evil—that man goes
> contemptible by the will of Zeus; ravenous
> hunger drives him over the wondrous earth,
> unresting, without honor from gods or men.

"Contemptible," like "infamous," draws attention to the "insult" in this "shame," i.e., the public character of the personal injury that is common to all four passages. Looking to the present passage, then, we can infer that Hektor's insult has two aspects: he has killed Akhilleus' henchman and has seized and wears Akhilleus' armor. Hektor's success, like Agamémnon's seizure of Briséis, is a defamation of Akhilleus in that the loss makes Akhilleus contemptible to other men. By avenging the death of Patróklos he will reassert that his honor is from the gods and that honor is due him from men. He will have, so far as is possible, erased the shame he associates with the death of his companion. In much the same manner Meneláos feels that the theft of Helen has tainted his honor,

> You don't lack vileness otherwise, or crime [lôbê]
> committed against me, you yellow dogs;
>
> XIII 622f. (p. 318)

464　　　**Odysseus answered:** no new arguments are advanced in this speech, yet Akhilleus silently acquiesces. If Odysseus' use of the contrast between judgment and valor impresses Akhilleus, no indication of its cogency is given in the narrative (for that motif see p. 275).

　　　　　Lykomêdês: before only p. 206; Melánippos appears only here. The gifts are the same as those offered in Book IX (see p. 207), but the description is amplified there.

465　　　**Now Agamémnon rose:** cf. the ceremony and prayer in Book III (p. 77f.) and the note there.

　　　　　flung the victim/into the offshore water: at III 310 (p. 78) Priam carries the victims back to town. Whereas most sacrifices are followed by a feast in which the gods are allotted their share, in the sacrifice that accompanies an oath the victim is not eaten, perhaps because it is consigned to the spirits of the underworld (which does not explain why Priam carries the victims back to the city).

　　　　　Father Zeus, you send mankind/prodigious follies: Akhilleus accepts Agamémnon's apology. He tells the others to eat, but he will abstain.

466　　　**Patróklos, very dear:** cf. the laments of Hékabê and Andrómakhê p. 529ff. For "royal Mynês" see p. 57f.; the context seems to imply that Mynês was her husband, but this is not certain. There is no other evidence for her suggestion that Patróklos urged a marriage between her and Akhilleus, although Akhilleus' language at IX 336 (p. 214) describes her as a wife ("He [Agamémnon] holds my bride, dear to my heart"). Brisêis is mentioned only once after this scene (XXIV 676; p. 590).

I'll hold out/till sundown without food: just as sundown was stipulated by Zeus as the terminus for Hektor's *aristeia*, so Akhilleus makes it the end of his fasting, and, implicitly, the last day of Hektor's life. Cf. "Have a feast, I'd say,/at sundown, when our shame has been avenged" (XIX 207f.; p. 463).

467   my son . . . on Skyros, Neoptólemos: according to later legend (Homer does not mention it), Akhilleus was reared in the court of King Lykomêdês of Skyros, where he was sent by Thetis and disguised as a girl because she feared he would be drafted for the Trojan war. While there he had a child, Pyrrhos or Neoptólemos, by the king's daughter Deidameia. This son is alluded to in only one other passage in the poem (XXIV 467; p. 583).

My heart's desire had been: cf. the notes to pp. 420 ("This time . . .") and 435.

468   his eyes blazed: the following passage is especially rich in light imagery, some of which has earlier been associated with Hektor; cf. XV 605ff. (p. 368f.) and the note to p. 301.

The beautiful greaves: cf. III 330–35, with which five lines are shared.

469   this great Pêlian shaft: according to tradition, besides the spear from Kheirôn and the armor Akhilleus brought to Troy (p. 438), Pêleus received the team of Xánthos and Balíos as wedding gifts from Poseidon. Cf. the references to the gifts at XVII 443 (p. 421) and XXIII 277f. (p. 544).

Álkimos: a shorter form of the name Alkimédôn, for whom see p. 383.

the blinding Lord of Noon: Hyperion, the sun god; the line is used of Paris at VI 513 (p. 157f.).

470   the Furies: this is an extraordinary function for the Furies, who are usually connected with wrongs committed within familial or social groups and with the vengeance of

the dead. Dodds (p. 7) observes: "The explanation is perhaps that the Erinys is the personal agent who ensures the fulfilment of a *moira* (fate or portion). That is why the Erinys cut short the speech of Achilles' horses: it is not 'according to *moira*' for horses to talk."

far away from my dear father: references to Pêleus (pp. 467 [is he dead?], 469 [the spear a gift from him], 449 [his old age], 438 [his wedding the beginning of misfortune]) foreshadow the role of Priam in Book XXIV and the analogy the Trojan king draws between himself and Pêleus (p. 583).

BOOK TWENTY

𝕽𝕽𝕽𝕽𝕽𝕽𝕽𝕽𝕽𝕽𝕽𝕽𝕽𝕽𝕽𝕽𝕽𝕽𝕽

THE RANGING OF POWERS

The reader familiar with Homer's style will not expect an immediate confrontation between Akhilleus and Hektor. It is the poet's way to bring events to a height of excitement and tension and then to introduce scenes and episodes which provide strong contrasts in theme and tone. A number of lines and scenes in Book XX look forward to later events in XXI and XXII, but much, and particularly the preparation for the theomachy and the duel with Aineías, has little to do with Akhilleus' revenge. These two episodes have vexed modern scholars, both for their form and their content, and they merit special comment.

Book XX is in a number of respects one of the least self-contained portions of the poem. Not only is the battle of the gods (the "theomachy") announced only to be postponed until Book XXI, but Akhilleus' two brief encounters with Hektor and his slaughter of a number of Trojans, in particu-

lar Polydôrus, a brother of Hektor's, link this book with XXI
and XXII. The death of a brother, kinsman, or friend has
motivated many battlefield vendettas, and we see the poet
using the deaths of Polydôrus and Lykáôn (in XXI), as well
as the other Trojans and allies, to substantiate Hektor's
reasoning at XXII 99ff. (p. 518), where he blames himself
for the Trojan losses. These and other signs (e.g., Athêna's
aid p. 487), appear, then, to indicate a narrative plan directed toward a climax in Book XXII. Yet scholars have
been troubled by the way the several incidents are handled:
the grand preparation for the theomachy (pp. 473–75) is
abruptly terminated, and when it is resumed (in XXI; p.
505) the gods engage in something less than a grand display
of power and ethos; Akhilleus' challenge of Aineías is curiously tentative for a hero so wild for battle, and the response
of Aineías, a long-winded account of his genealogy, is followed by a duel more remarkable for its brevity and the
intervention of Poseidon to save Aineías than for any apparent pertinence to Akhilleus' return to battle. Various ex-
pedients have been tried in an effort to explain the poet's
method, and of course numerous scholars have argued that
much here is interpolated by a later poet. For some time,
e.g., scholars have assumed that the duel with Aineías,
which is paralleled in some respects by Diomêdês' duel
with Aineías in Book V (p. 119ff.), is the work of a
local poet who intended to celebrate princes of the Troad
claiming descent from Aineías. On this account Poseidon's
intervention to help the Trojan hero would be explained
by later historical affinities between this god and the princes
of the Troad, affinities at odds with Poseidon's role in
the rest of the *Iliad.* Recently the grounds for this assumed
historical connection have been questioned; in any case this
hypothesis does not explain why the episode was retained in
the *Iliad.*

Modern readers will probably find some awkwardness in
this book (even Owen, one of Homer's most sympathetic
readers, speaks of "apparent ineptitude"). Most explanations
of Homer's technique through the first part seem strained, but
what follows after the duel with Aineías is both more dramatically and thematically coherent. Furthermore, the genealogy Aineías offers fits after a fashion into the theme of di-

vine descent, which is to be elaborated extensively in the later books (see the note to p. 477).

473 **gave command to Themis:** the goddess Themis (also mentioned p. 352) is described by Hesiod as the second wife of Zeus: "Next Zeus married bright Themis, who bore to him the Hours, Order (Eunomia), Justice, and flourishing Peace, who survey the works of man, and she bore the Fates, Klotho, Lakhesis, and Atropos, to whom thoughtful Zeus gave the greatest honor, for they give to men their portion of good and ill" (*Theogony* 901–6). In the *Odyssey* Telémakhos appeals to the suitors by invoking "Olympian Zeus and holy Justice [Themis]/that holds men in assembly and sets them free" (Book II 68–69).

474 **You know/what plan I have in mind:** Zeus has fulfilled his promise to Thetis and now takes precautions that Akhilleus in his zeal and strength will not prematurely sack Troy. Given the relative strength of the Akhaian and Trojan partisans, Zeus's logic is not compelling. Perhaps he is thinking of the kind of personal aid Apollo gives Aineías (p. 476). Of the divinities who join the battle, Hermês, Hêphaistos, Artemis, and Lêto have not taken part in the earlier fighting; Hêphaistos and Xánthos are introduced by way of anticipating their conflict in the next book (pp. 503–5).

475 **Strife:** cf. the beginning of Book XI (p. 251) and the note on p. 103.

Kallikolônê: the word means "fair hill" and was thought by some ancients to be the site of the judgment of Paris; but there is no evidence for this inference.

Aïdôneus,/lord of shades: i.e., Aïdês, which is the more common Homeric form.

These were the divine adversaries: Leaf's comment is typical of much older criticism: "There is in XXI a real battle of the gods; but all that we have here is a bombastic introduction (1–74) which leads to nothing whatever, and is in quite ludicrous contradiction to the peaceful mood of 133ff. It is likely enough that the prologue here really belongs to the battle in XXI; for XXI 385 or 387 ["Now they attacked in uproar," p. 505] might follow on XX 74 with much gain to the significance of 55–74." "Bombastic" gives the show away, for when Leaf writes the introduction to Book XXI the "real battle" has become a "ridiculous harlequin-

ade." Victorian prejudice cannot accept Homer's divine burlesque. More germane to criticism is the assertion of a "contradiction to the peaceful mood of 133ff." Poseidon does
restrain Hêra, and we note at 153ff. (p. 478) that "neither
(side) cared/to take the initiative toward wounds and war."
The poet has promised a battle of the gods, then withheld it,
while keeping the adversaries facing each other, poised to
help their favorites among the mortals; in effect he has ringed
the Trojan plain with expectant divinity and thereby enhanced the spectacle in which Akhilleus and Hektor act the
chief parts.

476   **Lykáon:** he is mentioned previously only at III
333 (p. 79) and is killed by Akhilleus in XXI (p. 494ff.).

          Lyrnessos . . . Pêdasos: another (see p. 466 and
note on p. 57f.) reference to the raid on Lyrnessos, and
Akhilleus will remind Aineías of it on p. 479. This action was
treated in another poem, the *Cypria,* of which we know a little from ancient commentators. Pêdasos on the river Sat-
nóeis, inhabited by the Lélegês (cf. p. 496), was also south
of Troy, about one day from Lyrnessos, as Eustathius tells us,
though the actual location of these towns of the Troad is not
now known.

477   **Akhilleus comes of a goddess not so high:**
A. W. H. Adkins has recently pointed out the prominence of
this theme, i.e., that of birth and standing with the gods, in
the last five books of the *Iliad.* The culmination of this theme
comes with the duel between Hektor and Akhilleus, when the
gods aid the Akhaian hero and abandon Hektor, but before
that it is introduced at some length in this episode and
amplified in XXI during Akhilleus' fight with the river and
his duel with Asteropaíos (see the victor's comments on p.
499). Adkins does well to remind us that the Homeric gods
were not creatures of the poet's fancy but real and powerful
divinities in the minds of Homer's audience. Despite the humorous scenes and petty deceits of everyday life on Olympos,
the gods' regard for man and man's standing with the gods,
whether by descent or by divine aid, were a vital concern to
the archaic Greeks. Much of the talk in these later books, and
the entire episode between Akhilleus and Aineías, has seemed
to modern critics aesthetically pointless, and consequently
many lines and passages have been condemned as un-

Homeric. But the present scene, though it slows the impetuous attack of Akhilleus and proves altogether inconclusive as a piece of action, initiates a topic not only of undoubted interest to Homer's audience but also of more than tangential relevance to the fates of his characters. Cf. Aineías' comments p. 481, Poseidon's rebuke of Aineías p. 483, and Akhilleus' comment on Aineías' escape p. 484. (A. W. H. Adkins, "Art, Beliefs, and Values in the Later Books of the *Iliad*," *CP* 70 [1975], 229–54.)

the sea's Ancient: Nêreus cannot compare with Aphrodítê in the hierarchy of divinities. But better than divine descent is divine aid: Hêra's concern is predicated on Apollo's aid and the reasonable fear his presence might be expected to inspire in Akhilleus.

on his life's thread: traditionally the Fates are represented as three old women who spin, measure, and cut wool, which symbolizes the thread or portion of life allotted to each mortal. See the note on Themis, p. 473. Homer does not use the Hesiodic names, although he obviously knows the metaphor; in the *Odyssey* he refers to them as "Spinners" (Book VII, 197–98; see note to p. 585).

dream-voice of gods: the word translated here expresses any sort of divine inspiration; it is "the dream voice ringing round him still" which Agamémnon hears in Book II (p. 36). Cf. Poseidon's "great directive" to Akhilleus (p. 502).

no need for senseless anger: Hêra has called upon Poseidon as a partisan of the Akhaian cause, and while he is reluctant to battle unnecessarily with the other gods, he accepts the role of guardian of Akhilleus. Later he intervenes to save Aineías (p. 482), not because of any sudden change in his loyalties, but because Aineías is personally "blameless." Perhaps an anecdote in the life of Aineías or his clan would have made apparent to Homer's audience Poseidon's reason for the special protection of this Trojan.

478 **the Wall of Hêraklês:** Apollo and Poseidon worked for Laomédôn for a year (cf. p. 176 and 507), at the end of which the king refused to pay their wage. In retaliation Poseidon sent a sea monster to ravage the coast of Troy. Hêraklês undertook to rid the Troad of this monster, and eventually was able to kill it. This reference to a wall built for

the hero's protection implies he experienced some difficulty in this task.

479 **Hoping to lord it over Trojan horsemen,/heir to Priam's dignity:** as Aineías' reply indicates, he is a descendant of Trôs and hence of royal blood. Perhaps the line from Assárakos had asserted a claim to the throne (cf. Aineías' manner, p. 313). Homer knows of Aineías' survival after the fall of Troy and the fate of the house of Aineías to "be lords over Trojans born hereafter" (see p. 432). This tradition offered Vergil a connection between Troy and Rome; Aineías becomes the protagonist of Vergil's epic.

    retire/on your own people: in such exchanges one of the speakers normally tries to induce his opponent to retreat, and Akhilleus follows this pattern. The last lines of his speech were used by Meneláos in XVII (196–98=XVII 30–32). Akhilleus is not so impetuous that he does not follow the usual norms of heroic speech. But Homer does vary the content of such speeches at least once, as Fenik (p. 66) notes in the case of Tlêpólemos' challenge to Sarpêdôn (V 633–46; p. 129). Cf. Akhilleus' brief challenge of Hektor (p. 486), where the Trojan answers with the same lines that open Aineías' speech (200–2=431–33).

480 **But if you wish to learn such things as well:** the two lines introducing this section were also used by Glaukos (VI 150–51; p. 146); both Glaukos and Aineías preface their genealogies by minimizing the importance or relevance of the information.

    the story of our race: Dárdanos, Trôs and Ilos all give their names to places and tribes. Erikhthónios has been suspected because this is the name of a legendary king of Athens. Apollodorus, however, includes him in the royal line, though not with exactly the same connections Homer gives (*The Library*, III.12.2). The digression on the blood line of his horses picks up a motif mentioned earlier (e.g., p. 129), i.e., the famous horses of Troy. The other mention of Ganymêdês in the *Iliad* (p. 118) speaks of the horses Zeus gave Trôs in fee for Ganymêdês. For Tithonos see p. 251. Lampós, Klytíos, and Hiketáôn are counselors of Priam (p. 72).

481 **for fear/Aineías' shaft might cleave:** the most natural interpretation of these lines suggests Akhilleus is afraid for himself, but Owen (p. 206f.) apparently interprets them to mean that Akhilleus is afraid for the shield. The frustration experienced by Akhilleus in this duel is paralleled subsequently in his encounters with Apollo and Skamánder (pp. 487, 501f., and 512). We expect Akhilleus to sweep all before him, but he is not so successful. Such scenes not only retard the action but also render the ultimate confrontation with Hektor more problematic.

482   **Akhilleus closed with him:** the next three lines (285–87) appeared at V 302–4 (p. 119), with the substitution of Diomêdês for Aineías as the warrior using the boulder. Usually the warrior who casts the boulder has the best of the duel, so Poseidon's concern for Aineías is also surprising on this count. Akhilleus' reputation once again has its effect. A number of commentators draw attention to parallels between Books XX–XXII and Diomêdês' *aristeia* in Books V–VI: see Owen, p. 203f.; Nilsson, *HM*, p. 258f.; and introduction to Book V.

     Here's trouble for Aineías' sake: there is no indication in the preceding that Aineías is losing, save perhaps for the attention called to the difference in their shields. No one seems to have offered a satisfactory reason for Homer having given this speech and intervention to Poseidon rather than the pro-Trojan Apollo.

     His fate is to escape: many scholars have noticed the inclusive nature of the epic, i.e., how the poet through the incorporation of scenes such as the catalogue in Book II and through allusion and reference such as the present passage seeks to place the few days of the *Iliad* into a larger context of the entire war. Compare Poseidon's claim for the special status of Dárdanos with Akhilleus' assertion that Hêraklês was dearest to Zeus (XVIII 118; p. 439).

483   **pulled his ashwood shaft/out of the round shield:** at lines 279–80 we are told the spear "stuck fast/in the battlefield."

     the Kaukônês: otherwise mentioned only on p. 242.

     Remember, after Akhilleus meets his doom: for a similar stipulation and encouragement compare Iris' message to Hektor p. 257.

     magic battle-haze: the noun used here more often

occurs of the mist that pours over the eyes at death; but cf. V
127 (p. 113), where Athêna clears the mist from Diomêdês'
eyes that he may distinguish god from man.

484   **Strong as I am,/it's hard for me:**=XII 410 (p.
293); Sarpêdôn exhorts the Trojans. Such touches, since they
implicitly compare Akhilleus to his fellows, limit his battle
prowess more than might have been expected.

though he thrusts like fire, bladed/fire: the repetition of the clause (in Greek) is very rare in Homer. Hektor
dwells, for a moment, on the deadly hands of Akhilleus,
which are associated by him with consuming, triumphant fire
(see the index). The culmination of this imagery comes at
XXIV 478f. (p. 583) when Priam kisses "the hands of wrath
that killed his sons." (See the note there for Homer's transference of "man-killing" from Hektor to the hands of Akhilleus.) So at XXI 294 (p. 502) Poseidon advises Akhilleus
not to let his hands rest from war, and at XXI 548 (p.
510) Apollo strengthens Agênor that he may escape the
heavy hands of death. Iron and fire are again connected at
XXIII 177 (p. 541): "the pitiless [i.e., "of iron"] might of
fire." At XXII 357 (p. 527) the dying Hektor says to
Akhilleus: "Iron in your breast/your heart is." See the note
on "iron" p. 574.

485   **first he killed . . . brave Iphitîôn:** Beye notes that
of the fourteen Trojans slain by Akhilleus during his *aristeia*
(XX 381–503) "eleven—a high number—appear only here.
Three were slain before, two by Patroklos in his aristeia"
("Homeric Battle Narrative and Catalogues," *HSCP* 68
[1964], 364).

born by a naiad: i.e., a water nymph. Mount
Tmôlos is near Sardis, which is inland from Ephesos in the
valley of the river Hermos. In antiquity Hydê and Sardis, the
later capital of Lydia, were identified as the same town.
Gygaiê lake is another reference to this district.

Terror of all soldiers: this phrase was used at I
146 ("fearsome as you are") by Agamémnon of Akhilleus,
and at XVIII 170 (p. 441: "who strike cold fear/into men's
blood") by Iris addressing Akhilleus. All three passages—the
only uses of the superlative form of this adjective—admit of
some sarcasm in the tone of the speaker. Although Iphitîôn is

otherwise unknown, Akhilleus is given the poet's full knowledge of his background.

He hit him on the temple . . . Akhilleus downed him: lines 398–400=XII 184–86 (p. 286f.).
486 **lord of Hélikê:** cf. p. 188. Herodotus (I 148) tells us that Poseidon Helikonios was worshiped by the Ionians at Mýkalê.

Polydôros: he is first mentioned here. Both Lykáôn (p. 496) and Priam (p. 517) later recall his death. A fallen brother or comrade often motivates a warrior to action: cf. Koôn (p. 259), Sôkos (p. 264), and Glaukos (p. 393).

and mist of death veiled Hektor's eyes: cf. "magic battle-haze" p. 483.
487 **Athêna turned/the spearhead from Akhilleus:** this brief encounter anticipates the final duel in Book XXII (p. 522ff.). Both Apollo and Athêna are present there, but Apollo leaves the field to Athêna's control. Commentators have compared the duel of Diomêdês and Aineías in Book V: see especially p. 123, where Diomêdês charges three times, then a fourth, and is repelled by Apollo, who then catches up Aineías and takes him into Troy. Cf. also Patróklos' *aristeia* and the note to p. 398 (for a different use of "three times and . . . fourth" see XXI 176f.; p. 499). For the cloud protecting the hero see the note to p. 415.

You got away from death again, you dog: this speech (lines 449–54) appeared earlier at XI 362–67 (p. 262), where Diomêdês abuses the fleeing Hektor. The various parallels between scenes involving Akhilleus and Diomêdês have suggested to some scholars that Homer intends to draw a contrast between the two warriors, showing in Diomêdês youthful valor and discretion, in Akhilleus the extremity of heroic energy and fury. Both have a fair amount of business with Agamêmnon, and generally speaking they differ in every point in their manner toward the king (note, however, Diomêdês' outspoken advice and rebuke at the beginning of Book IX). Many of the parallels between their careers obviously result from the use of typical scenes, stock motifs, and formulae (see, e.g., the note to p. 494). The differences in the two *aristeiai* are discussed in the introduction to Book V.
488 **How witless, to imagine/Akhilleus could be**

swayed: such comments are a stock motif: cf. II 38 (p. 36): "Oh childish trust"; XII 113 (p. 284): "idiot"; XVI 686 (p. 398): "the blunderer"; and more recently XX 264 (p. 481): "a foolishness." All these passages, and there are others, translate the same Greek adjective; all represent the poet's comment on a mistake of judgment.

No moderate temper/no mild heart was in this man: Homer's understatement is expressed through two adjectives which occur only here. A noun formed from the same compound stem as the second does, however, occur in Helen's description of Hektor: "Your kind heart and gentle speech" (XXIV 772; p. 593).

Ekheklos, Agênor's son: is this the Ekheklos killed by Patróklos (p. 398)?

A forest fire will rage: cf. the simile on p. 256 describing the victorious course of Agamémnon and the prairie fire simile at the top of p. 494.

489   His axle-tree/as splashed with blood: this description is similar to one of Hektor's advancing chariot at XI 534ff. (p. 267). The last line of this book (503) also describes the bloody Agamémnon at XI 169 (p. 256).

BOOK TWENTY-ONE

THE CLASH OF
MAN AND RIVER

With the slaughter concluding the last book we move much nearer to the Akhilleus expected from earlier descriptions. And "like a wild god" Akhilleus rampages through Book XXI. Until line 513 (p. 509) the incidents of XXI look back to preceding episodes and themes: the supplication of Lykáôn is specifically tied to the death of his brother Poly-dôros; the duel with Asteropaíos incorporates thematic lines concerning divine descent found in XX; and the duel with the river god, followed by the general engagement of the other divinities, picks up a scene promised in XX (p. 475). The introduction of Priam and Apollo's intervention in behalf of the Trojans (pp. 509–12), however, clearly anticipate events of Book XXII. Although Book XXI is hardly seamless—few stretches of any length in the *Iliad* are—the surge and tempo of its action have occasioned less anxiety for the critics than many others.

493   when Hektor raged: since Books XI–XVIII comprise a single day of fighting, the reference need not take us to a specific episode. Hektor's reputation (see the note to p. 301) exceeds his performance: Akhaians and poet alike attribute a passionate battle fury to him which his speeches, and perhaps even his actions, hardly bear out.

494   like a wild god/he leapt: just used of Akhilleus (XX 493; p. 489) and repeated again at XXI 227 (p. 500). But it is also used of Diomêdês in V ("beside himself" p. 123; "like a fury" p. 124 and p. 137) and of Patróklos ("more than human in fury" p. 398; "the fourth demonic foray" p. 401). So the phrases characterize the warrior who would fight even the gods.

          picked twelve young men alive: see p. 446, and for their sacrifice p. 541.

          At this point he met/a son of Priam, Prince Lykáôn: this scene has been much admired for its dramatic values, the restrained pathos, and integration of a variety of thematic lines. Commenting on the place of genealogies, e.g., Charles Beye observes: "The world of order, of connection, of human care and human bonds can be seen in these histories of families, friends and relations. The fighting in this episode more than ever seems antithetical to this human fabric, and Achilles' response to Lykaon grows out of the poet's use of the genealogical motif. Patroklos' death has nullified human relations for Achilles. Again the dying Patroklos is a symbol of death, itself, and Achilles seems to be fighting still against its inexorable finality. The speech to Lykaon shows that underlying all this is Achilles' sense of isolation." (*The Iliad, the Odyssey, and the Epic Tradition*, p. 143.) This isolation may be seen not only in the speech, but also in Akhilleus' rejection of the supplication and ransom which he had previously accepted (see on p. 254), and which he will again accept when Priam treats for the body of Hektor. Lykáôn's language ("show respect, and pity me": XXI 74; p. 495) is echoed numerous times, e.g., in Apollo's "The man has lost all mercy;/he has no shame" (XXIV 44; p. 568). Until the end of the poem Akhilleus' sense of shame (i.e., his respect for social conventions and the opinion of his fellow man) is as dead as his friend. Rather than say Akhilleus is fighting against its finality, one might argue that Akhilleus is, until Priam's supplication, so committed to the acceptance of death that all humane and civilizing forces are in abeyance.

Lemnos . . . Imbros . . . Arísbê: the second island lies between Lemnos and the Troad; Arísbê is on the coast of the Hellespont. Euneôs (Iêson's son) was mentioned on p. 176 as a supplier to the Akhaians. This Eëtíôn is not mentioned elsewhere.

495 the first Akhaian at whose hands/I tasted the bruised barley of Dêmêtêr: Lykáôn would like to present himself as if he had been a guest of Akhilleus rather than his prisoner.

496 Laóthoê: see Priam's speech p. 517. This would appear to be the same Pêdasos described by Aineías as "plundered" by Akhilleus (p. 476). Both here and in VI (p. 142) it is described as if it were still held by these Trojan allies.

noble Polydôros: see p. 486.

My father is noble,/a goddess bore me: cf. his vaunt over Asterpaíos (p. 497). The tone passes from sarcasm (this "friend" has no ransom that can buy pity) to irony (divine parentage is as useless to Akhilleus as Lykáôn's tenuous relation to Hektor is to the suppliant) to fatalism (we shall all die, so why make anything of it).

497 when someone takes my life away: see Hektor's dying prophecy, p. 527. Akhilleus' death was related in an epic poem, the *Aithiopis,* by Arctinus. The primary tradition was that he died of an arrow wound inflicted by Paris and Apollo (see Apollodorus, *Epitome* V.3, and Frazer's note there), but on p. 502 Akhilleus speaks of his death "from the flashing arrows of Apollo," which does not necessarily contradict the tradition of Paris' part in his death. Like Patróklos, Akhilleus may prefer to think of himself as dying at the hands of a god rather than a mortal.

Asteropaíos: this leader of the Paiônês is not mentioned in the catalogue, but does appear briefly elsewhere (pp. 284, 414, 418). His people are the westernmost European allies of the Trojans. The Áxios is identified with the modern river Vardar.

498 why do you ask my birth: so Glaukos p. 146. Asteropaíos' connection with the river god Áxios provides a natural tie to the river god Skamánder, who will attack Akhilleus in the next scene. The transition is made still easier by

Akhilleus' vaunt (p. 499), in which he denigrates the origins of the Paionian hero and the powers of river gods generally.

499   Akhelôïos: a large river of Aitolia in northwestern Greece which flows south into the Gulf of Ambracia. The scholiast remarks on the special veneration given this river. One may wonder if in this context there is not an oblique allusion to Hêraklês' wrestling bout with Akhelôïos for the hand of Deianeira.

500   Aye,/Skamánder . . . as you require: no satisfactory explanation for this response has been offered. Perhaps it comes down to an absent-minded "whatever you say," though Akhilleus' actual intention follows decisively.

You could defend them until sunset comes: Skamánder has two motives: he is personally offended by the havoc Akhilleus causes in his waters; and as a river divinity venerated by the inhabitants of the place, he naturally sides with the Trojans. So on p. 501 he pursues the hero beyond his own banks.

501   as gods are stronger than men are: see the note to p. 477. But the theme of due order pervades the *Iliad.* See Agamémnon's claims to be "stronger," i.e., of more authority (p. 17); Odysseus' rebuke of officers and especially of the commoners (p. 41f.); Helen's rebuke of Paris, who is bested by a better man (p. 82); Diomêdês' reluctance to assail a god (e.g., p. 145); Agamémnon's obstinate insistence that Akhilleus should bow to him because of his higher rank (p. 208); Zeus's frequent assertions of his pre-eminence (e.g., the message to Poseidon [p. 354f.] and Poseidon's contentious response). The entire *Iliad,* especially for the Akhaians, moves from order to disorder and back to order and is marked by disputes over personal rank and honor involving both the gods and men of all ranks and both parties.

502   In returning to battle Akhilleus first turned to the gods (Thetis, Hêphaistos), then to the assembly of the Akhaians (Book XIX), and finally to the field he had dominated for years. Unlike Diomêdês, however, who has seemed to many to represent Homer's norm of integrated heroic behavior, Akhilleus in his passion disregards the cosmic order, first by desecrating the river and then by treating the Skamánder's power as inconsequential. Overwhelmed by the river he appeals to Zeus, invoking his own destiny as a mortal, and

like Odysseus when he is beset by the wrath of Poseidon
(*Odyssey* V 306–11), he prefers an honorable death at the
hands of a great warrior. No sooner has he checked himself
and recognized his mistake than the gods themselves reassure
him and invoke Hêphaistos' aid against "the great raging
stream."

503   the broad flooded river could not check him: just
as Diomêdês was able to wound Arês and Aphrodítê with the
help of Athéna, so Akhilleus is able to threaten Skamánder
when he is directed by the Olympians. But the two river gods
together may prove too much for him; consequently Hêra
summons the aid of yet another Olympian, Hêphaistos.

504   Am I/a party to that strife: "strife" translates the
same word used to describe the quarrel between Agamémnon
and Akhilleus (e.g., p. 439). The river god finds it easier to
withdraw with honor than do men in similar situations.

505   and Zeus . . . laughed in his heart for joy: Zeus
maintains his distance from the battlefield throughout the
poem, and often he takes the role of the supreme spectator
observing the theater of the world. Like the director of a
play, he instructs the actors, whether by command, persuasion, or duplicity, and occasionally he is affected by the events
he has himself arranged (e.g., the death of Sarpêdôn, p. 390).
See the note to p. 254 and cf. "as all the gods looked on"
(XXII 166; p. 520) and "Here with delight they [Apollo and
Athêna] viewed the sea of men" (V 61; p. 163).

        now Arês the shield-cleaver/led them: the poet
now returns to the engagement of the divinities promised and
introduced in Book XX (p. 475). The same pairs are
matched that were aligned against one another there.

**506   Laughing at him,/Athêna made her vaunt above
him:** this line and several others in the passage are used elsewhere in the poem to describe the duels of the mortal warriors. The entire passage carries burlesque so far that some
readers have felt it beneath the dignity of its context and the
art of Homer. But the wounding of Aphrodítê and Arês in
Book V and the manner in which they are treated by the
other divinities imply that a lighter tone was permissible in a
long *aristeia*. (Owen, p. 204, note 1, lists some of the parallels
between XXI and V.) Though Akhilleus is temporarily
offstage, Homer has incorporated this theomachy by way of

enhancing the prestige of his continuing *aristeia*. The scene obliquely indicates Hektor's fate, for the Trojan gods are no match for the Argive divinities led by Athêna and Hêra.

your mother's curse: Ares' mother is Hêra. "Curse" appropriately translates a noun elsewhere rendered "Furies." See the note to p. 217 and index.

But Hêra saw her: cf. Hêra's speech to Athêna p. 131f. Aphrodítê was not mentioned at the marshaling in XX.

507   Idiot, but how/forgetful you have been: Poseidon alludes to his labor for Laomédôn at the end of Book VII (p. 176).

508   Ephemeral as the flamelike budding leaves: cf. Glaukos' preface to his speech VI 146ff. (p. 146). Apollo retires with less fuss than Skamánder, but then he has never shown the zeal for the Trojan cause that the partisans of the Akhaians have displayed. That Artemis, who has had no part in the action to this point, should abuse him demonstrates once again how frail divine support for the Trojans is.

509   as a wild dove: cf. the simile p. 519f., where Akhilleus pursues Hektor.

Hermês . . . Lêto: like Artemis, Lêto appears only here in the action of the poem. Hermês' facetious reply suits the trickster divinity portrayed in the Homeric *Hymn to Hermes* and recalls his lines at *Odyssey* VIII 339.

at her father's knees/sank down, a weeping girl: cf. the scene at V 370ff. (p. 121), where Aphrodítê is consoled by Diônê.

510   aging Priam/gazed at huge Akhilleus: Homer has moved Paris and the other Trojan chiefs from the stage. Only Priam remains, who cannot help Hektor so long as he lives. The gates will remain open. Hektor could escape, as Priam's appeal shortly shows (p. 516).

Akhilleus,/wrought to a frenzy: all earlier uses of this noun ("frenzy") are of Hektor (see on p. 301). Note the connection between "frenzy" or "madness" and glory (lines 542–43).

Prince Agênor: See p. 103. He was mentioned last in XVI (p. 393).

the shapes and weight of death: most editors accept the reading translated here, which is preserved by a single manuscript and the commentary of Eustathius. Leaf follows the reading of the rest of the mss. with a line which may be translated: "to guard him from the heavy hands of death." See the note on p. 484 for the imagery. For "shapes . . . of death" see notes to p. 291.

511 **This is the end of me:** this is a familiar type of monologue in which a warrior debates whether he should flee or face his opponent (cf. Meneláos at XVII 91ff.; p. 410 and note). A comparison of these monologues (e.g., Hektor's at XXII 99ff. [p. 518]) will show that the poet has a standard format within which he exercises considerable freedom. The warrior weighs alternatives, then chooses one which, typically, he views as pre-emptive. The line translated in this speech as "Why say it?" occurs in five speeches and marks the transition from deliberation to decision (XXI 562=XI 407=XVII 97=XXII 122=XXII 385; only this last occurrence is an exception to the usual context).

512 **Apollo . . . whisked away Agênor:** cf. Apollo's intervention to save Aineías p. 123. There too a "figure of illusion" is created to delude the crowd.

This last scene of Book XXI teases the reader as well as Akhilleus, since Agênor's speech is much like, in form and content, Hektor's longer deliberation on p. 518f. Both warriors dismiss immediate flight, consider a less obvious mode of escape, and reject the second as well. Both think there is a chance of winning the victory, but both are pessimistic and afraid of the "prodigious" Akhilleus (Agênor, p. 512; the same word is used by Hektor, p. 523: "terrible as you are"). Yet Apollo's presence and active aid seem to hold out some chance for Hektor, as they have for Agênor. Of course the Greek auditor knew that Akhilleus killed Hektor, but such knowledge did not keep Homer, any more than it did the Attic tragedians, from playing on the possibilities. The gods are fickle, but what they will do they can do.

BOOK TWENTY-TWO

DESOLATION BEFORE TROY

Although Book XXII continues the *aristeia* of Akhilleus, the culmination of which is Hektor's death, its pathos derives from the speeches of Hektor and of his parents and wife. Structurally, the book is introduced by a link with the last incident of XXI, the deception of Akhilleus by Apollo, but after that it is a self-contained episode divided into three large parts: the first section is composed of speeches by Priam, Hékabê, and Hektor, all of which bear on the possibility of Hektor retiring within the walls; the third section is comprised of three lamentations (Priam, Hékabê, and Andrómakhê); the middle section contains the duel, in which narrative and first-person speech are carefully balanced:

1) pursuit
2) deliberation on Olympos
1′) pursuit

2′) return to Olympos
3) intervention of Athêna a) to aid Akhilleus and
                                 b) to deceive Hektor
4) the combat, in which we find a) speeches, b) attack,
    a′) speeches, b′) attack, a″) speeches.

Just as Hektor's first speech in the book (p. 518) is both a response to his parents and introductory to the duel, so the last
two incidents of the middle section (the stripping of the
armor and the mutilation) both mark the climax of Akhilleus'
victory and motivate the lamentations of the third section.
The portrait of Hektor as he deliberates, flees, takes his stand,
and recognizes his doom, has won for him so much sympathy
from modern readers that many have felt him the "hero" of
the poem. Add to this the savagery of Akhilleus' triumph
("That kept the dogs in their place," observes Gilbert Murray, not a little disgusted by the butchery and mutilation),
and one must wonder if even Homer's audience may not have
felt sympathy, if not admiration, for the greatest of the
Trojans. But Akhilleus' manic violence has too many parallels
in the *aristeiai* of the other heroes, even of the gentle Patróklos, to be dismissed as barbaric and primitive; his victory is
celebrated by his comrades, who are all too ready to mutilate
and taunt the corpse themselves. Hektor's request for fair
treatment is not unreasonable, as we see from the decision of
the gods at the beginning of XXIV, but it is made from weakness. He knows he has no hope, and we are likely to forget
that Hektor fought to "behead [the corpse of Patróklos] and
give the trunk to Trojan dogs" (XVIII 126f.; p. 411).

515   **fatal destiny pinned him where he stood:** the language is not unusual, though some texts capitalize Destiny
(Fate). Pitted against this apparently mechanical conception of destiny are the speeches which follow (pp. 516–19),
all of which imply that Hektor might yet escape if he chooses
to do so. But, as Hektor's reasoning shows, it is not in the
scheme of things for him to refuse this engagement.

516   **like a racing chariot horse:** cf. the more elaborate
simile at VI 506–11 (p. 157); the stallion is a symbol of
power.

           bright as that star . . . Oríôn's dog: Sirius, which
is also thought to be alluded to at V 5 (p. 109), where

Athêna kindles fire like a flaming star on Diomêdês' armor. The comparison is common, e.g., p. 253 (Hektor) and p. 306 (Idómeneus like a lightning bolt). The striking point about this simile is that the poet tells us what Akhilleus appeared like *to Priam,* whereas most similes are introduced in a more objective fashion.

more powerful/by far than you, and pitiless: the word for "pitiless" here connotes a certain hardness and stubbornness ("ironhearted/son of Pêleus," p. 383, where Akhilleus recognizes it as a reproach against himself), but it is also used affectionately. Cf. Patróklos' assessment of his friend on p. 378 and Hékabê's "He has no pity" (p. 518), and Hektor's "no quarter, no respect" (p. 519). This theme is especially prominent in Book XXIV.

517   Wild dogs and kites would eat him where he lay: mutilation is the greatest fear of the warrior, the most savage threat one warrior can bring against another. Later (p. 526) Akhilleus will say: "The dogs and kites/will rip your body" and the dying Hektor pleads: "do not let the dogs feed on me," for which request he is called a "whining dog" by Akhilleus. Dogs are vile creatures whose desecration of the corpse not only makes it an ugly thing of shame but endangers the rites of burial. Eating in the poems is a sacral occasion: libation and sacrifice precede the meal, and the feast which follows celebrates the community of men and their mutual respect and goodwill. Consequently, to be eaten by dogs and birds of prey represents a total inversion of normal standards; rather than sharing with his fellow man the warrior denies the humanity of his enemy and abnegates his own humanity by making a feast with and for the lowest of animals. Both Akhilleus (p. 526) and Hékabê (p. 574) reach their lowest moral depths when they express a desire to eat the raw flesh of their enemies. Cf. Hesiod, *Works and Days,* 275–78. See Charles P. Segal, *The Theme of the Mutilation of the Corpse in the Iliad* (Leiden, 1971).

Lykáôn . . . Laóthoê: cf. the variation on these particulars on p. 496.

Everything done/to a young man killed in war becomes his glory: these lines have seemed to several modern commentators an interpolation based on an imitation of lines by the Spartan poet Tyrtaeus. Priam's argument is certainly double-edged, but he depends on the pathos evoked by his prospective humiliation to move his son.

518   **Here I am badly caught:** see the note on monologues p. 511. The speech has three movements. In the first Hektor reflects on escape into the city, and realizes that if he runs he will be subject to reproach by Poulýdamas and others. He concludes that an honorable encounter, even if it means his death, is preferable. In the second movement ("Suppose, though . . .") he considers approaching Akhilleus as a suppliant and promising Helen and half the city's wealth. Hektor puts all this in the form of a condition, but before he can reach the conclusion he breaks off ("Ah, no,/why even put the question to myself?"). He knows Akhilleus will have nothing to do with treaties, and so the last section turns on the imagined contrast of dying "defenseless as a woman" or with some honor in a duel. The reasoning of the central section is pathetically hopeless, as Hektor himself realizes. Akhilleus wants neither ransom nor Helen, only Hektor's life. In imagining an unarmed suppliant's role Hektor clearly projects his own helplessness. He knows that, compared to Akhilleus, he is no warrior at all, and that such an appeal would be as incongruous as the courting speech of a young lover.

The poignancy of this speech derives from the mingling of objective self-reproach and exhortation with wistful self-deception. He begins by recognizing the facts, his responsibility and failure; then he imagines the just censure he has earned, and prefers the duel. But he cannot really face Akhilleus, so he immediately turns to an alternative and altogether hopeless proposal, which he dwells on till the illusion breaks. While he concludes with a second resolve to duel, he has so vividly exposed his sense of inadequacy that we can only pity him.

          Poulýdamas: Hektor refers to the advice in Book XVIII (p. 443f.).

          for my foolish pride: the word translated (line 104) is particularly strong self-condemnation. Elsewhere in the *Iliad* (four times) it is always used of the folly or outrageous behavior of others, and in the *Odyssey* it characterizes Odysseus' crew (Book I, 7) and the suitors who conspire against him.

519   I am ashamed to face: = VI 442 (p. 155), where Hektor speaks to his wife.

Someone inferior to me may say: see the note to p. 94.

fighting him to the end before the city: the Greek (line 110) contains the adverb "gloriously" or "honorably," i.e., winning a good name even in defeat. Cf. his determination not to "die ingloriously, but in some action/memorable to men in days to come" (XXII 304f.; p. 525).

No chance, now, for charms from oak or stone: many explanations have been offered for "from oak or stone," which is found in a number of passages in ancient literature (at *Odyssey* XIX 163 it clearly refers to birth from oak or stone), but none has satisfied a majority of modern scholars. Some have thought the line means "why talk of old topics?" Others have thought that "why bring up origins and genealogies?" suits the sense, while Fitzgerald and others have construed it closely with the following comparison. The answer is lost in antiquity, but the vagueness is not altogether unsuited to Hektor.

An interesting problem, and one peculiar to oral epic, may be noted in connection with lines 127f., where a repeated verb (translated through the combination of "charms" and "enchant") has seemed to some critics to have special poignancy, not only because of its meaning, but especially because its only other appearance in the *Iliad* (VI 516) comes at the end of Hektor's interview with Andrómakhê ("he had discoursed with his lady"; p. 158). While no one would doubt that such rare diction was used self-consciously by Vergil or Milton, one must wonder if an oral poet would plant, or his audience remember, such a nuance, when several thousand lines, and perhaps several days of recitation, intervened.

He ran,/leaving the gate behind him: the following scene, so often admired, is described dispassionately and as far as the race itself is concerned, obliquely. Hektor has talked himself into facing Akhilleus, but talk will not do now, and he has not the courage to attack. Not the thoughts of either warrior, which we learn only from their speeches, but comparison and selective description of the landscape comprise the twenty lines within which they run around the city three times. First a simile of hawk and dove, which stresses both the difference in power and in manner, then the figtree and road are described, before they come to the springs, mentioned here for the first time in the poem. Unlike the similes which frame the race, the hot and cold springs tell us nothing of the warriors or their purpose: for nine lines Homer ignores the immediate context to describe the world before the war. Again the runners: one is noble, but the other still greater. Their race is compared to an athletic event, first in an informal way (in peacetime men also race, and for prizes; here the prize is a man's life), then in a formal simile from chariot-racing. No exertion and but little emotion is suggested, for the course is seen from a distance, "as all the gods looked on."

520 **My heart/is touched for Hektor:** cf. the arguments of Apollo and Zeus p. 568f. For Hektor's piety see p. 150.

521 **The man/is mortal:** these three lines (179–81) were used by Hêra at XVI 441–43 (p. 391) in protesting Zeus's inclination to save Sarpêdôn.

As in a dream: the simile is extraordinary for its psychological origin. Cf. XV 80ff. (p. 352): "quick as a thought in a man's mind . . ."

How could he/run so long: these lines have been suspected as an interpolation because they have the look of an explanation for the curious fact that "swift-footed" Akhilleus fails to catch his man in the only race for him in the poem. Such sudden epiphanies of the gods, however, are not un-Homeric.

522 **the Father poised his golden scales:** see the notes to p. 183. On "shapes of death" see notes to p. 291.

Then came Athêna: Athêna's dual role in this scene may be compared to her deception of Pándaros and saving of Meneláos in Book IV (pp. 90–92). Modern readers are likely to object to her intervention on either, or both, of two counts: the greatest hero of the poem should not need divine help, and secondly, the mean deception of Hektor is neither necessary nor morally satisfying. To the first point it should be noted that no hero finds his efforts less glorious for divine aid, which is on the contrary always welcome (cf. Diomêdês' prayer to Athêna p. 113, and the reason for the failure of Teukros p. 562). In fact the proximity of the gods demonstrates the stature and glory of the hero (Akhilleus

ves credit to Athêna: "Pallas Athêna/will have the upper
and of you"; p. 524). As for the second point, these are
odern scruples, not ancient; even Hektor is content with
Athêna tricked me" (p. 525) and accepts the fact of his
nminent death. The gods, like mortals, differ in their powers,
nd since the immortals exercise their powers in every aspect
f life and death, inevitably discrepancies in power will ap-
ear to affect the lives of men. For some readers this trick-
ry will seem to offer Hektor an opportunity for achieving
ven greater glory, for rather than cower and whine he ac-
epts his fate and closes on his enemy with a will for "some
ction/memorable to men in days to come" (p. 525).

23   This way, by guile, Athêna led him on: the word
r "guile" is otherwise used only of Odysseus, and only in
ie *Odyssey* (two times); a less abstract form from the same
ot is used on p. 551 (XXIII 515), "by guile, not speed,"
hich may be slightly pejorative, but Nestor's use at XXIII
22 (p. 545: "But a skilled charioteer . . .") commends the
ord.

        terrible as you are: other uses of this adjective usu-
lly imply a degree of sarcasm or irony. Hektor seems to ask
r favorable terms, but his request does not differ in sub-
tance from that which preceded the duel with Aías (p. 164).
Ve should also remember Akhilleus' generous treatment of
ie father of Andrómakhê, Eëtíôn (see her description p.
55). These last lines may not, then, reflect a fearful spirit
iore than reasonable and even customary conditions with
hich Akhilleus will have no part now.

24   By god,/you'd better be a spearman and a fighter:
ie line (269) is used by the dying Sarpêdôn (XVI 493) in a
ifferent context (p. 392). It is odd that Akhilleus speaks of
ie suffering of his "men" rather than of Patróklos
pecifically.

        **hitting his enemy mid-shield . . . the spear re-
ounded:** the armor of Hêphaistos has already proven invin-
ible; cf. Akhilleus' reaction to Aineías (p. 481) and the fu-
le blow of Agênor (p. 512). The difference in their armor
nd weapons might alone account for the superiority of Ak-
illeus, but that difference also reminds us of the ultimate
eason for the duel: Hektor stripped Akhilleus' armor from
ie slain Patróklos.

526   **All childishness:** the reference is to Hektor.

            I beg you by your soul: the translation of psycho-
logical terms is particularly difficult. In Homer "soul"
(*psyche*) is the living, vital spirit breathed forth at death, usually through the mouth or from a wound. Homer does not
refer to any function of the "soul" in the living person, nor
does it appear to be an organ. So in a sense Hektor is saying
"by your mortality, for you too have a *psyche* and must lose
it, which will be a grief to your parents." (See the discussion
in the first chapter of Bruno Snell's *The Discovery of the
Mind*.) The last sentence of this speech also occurs in the
terms Hektor offers Aías before the duel in Book VII
(342f.=VII 79f.).

            to slaughter you and eat you raw: cf. the hatred of
Hékabê p. 574. The concentration of references to mutila-
tion by dogs and birds reaches its greatest intensity in the
Iliad on this page.

527   **this may be/a thing the gods in anger hold against
you:** Hektor's warning is not vain, for the gods are angered
by Akhilleus' treatment of the body (see p. 568). But the line
also occurs at *Odyssey* XI 73, where the shade of Odysseus'
companion Elpênor admonishes his commander to return to
Circe's island and bury him:

there, O my lord, remember me, I pray,
do not abandon me unwept, unburied,
to tempt the gods' wrath, while you sail for home.
                                      Fitzgerald's version, p. 187

Since the worst Odysseus could be accused of in Elpênor's
case is negligence, for there is certainly no malice, Hektor appears to claim a fundamental sacral obligation due the dead,
which the gods have a particular interest in overseeing. This is
not a claim for which there is extensive evidence in the *Iliad*,
perhaps because the poet chose to conserve the theme for development in these later books. With Hektor's last lines compare Patróklos' prophecy of Hektor's death (p. 403).

            and no one came who did not stab the body: mod-
ern readers tend to notice the savagery of Akhilleus and ignore the attitude of his peers, no one of whom blames
Akhilleus for desecrating the corpse.

528   **I shall not forget him:** cf. the reproach of the shade of Patróklos p. 537.

He may feel shame before his peers: i.e., as Leaf interprets, he "may feel disgraced among young men if he does not respect the aged." But it is the analogy between himself and Pêleus which Priam will pursue in Book XXIV (p. 583).

529   **But Hektor's lady:** Andrómakhê last appeared in Book VI. Hektor's last words bid her "Go home, attend to your own handiwork/at loom and spindle, and command the maids/to busy themselves, too" (p. 157).

530   **sighing out her life:** i.e., her *psyche* (see the note on "soul" p. 526) left her for a moment (below: "when she breathed again").

at Thêbê in the home of Eëtíôn: cf. her remonstrance to Hektor p. 154f. The fate of Astýanax also figures in that speech, though it is given more prominence by the actions and words of his father (p. 156f.).

531   **another's khiton:** the khiton is a light tunic or shirt. The pattern of this lament is as follows; 1) lament for Hektor and herself; 2) the fate of Astýanax; 3) the fate of any orphan; 2′) the fate of Astýanax; 1′) lament for their marriage. The uselessness of the garments "delicate and fine" points to the motif of clothing, and especially to the armor which has gone from Akhilleus to Patróklos to Hektor. Even Akhilleus' new armor, brilliant as it is, was only gotten when he was willing to give up his life. The poet has identified a man's life with his clothing and armor.

BOOK TWENTY-THREE

⌦⌦⌦⌦⌦⌦⌦⌦⌦⌦⌦⌦⌦⌦⌦⌦⌦⌦⌦⌦⌦⌦⌦⌦⌦⌦⌦⌦⌦

A FRIEND CONSIGNED
TO DEATH

The first section of XXIII describes the funeral of Patróklos, the second the games celebrated after those rites. Akhilleus has already announced that the Akhaians must attend to the burial (XXII 385ff.; p. 528), so that this first quarter of XXIII follows from XXII and complements the lamentations for Hektor which conclude that book. In the last and longer section Akhilleus presides over the games for which he offers the prizes and acts as arbiter. Some incidents in the contests bring back a bit of Homeric humor, and despite a pair of altercations the games mark a return to normality and goodwill in the camp, which are epitomized by Akhilleus' final gesture of offering the prize in the javelin throw to Agamémnon without competition.

Though funeral games were probably a traditional topic of oral poetry, these have a special function in that they enable the poet to show his hero once again a respected leader and member of the warrior society from which he had separated himself through much of the poem. Since Book XXIV is devoted exclusively to Akhilleus, the gods, and the Trojans, this is the last time we see the hero among his fellows. The tradition knew that Akhilleus continued to fight until his death, and that at his death he was mourned as the most valiant and formidable of the Akhaians. Book XXIII accomplishes this return and more, for in it Akhilleus moves from grief for Patróklos to an active attempt to conciliate Agamémnon. This tempering of his passion and redirection of his energies mitigate the spiritual alienation he has suffered. Book XXIV remains to solve the moral and spiritual dilemma posed by Akhilleus' possession of the body of Hektor.

536   **Thetis roused their longing to lament:** Kakridis (*Homeric Researches,* p. 84) has argued that this reference to Thetis together with other anomalies in this scene indicates that the poet has adapted the burial of Patróklos from the burial of Akhilleus himself. See the discussion in the note to p. 541.

     Shameless abuse indeed he planned for Hektor: line 24=XXII 395 (p. 528). These lines and 176b (=XXI 19b; p. 494: "he leapt in savagely for bloody work"), "he willed their evil hour," are often cited as the poet's condemnation of the sacrifice of the Trojan youths. As the context of XXI 19 shows, however, line 176 may mean no more than "he intended them harm." So in the present context "shameless" may also mean "shameful" (for Hektor), i.e., the kind of abuse which is shameful to any man who suffers it. To suffer at the hands of your enemy is in itself shameful, and the line need not represent a moral judgment of the poet.

     Akhaian peers induced Akhilleus now: the book marks a gradual return of Akhilleus to the fellowship of the camp. He has already (line 11) accepted the need for eating (contrast his attitude in XIX, p. 463), and after the ritual of the funeral he will preside over the games. That he will not bathe is probably due to the proprieties of mourning, but it also implies that his grief still separates him from the group. Normally an Akhaian would bathe before eating (cf. *Odyssey* IV 48ff.; p. 54 of Fitzgerald's translation).

537   **reach the gloomy west:** i.e., Hadês, often described as being on the edge of the world. Below, in "gates of Death" and "hall of Death," Hadês is explicitly mentioned.

let me pass the gates of Death: according to Greek belief the spirit of the dead was not at rest and received into Hadês until the proper ceremonies were performed. Though Homer speaks of Patróklos' "shade" (*psyche*), the passage reads very much like a dream, for it has the subjective color of Akhilleus' concern.

538 **The day/of wrath:** for the meaning of this phrase see the note to p. 291.

Menoitios/from Opoeis: see also p. 446. Accidental and intentional homicide were not distinguished in archaic Greece. So even a child must flee his native land if he has killed his fellow. Cf. Deuteronomy 4:41–43.

Patróklos' shade like smoke: when Odysseus sees his mother in the underworld and tries to embrace her, she flies from his hands "like a shadow or a dream" (*Odyssey* XI 207); cf. the imitation at *Aeneid* II 790ff. and VI 740ff.

540 **Apart/from the pyre he stood and cut the red-gold hair:** the usual offering to the dead, as Peisístratos, the son of Nestor, observes at *Odyssey* IV 198 (cf. also Orestes' sacrifice at the beginning of Aeschylus' *Libation Bearers*). Homer's comment that "he had grown (it) for the river Sperkheios" and Akhilleus' address to that river god call our attention to ambiguities in this usage, especially as found here. Hair is associated with strength, and in this context with the survival of Akhilleus. He and the Myrmidons not only make the usual sacrifice, but in announcing that it was intended for the river god (river gods are often considered the founding fathers of clans) he indicates his full acceptance of his death and the fact that he will not return home. Having already accepted Thetis' prophecy that he must die if he kills Hektor, he now dedicates his strength in what amounts to a vow.

Gilbert Murray thought that "long-haired Akhaians" contained an allusion to a vow to take Troy: "In modern language they were *taboo* while on the war-path, and the duty of never cutting, combing, or washing the hair was the visible sign of various other abstinences" (*Rise of the Greek Epic*, p. 132f.). While this interpretation has been disputed by D. L. Page, who notes that historically the Mycenaeans were long-haired, should Murray be right, then Akhilleus by this act renounces the possibility that he will take Troy (Page, *History and the Homeric Iliad,* p. 242f.).

I would confer my hair upon the soldier/Patró-klos: and Patróklos will carry that token with him to Hadês.

Taking fat from all . . . (he) sheathed the body head to foot: this is done to make the body burn more readily. The significance of the sacrifices here, and especially of the Trojan youths, has been disputed. George Mylonas argues: "The immolation of the twelve Trojan youths, often taken to be a remnant of a barbaric ritual that had become obsolete and that demanded human sacrifices over the grave of a hero, is explained by the poet as 'to pay the price/for dead Patróklos' [Fitzgerald's translation of XXI 28; cf XVIII 91–3, 336–37, etc.]. Thus it should be placed in the same category as the killing of an enemy in revenge for a friend lost. . . . Deiphobus's statement that he killed Hypsenor, son of Hippasos, first to avenge the death of Asios and then to provide to his friend a *pompon*—'one to escort him on his way' (XIII 414ff.), seems to explain both the killing of the Trojans and the true meaning of the gifts placed on the pyre; these were to provide for the journey to the house of Hades." (*A Companion to Homer,* p. 480.) On the other hand, Déíphobos' vaunt is one of several in a sarcastic vein, and perhaps should not be taken too literally. Also, Hektor was particularly nominated by Akhilleus to "pay the price" for Patróklos, and these anonymous Trojans seem a poor thing after all the carnage on the plain and in the river. The horses, dogs, and youths are probably killed as companions for the dead, but this hardly makes the act less barbaric. For the poet's "as he willed their evil hour" see the note to p. 536.

For an eighth-century parallel to the burial of Patróklos see J. N. Coldstream, *Geometric Greece* (New York, 1977), p. 349. Coldstream argues that burials in royal tombs at Salamis in Cyprus reflect the influence of the *Iliad.* Fig. 111 on p. 348 of his text shows a chariot reconstructed from the parts found in one of the tombs.

541   he shall not be eaten/by fire but by wild dogs: see the note on imagery to pp. 484 and 526.

oil/ambrosial: cf. the treatment of Patróklos' body (p. 458) and the care of Apollo for the body noticed at the beginning of Book XXIV (p. 568).

And now, too,/Patróklos' pyre would not flame up: the following scene has provoked much speculation: why will the winds not come unsummoned? why does Iris, to whom Akhilleus does not pray, answer his prayer and summon the winds? why does she make excuses and refuse their invitation, alleging a prior engagement with the Ethiopians? J. Th. Kakridis (*Homeric Researches,* pp. 75–83) offers the following explanation. The refusal of the winds results from a "pale imitation" of another narrative describing the funeral of Akhilleus himself. Since Akhilleus had killed Memnon, brother of the winds, only a little before his own death, they refused to come to his funeral pyre. Consequently, the gods (here Iris) intervened to summon the winds that the hero might be honored properly. This interpretation is admittedly speculative. As for the Ethiopians, Kakridis compares the refusal of Hektor in Book VI (p. 153) and Patróklos in Book XI (p. 271) to stop for rest and refreshment: Iris is also busy, and like Thetis in Book I (p. 25) she refers to the gods' engagement with the Ethiopians, a banquet which in both contexts is inconsistent with other immediate activities of the divinities. The preceding explanation does not tell us how the poet was led to the transposition of these assorted motifs.

The entire scene foreshadows later developments: a) Akhilleus says he will honor Patróklos with fire but will dishonor the body of Hektor; b) the gods protect the body of Hektor; c) Akhilleus must appeal to the gods for aid, even in the honoring of Patróklos; d) Akhilleus is able to rest (p. 543), and when he awakens is concerned only with the care for the ashes of Patróklos. The anger which has prompted him to further desecration of Hektor's body has temporarily passed. Once the poet has selected this mode of demonstrating the limitations of Akhilleus' power, he is not reluctant to include details concerning Iris' visit and the journey of the winds.

542   **to the country of the Sunburned:** see the note on p. 25; here, as there, the poet is indifferent to the fact that the gods have just been involved in the events of Troy and will be equally involved the next day.

    calling Patróklos' feeble shade: so long as the body is not consumed by fire, the shade of the dead is believed to be in the vicinity.

543   **for their mildhearted friend:** "mildhearted" trans-

lates an adjective the poet thought particularly suitable for
Patróklos. Cf. Meneláos' "his warmth of heart" (XVII 670;
p. 428); Zeus and Lykáôn characterize Patróklos as "gentle
and strong" (XVII 204=XXI 96; pp. 413 and 496). The
only time in the *Iliad* the adjective is not used of Patróklos comes at XXIII 648, when Nestor uses it of himself as
"well disposed" toward Akhilleus. Cf. Akhilleus' "The kind
man" (XXIII 281; p. 544).

      but now/Akhilleus held the troops upon the spot:
there has been no previous announcement of the games, but
they are the usual culmination of the funeral rites (cf. Nestor, p. 555), and like the mound raised over the pyre the
games are intended to perpetuate the fame of the dead
warrior (see Hektor's speech at VII 89–91 [p. 164] and Akhilleus to Nestor p. 554).

544   **Poseidon/gave them to Pêleus:** Poseidon is regularly associated with horses in Greek art and myth; presuma-
bly these were given to Pêleus as a wedding present (cf. p.
438).

      Eumêlos: he is the son of Admêtos, who is the son
of Pherês (so on p. 547: "The mares/of Pherês' son").
Eumêlos has not been mentioned since the catalogue in Book
II (pp. 58 and 60), where his team is singled out as the best
in the army because "Apollo of the silver bow had bred
them" (p. 60).

      **yoking the Trojan horses he had taken/from
Aineías:** see pp. 119–20.

      Ekhepôlos Ankhísiadês: see the note to p. 103. His
home, Sikyôn, is on the Corinthian gulf.

545–546 **his father halted, with a word to the wise:** Nestor's
counsel gives him a place in the games, even though Antílokhos does not gain his advantage from careful manage-
ment at the turn. In fact, after his description of the marker,
of proper equestrian procedure, and of the assigning of a ref-
eree at that critical juncture, the drama of the race develops
in the homestretch, where Antílokhos recklessly makes a
move at a narrow point in the track.

546   **joy to your adversaries,/humiliation to you:** the
converse of this line epitomizes the rough ethics of archaic
Greece. Cf. Hektor's abuse of Paris p. 68f.

      the great horse of Adrêstos,/fleet Aríon: Adrêstos

was one of the Seven who attacked Thebes in support of Polyneikês (see on p. 100f.). According to Apollodorus, Adrêstos was the sole survivor, saved by his horse Aríon. "That horse Poseidon begot on Demeter, when in the likeness of a Fury she consorted with him" (Apollodorus, III.6.8; see Frazer's note there).

547   had not Apollo in a fit of anger: the god's resentment would seem to be motivated by the fact that he bred the stock Eumêlos drives (p. 60). Athêna has a personal attachment to Diomêdês (p. 109ff.) and less interest in the horses.

549   unless/you take oath for it: see below p. 553.

550   A rude reply he got from the runner, Aías: this scene is designed, like the dispute between Meneláos and Antílokhos, to provide an opportunity for the arbitration of Akhilleus, whose good sense and courtesy present the strongest contrast to his recent morbid fury.

551   by guile, not speed, outrunning Meneláos: Nestor has recommended "guile" (line 322; p. 545), and Antílokhos' move has seemed to Meneláos "madness." The noun used here is ambiguous as a value term in the epics, but "guile" and "cunning" are in every case more valued if they are effective. Cf. Antínoös' censure of Telémakhos' "own dear, incomparably cunning mother" (*Odyssey* II 88; p. 21 of Fitzgerald's translation). Her cunning has served her well, but the suitors can complain of it.

552   The best man is the last: in a variety of ways the chariot race presents a microcosm of the values and tensions inherent in the heroic society. Akhilleus' judgment recognizes absolute merit, merit to be valued regardless of the issue of a single race whereas Antílokhos' claim is based on competitive results. The divinity of Eumêlos' team ought to guarantee victory, but when a goddess intervenes his best efforts are thwarted. When Antílokhos says,

if you go through with this thing you've announced,
I'll be furious! You mean to take my prize,

XXIII 543f. (p. 552)

we hear echoes of the quarrel between Agamémnon and Akhilleus in Book I: Agamémnon insists upon the honor due his position, on the propriety and decorum that bring the

finest prize to the king even though he has not personally
carried the sword; Akhilleus insists on the honor due his vic-
tories and his acknowledged pre-eminence among the warriors. For Antílokhos or Akhilleus to yield is difficult because public standing is thereby jeopardized. In this scene
Akhilleus is more magnanimous than Agamémnon in Book I,
and smiles at the youthful aggressiveness of Antílokhos.

But Meneláos' complaint is a different matter. Antílokhos'
tactics shame Meneláos' skill (his *aretê*, line 571; p. 553)
and make him seem less worthy than he is. He must have compensation, but by imitating the good sense of Akhilleus and
proposing an oath rather than a duel—only Athêna's intervention saved Agamémnon in Book I—Meneláos finds an
equitable and chivalrous solution. Such oaths were an accepted method of resolving disputes, and their efficacy is
demonstrated by Antílokhos' apology (if he forswears himself
he risks living "as an offender before the powers unseen").

These themes probably explain the argument between Idómeneus and the lesser Aías (p. 549f.). Aías' gratuitous insult of Idómeneus before the crowd promises a quarrel, until
Akhilleus' cooler head reminds them of the "occasion" and
public respect for seemly behavior (line 493f.). This incident,
like the granting of a memorial prize to Nestor (p. 554),
shows how effective an authoritative insistence on decorum
can be. The pride and egocentricity of the younger men are
always ready for a test; like Akhilleus in his wrath, they care
little for social order, if that order in any way limits their self-
assertion. That Akhilleus should be the arbitrator and sponsor
of decorum now, after his complete disregard of all ceremony
in XIX, is a master stroke of dramatic contrast. Yet he is still
capable of passion, as the poet shows in XXIV, and his
civility and calm in this scene are best attributed to a desire to
provide a suitable memorial to his comrade.

555   **Would god/I had my young days back:** line
629=XI 670 (p. 272)=VII 157 (p. 166).

          Amaryngkeus: he is the father of Diorês, one of
the leaders of the Epeioi in the present expedition (p. 55).

          Angkaios the Pleurônian: one of the Aitolians (p.
56). Angkaios' name is appropriate to a wrestler, meaning
"taking into the arms."

          Phyleus: he is the father of Megês (p. 55); the

sons of Aktor are also mentioned in the same passage in the catalogue. They were perhaps Siamese twins (see the note to p. 273).

556   **Epeiós, a son of Panopeus:** that this is the same Epeiós given credit in legend for building the wooden horse, "the ambuscade Odysseus filled with fighters/and sent to take the inner town of Troy" (*Odyssey* VIII 494–95; p. 140 in Fitzgerald's version), seems unlikely.

Eurýalos: he is listed in the catalogue (p. 53) and appears in battle only on p. 142. His father Mêkisteus was a brother of Adrêstos' (see note to p. 546), who was the grandfather of Diomêdês.

Oidipous: apparently the poet thinks of Oidipous as having died at Thebes; later legend placed his tomb in Attica (see Sophocles' *Oedipus at Colonus*). For Homeric knowledge of the story of Oidipous see *Odyssey* XI 271–80 (Fitzgerald's version, p. 193f.).

557   **huge Aías Telamônios, then Odysseus:** the contest brings to mind their later competition for the arms of Akhilleus after that hero's death. Both warriors had helped to defend and save Akhilleus' body on the field. Subsequently his arms were offered to the bravest hero in the army, and Odysseus won them. (The nature of the judgment and judges differed according to ancient legend: see Apollodorus' *Epitome* V 4–7 and Frazer's notes there. Sophocles' *Ajax* takes its impulse from the judgment of arms.)

558   **artisans of Sidon:** see p. 150.

Thoas: see p. 337. For Eunêos, son of Iêson, see p. 176f.

559   **Odysseus/prayed in his heart to the grey-eyed one, Athêna:** see Diomêdês' comment on their affinity p. 237; her association with Odysseus is familiar to all readers of the *Odyssey*. Ten years later, not yet home, and feeling pressed by time and hostile competitors, Odysseus says to the assembled Phaiakians:

Only in sprinting, I'm afraid, I may
be passed by someone. Roll of the sea waves
wearied me, and the victuals in my ship
ran low; my legs are flabby.

(p. 131 of Fitzgerald's translation)

560   **Fresh in age, they call him:** curiously, the adjective rendered "fresh in age" occurs only here in the epics, though it certainly suits the hero of the *Odyssey*.

561   **that I took from Asteropaíos:** thus the armor of the three most notable Trojans killed since XVI, Lykáôn, Sarpêdôn, and Asteropaíos, has now been offered for prizes. No one seems to know how the warriors will hold armor "in common."

          Polypoitês . . . Leonteus: these are the Lapiths who last appeared defending the gates of the camp (p. 285ff.). Polypoitês is the son of Pieríthoôs; in the catalogue (p. 59) Leonteus is named his co-commander.

562   **also without a vow/of rams in hekatomb to Lord Appollo:** cf. Athêna's advice to Pándaros p. 91.

563   **Son of Atreus,/considering that you excel us all:** Akhilleus has been careful to preserve the honor of all concerned, and perhaps even the life of Aías in the duel with Diomêdês. Now he makes a final gesture of conciliation.

BOOK TWENTY-FOUR

A GRACE GIVEN
IN SORROW

The last book of the *Iliad* is concerned with the ransoming of Hektor's body and with his funeral. In its drama and thematic resources it not only concludes the poem but summarizes it. Akhilleus' wrath, and more particularly the second stage following the death of Patróklos, is finally placated; he does not forget his friend, but he does obey the dictates of the gods as well as his own generous spirit. For once in the poem divine intervention has a benign influence on all parties. Homer is not content, however, to let the command of Zeus resolve the moral dilemma, and so we see Akhilleus, still troubled and quick-tempered, recognize in Priam the image of his own father's eventual suffering. In acceding to Priam's supplication the Akhaian hero once again thinks of his mortality, and on this occasion of its consequences for those who depend on him. The book is, moreover, one of reversals, not the least of which finds Akhilleus persuading Priam that he must come to terms with his grief and accept his mortal lot.

Parallels between Books XXIV and I have been noticed by many modern critics (see Whitman, p. 259ff.). In both episodes an old man makes supplication for the return of a child; in both the gods play an active part in achieving the return. Other motifs include death and funerals, quarrels among the gods, Thetis as emissary between Akhilleus and Zeus, and the journey. Whitman may have stressed too much the analogy with geometric art, but he is surely right to emphasize the prominence of contrast and antithesis in the art of the *Iliad*. Book I utilizes supplication, divine intervention, and exchanges between gods and mortals to effect the divisions which animate the poem. By contrast, Book XXIV resolves quarrels and appeases the passions through a successful journey and supplication. The shift from divisions within the Akhaian camp to divisions between Akhaian and Trojan is not only an obvious difference between the two books but also reflects the shift in the wrath theme from a purely social and personal schism within the Akhaian camp to the revenge motif which activates Akhilleus in the last third of the poem.

Yet some matters remain open and permanently changed, and while the book concludes, it also leaves us with the lasting impression of a city irrevocably doomed. Hêra's arguments for not returning the body may be put aside, but her enmity remains. Priam may have the body of Hektor, but Troy has lost her chief bastion. Akhilleus may acquiesce in the will of the gods and genuinely pity the aged Priam, but he will die, never to see his homeland and father again.

567   But Akhilleus/thought of his friend: none of the spiritual agitation over the death of Patróklos, evident still in this book, was present in the funeral games. We may look for the marked difference of mood in scenic parataxis, or we may say that the social responsibility of the games distracted Akhilleus for a while.

He tossed and turned/remembering with pain Patróklos' courage: sleeping, eating, and remembering continue to be prominent motifs associated with psychological and social adjustment. That the poet has consciously developed these relationships is suggested by Priam's urging of Akhilleus to remember his father, and by Akhilleus' urging of

Priam to "think of supper" (p. 587f.) and of sleep (p. 589f.).

  cutting through ranks in war and the bitter sea: the line occurs three times in the *Odyssey,* more appropriately of the old mariner Odysseus. Some ancient critics condemned lines 6–9, but the entire book shows stylistic affinities with the *Odyssey.*

568 **great shield's flap of gold:** this is the *aigis* (see p. 40 and note). This is the only passage where a part of it is described as golden.

  the day Aléxandros/made his mad choice and piqued two goddesses: this is the only allusion in the *Iliad* to the judgment of Paris. See Introduction, p. 6. Poseidon's animosity must apparently be reckoned from his service to the abusive Laomédôn (see p. 507).

  Did Hektor never make burnt offering: see pp. 89, 150, and 520 for this motif.

  The man has lost all mercy;/he has no shame: "shame" normally means regard for the opinion of other mortals, but Apollo argues that Akhilleus fails to respect the opinion of the gods. Cf. Priam's appeal: "Akhilleus,/be reverent toward [i.e., respect the feeling of] the great gods! And take/pity on me . . ." (XXIV 503; p. 584). Apollo's example ("A sane one may . . .") is similar to the argument of Aías at the end of the embassy (IX 628–42; p. 223).

569 **The Fates have given patient hearts to men:** this is the only passage in Homer where "fate" (*moira*) appears in the plural, although the personification of the three fates is certainly present in Hesiod. At *Odyssey* VII 197 they are the Spinners:

<blockquote>
his fate
he shall pay out at home, even as the Spinners
spun for him on the day his mother bore him.
</blockquote>

(Fitzgerald's translation, p. 116f.)

Cf. Hékabê's "Almighty fate spun this thing for our son," (XXIV 209f.; p. 574) and the note to p. 585.

  brave as he is, we gods will turn against him: the idea here is that the indignation (*nemesis*) of the gods may be turned against Akhilleus despite his standing with them.

if one had a mind to honor/Hektor and Akhilleus equally: see the note to p. 477 for a discussion of this theme. Hêra's personal attachment to Thetis is not elsewhere mentioned in Homer, and may have been invented for this argument (Apollonius of Rhodes [*Argonautica* IV 790ff.] makes Hêra elaborate this point).

570   **Midway between/Samos and rocky Imbros:** This is the northern Samos, i.e., Samothrace.

571   **He must bring gifts/to melt Akhilleus' rage:** Zeus of course expects Akhilleus to comply, but he recognizes the hero's freedom to refuse and the propriety of offering him compensation. Cf. Athêna's promise at I 212–14 ("winnings three times as rich," p. 18).

572   **the Wayfinder:** i.e., Hermês.

He is no madman,/no blind brute: this may seem to contradict Zeus's "I . . . am angered at his madness" (p. 571), but the preceding references to "madness" and "rage" focus on immediate, and usually transient states, while the present lines describe permanent qualities of the man. They are also designed to reassure Priam, for Zeus anticipates the king's apprehension before the journey.

573   **caked in filth/his own hands had swept over head and neck:** cf. the immediate reaction of Akhilleus to the announcement of Patróklos' death (p. 436).

574   **Tell me/how this appears to you:** he has begun preparations but reflects his fear when he asks how she views the project.

Iron must be/the heart within you: line 205=521 (p. 585), where Akhilleus comments on the daring of Priam. Cf. Hektor's last words p. 527 (XXII 357). So iron may be used for what is "pitiless" or "obtuse" or "daring," the idea of hardness (of spirit) connecting the three. A special kind of irony results from the common use of formulae by characters as disparate as Akhilleus and Hékabê.

savage and wayward as the man is: Hékabê's estimation is the antithesis of Zeus's "He is no madman . . ." (p. 572). Everything in the book points to the interview between Priam and Akhilleus.

I could devour the vitals of that man: cf. Akhilleus, p. 526 (XXII 346–47). This is the ultimate perversion of eating, an expression not only of loathing but also of the potential depravity of man, who never entertains his fellow without first offering him a meal.

a raven crying/calamity at home: the commentators compare XII 243 (p. 288), which is not quite the same, though in both passages the speaker condemns the pessimism of another: "Don't," says Priam, "be a bird of ill omen." The following lines reveal Priam's doubt and fear. Cf. Nestor's skepticism upon hearing Agamémnon's dream (p. 38).

575 **He lashed out/now at his sons:** of the nine, five (Agathôn, Pammôn, Antíphonos, Hippóthoös, and Dios) are mentioned only here; cf. Apollodorus, III.12.5.

576 **Mêstôr, Trôïlos:** the former is not otherwise known. Trôïlos is not mentioned elsewhere in the *Iliad*. Tradition made him a son of Hékabê and Apollo who was killed at an early stage of the war by Akhilleus (see Apollodorus, *Epitome,* III.30–32, where the death of Mêstôr is also accounted for).

they lifted out a cart, a cargo wagon: this is apparently the same "four-wheeled wagon with a wicker box" which he orders immediately after Iris departs (p. 573). The intervening scene with Hékabê and his sons has interrupted his preparations, which are resumed by the repetition of a line and a half (265f.).

a team the Mysians had given Priam: for the Mysians see p. 63; in antiquity they were given credit for first crossbreeding asses and horses.

577 **Zeus,/the father of gods:** in his role as father and king Priam would naturally invoke Zeus as father of the gods; as a man journeying over the plain of Troy he invokes Zeus as ruler of Mount Ida and the locality around it.

578 **and put an eagle, king/of winged creatures:** line 315=VIII 247 (p. 189); and see the note on p. 163.

driven by Idaíos: he last appeared in Book VII (p. 174).

as though for Priam's last and deathward ride: a number of motifs in these scenes suggest that the passage from Troy to Akhilleus' camp should be taken as a symbolic trip to the underworld. Priam is lamented and counted for dead by his family in Troy. He is accompanied to his destination by Hermês, one of whose functions was to act as a guide to the underworld. He travels through a desolate, unknown place during the night, passes through gates whose warders have been put to sleep (p. 582), and carries ransom in the hope of reclaiming his dead son from a warrior who has accepted death, who is a living lord of the dead. As Whitman notices (p. 217f.), one thinks of Orpheus and other Greek heroes who would conquer death by reclaiming something already consigned to the underworld. It is probably unnecessary to observe that for Homer's audience, who knew Sleep and Death as brothers (p. 337), the symbolism of such a passage was far from "literary"; for many it must have been as vividly concrete and realistic as their own breathing.

Argeiphontês: according to ancient interpretation this epithet means "killer of Argus" (see Apollodorus, II.1.3), but this etymology is unlikely. Elsewhere Fitzgerald has translated it and connected it with Hermês' function as a guide to the underworld.

sandals . . . ambrosial, golden: "ambrosial" is used loosely for "immortal," i.e., "unperishing."

the wand with which he charms asleep: according to the Homeric *Hymn to Hermes* (529ff.), Apollo gave this wand to Hermês; there it is described as "golden, of three leaves, which will keep you unharmed, accomplishing every task of word and deed." In classical art Hermês is often represented holding a herald's staff. Cf. *Odyssey* V 43ff. and X 277ff.

579   Old father . . . You remind me of my father: the ring composition of this speech has a special thematic and rhetorical point, the climax of which comes in Hermês' advice to "invoke his father, his mother, and his child" (p. 583). Hermês in fact poses as a kind of alter Akhilleus (he is a young Myrmidon of good family—his father's name means "wealthy"—who has seen the battle and knows the disposition of Akhilleus and the Akaians). Thus this scene initiates and serves to reassure Priam, who for all his courage is very much afraid. Hermês does not completely dispel the tension, however, for though "The blest immortal ones . . . care for every limb [of Hektor]," still Akhilleus acts "pitilessly" (p. 581).

581   and care for every limb: there is an extraordinary degree of verbal subtlety in this book. Here the gods' "care" reminds the Greek reader of "pitilessly" five lines earlier (verb and adverb derive from the same stem), and so suggests the contending interests of Akhilleus and the immortals. Priam may take some hope from this.

did my son exist? was he a dream: line 426ᵇ=III 180ᵇ (p. 73), "or was that life a dream?" This rhetorical construction does not deny the past so much as it suggests its remoteness.

Protect me, give me escort: the irony of the scene is developed in language altogether appropriate to Hermês. Traditionally Hermês is herald, guide, and escort, and particularly for the souls of the dead (for which see *Odyssey* XXIV 1ff.). So here Priam's request ("give me escort") touches the essential function of the god, whose reply ("You are putting a young man to the test") playfully treats Priam as more knowledgeable than he is and honorably refuses gifts, though the Hermês of the Homeric hymn is a thief eager for any sort of gain.

583   to be received with guests of mortal station: this is a curious objection, and the line has been suspected. To cite but one exception to this rule of dignity, in *Odyssey* Book I the disguised Athêna does not hesitate to be received and accept the hospitality of Telémakhos' house.

invoke his father, his mother, and his child: Priam invokes only his father. Neoptólemos, his only child, is mentioned at XIX 326 (p. 467).

Automédôn/and Álkimos: see p. 469.

the hands of wrath that killed his sons: see the note to p. 484. When the adjective translated here is used of Akhilleus (three times: XVIII 317=XXIII 18), it modifies his hands, but it is most frequently attached to Hektor (eleven times; also once of Arês and once of Lykourgos [VI 134]) and has usually been translated "Hektor, killer of men," as on p. 584. Non-formulaic usage at XVII 638 ("Hektor's rage,/his uncontainable handiwork") and the adaptation at XXIV 506 suggest that this epithet had not become a metrical cliché. The usual phrase for Hektor is *Hektoros androphonoio* ("Hektor, killer of men"). At XXIV 506 (p. 584) we find *andros paidophonoio* ("of the one [man] who killed my son"), a unique phrase occupying exactly the same position in the line, evidently modeled on the more common phrase, and grammatically linked with the suppliant's gesture of raising his hand in submission. Hektor since I 242 (p. 19, where Akhilleus refers to "the killer, Hektor") has been the distinctive proprietor of this epithet, but Priam now adapts the adjective to his personal situation and makes Akhilleus a "child-killer."

For other imagery associated with hands cf. Akhilleus' reassuring gesture at XXIV 671f. (p. 589): "He took the old man's right hand by the wrist/and held it, to allay his fear" and Patróklos' "Give me your hand, I sorrow" (XXIII 75; p. 537).

When, taken with mad Folly in his own land: the formal point of the simile turns out to be awe/wonder, but since that idea is not introduced until the end of the comparison, we are implicitly invited to view Priam's posture as inspired by Folly (*atê*), i.e., so extraordinary that only the goddess of Delusion (p. 460f.) could occasion it. For the motif see homicide in the index.

Remember your own father: for earlier references to Pêleus see the note to p. 470. This speech and Akhilleus' response exemplify the technique of ring composition: a) think of your father; b) he may be as hard pressed as I am; c) news of you would give him joy; b') I have lost so many sons; c') return Hektor (I shall never have good news of Hektor again); a') think of your father (I am more pitiful than he). Akhilleus responds directly: a) the unhappiness of Priam; b) one must endure; c) paradigm: the urns of Zeus; b') the mixed fortune of Pêleus, which he must endure; a') Priam's unhappiness, which he must endure.

Priam's suggestion that even Pêleus may be "hard pressed" recalls the portrait of Odysseus' father (*Odyssey* XXIV 225ff.), who has retired to a shabby and neglected existence on his farm. In the rough world of archaic Greece the situation of old Laërtês was probably typical of those who had no active sons to protect and care for them.

584   **fighting for his land, my prince,/Hektor:** Priam's phrasing echoes the words of his son at XII 243 (p. 288: "defend your fatherland") and XV 496 (p. 365: "defending his own land").

585   **This is the way/the gods ordained the destiny of men:** cf. the discussion of Fate in the notes to p. 183.

Onians (p. 395ff.) argues that the urns of Zeus may be connected with the threads that the Fates (*Moirai*) or the gods spin for man, for they are simply the storage jars in which the Greeks, and so their gods, stored their goods, in this case the product of their spinning. The probability of this interpretation for the present passage is enhanced by the fact that the word here translated "ordained" might also be rendered "spun." Cf. the notes to pp. 332 and 477. The words here translated by "good and evil" (the usual rendering in English) refer not to moral qualities so much as qualities of life (social standing, birth, wealth, etc.) which make a man's life happy or unhappy for him and which, consequently, assign him to a "good" or "evil" standing in the eyes of his fellow man. The enumeration of Pêleus' gifts and afflictions illustrate the point sufficiently.

I sit at Troy to grieve you and your children: perhaps no line in this book more succinctly illustrates the reversal Akhilleus has experienced in situation and temper. But cf. also his argument that Priam should eat (p. 587f.).

From Makar's isle of Lesbos/northward: Homer's description of Priam's realm is neither ample nor exact. Leaf would like to include Phrygia and Lesbos within the realm, though Akhilleus' expression implies they are taken as boundaries. Makar was a legendary king of Lesbos, perhaps drawn to this context because of his significant name ("Happy").

586   **Do not vex me, sir:** the temper that led Akhilleus into the quarrel with Agamémnon is still with him. Those who deny the Homeric agents freedom of will and action should have difficulty in explaining Akhilleus' threat to "trample on/the express command of Zeus." As if to reinforce this point and maintain tension to the end of the scene, the poet repeats this idea in the narrative (p. 587: the danger of Priam's rage and Akhilleus' furious response [lines 584–86]).

587   **Patróklos,/do not be angry with me:** Akhilleus' apology originates in his vow at the funeral not to permit the burial of Hektor (XXIII 182–83; p. 541). Akhilleus is no longer scornful of gifts, as he was in earlier episodes. Priam's ransom has assumed something of the significance of the prizes in Book I.

even Niobê in her extremity/took thought for bread: as J. Th. Kakridis has shown, Akhilleus' version of the Niobê story is altered radically in order to fit this occasion. Most significantly, Niobê, a famous example of grief, never eats in other versions. Here she is made to eat so that Priam in his grief will eat. (J. Th. Kakridis, *Homeric Researches*, Lund [1949], pp. 96–105).

The story begins at midpoint, with the death of her children, then moves back to the reasons for her loss. That her children were not buried for nine days was introduced to strengthen the analogy between Priam and Niobê. The explanation, i.e., that Zeus has turned the people to stone, is also novel, and in turn leads to the strange involvement of the gods with the burial of the dead. Kakridis supposes that this point does not reflect problems of improvisation, but that "in the end the gods take pity on Niobe and bury her children themselves, as Achilles takes pity on Priam and provides for the burial of his son's body. It is because Achilles pays this last tribute to his foe, after having misused him cruelly, that the gods are presented as having themselves buried Niobe's children, a thing which they had not done even for the heroes whom they loved." (p. 102)

The usual version may be found in Apollodorus, III.5.6. Niobê married Amphion of Thebes and retired to Mount Sipylos in Asia Minor, the home of her father Tantalos, after the death of her children. Apollodorus concludes: "there she prayed to Zeus and assumed the form of a stone, and day and night tears stream from that rock."

let us know the luxury of sleep: normally, eating precedes conversations with the guest, but the special status of Priam in this scene made an inversion of the usual order necessary. Having dined with his host, Priam, who like Akhilleus has been unable to sleep, feels secure enough in the present hospitality to ask for a bed.

589   to make a bed outside: Akhilleus feels obliged to explain this treatment, perhaps because Priam is an old man and a king, but in *Odyssey* Book IV Telémakhos and Peisístratos sleep on the porch and no one thinks it worth notice.

Then Akhilleus, defiant of Agamémnon: this passage poses a problem that has not yet found a completely satisfactory solution. In the Greek text "Agamémnon" is represented by a demonstrative pronoun, i.e., "him," which would most naturally be taken of Priam rather than of Agamémnon. "defiant" would in that case be rendered "provoking" or "speaking contemptuously of." Yet Akhilleus seems civil enough, and his mood would appear especially reasonable, since his concern for the delay which Agamémnon might cause may be assigned to his tacit recognition of Agamémnon's overlordship.

Fitzgerald's version strains the Greek while offering a suitable introduction to the speech; those who take the pronoun of Priam have difficulty in finding what is "defiant" or "mocking" in Akhilleus' address.

590   **Kassandra:** this is only the second reference to this famous daughter of Priam (see p. 310).

591   **Now she lamented:** Andrómakhê's lament here is similar to that one at the end of XXII (p. 530f.), particularly in the central motif of concern for their son. One detail added here, that Astýanax might be hurled from a tower, became the standard account of his death (cf. Euripides' *Trojan Women* 709ff.).

592   **Hektor, dearest of sons to me:** Andrómakhê has touched on Hektor's success as a warrior, but for the most part she laments a personal loss. Hékabê opens and closes her brief lament with the "favor of the . . . gods." Like Helen, she celebrates the dead hero.

593   **This is the twentieth year:** the ancient commentators observe that it took the Akhaians ten years to organize the expedition, but there is also a tradition that the first expedition went astray, landed in Mysia, and wasted ten years—even returning to Greece—before finally arriving at Troy. And these lines also occur at *Odyssey* XIX (222–23, which has led a few commentators to speculate that the present passage is a clumsy adaptation.

The funeral of Hektor follows the same lines and order as that of Patróklos, but in a much abbreviated form.

594   **Hektor, tamer of horses:** the memorable last line of the poem utilizes an epithet for Hektor which has also been applied to various other heroes, Trojan and Akhaian, e.g., Diomêdês and Antênor.

INDEX

With the exception of references to the Introduction to this volume (designated *Introd.* and set in italics), all citations are to the pages of Fitzgerald's translation., i.e., to the numbers in the left-hand margin of this volume. Most references are to pages on which notes will be found, out ff. indicates an extended passage in which the character or topic is prominent. Roman numerals after a name indicate the books in which the character is particularly active. References to the comments prefatory to individual books of the *Iliad* are made by citing the first page of that book in Fitzgerald's translation. An index of Greek words follows the general index.

INDEX OF GREEK WORDS